# MICROSERVICES
# IN CLOUD

*Doing it right in GCP,
AWS and Azure*

# HOW TO USE THIS BOOK

This book is designed to be flexible, allowing readers from different backgrounds and expertise levels to benefit from its content. Whether you're new to microservices or an experienced developer looking for cloud-specific implementations, here's how you can navigate the book:

### 1. If You're Starting from Scratch:

If you're new to microservices and want to build your knowledge from the ground up, we recommend starting from **Chapter 1** and working your way through to the final chapter. These early chapters cover the foundational concepts, architectural principles, and rationale behind microservices, giving you a strong base before diving into implementation details.

### 2. If You Already Have Some Background on Microservices:

If you're familiar with the basics of microservice architecture, feel free to jump ahead and start from **Chapter 4**. This chapter begins the in-depth discussion of microservice patterns and implementation strategies, giving you the practical insights you need without covering too much of the introductory material.

### 3. If You're Focused on a Specific Cloud Platform (AWS, Azure, GCP):

Each chapter in this book separates the implementation of microservices based on the three major cloud platforms: AWS, Azure, and GCP. If you're only interested in a specific cloud provider, such as AWS, Azure, or GCP, you can navigate directly to the relevant sections of each chapter to see how the concepts are implemented on your platform of choice.

## 4. Familiar Concepts and Repeated Explanations:

Certain key microservices concepts—like API Gateways, CQRS (Command Query Responsibility Segregation), and Event Sourcing—are discussed multiple times in different chapters to show how they're implemented in various contexts across different cloud platforms. If you're already familiar with these concepts, you can skip over them and jump to the next topic, focusing on new material or platform-specific implementation details.

## 5. Code Snippets and Configurations:

The code snippets throughout the book use a variety of configurations, including **YAML, XML, and JSON,** depending on the specific needs of the service or cloud platform being explained. Additionally, code examples are written in **Java, Python, and C#** to illustrate implementation strategies. These are chosen based on ease of explanation and can be treated as pseudo-code for learning purposes. Feel free to adapt these snippets to your preferred programming language or platform as needed.

## 6. Cloud Service Reference Appendix:

At the end of the book, you will find an Appendix that lists the key services used in AWS, Azure, and GCP. This section serves as a quick reference guide, summarizing the various cloud services you can use when implementing microservices on these platforms. It's a great resource for reviewing cloud-specific options as you work through the book.

By tailoring your journey through this book to your specific needs, you can make the most of the content and develop a solid understanding of how to build microservices in the cloud—whether you're focused on AWS, Azure, GCP, or a combination of all three.

# TABLE OF CONTENTS

# CHAPTER 1. HISTORY AND EVOLUTION OF MICROSERVICES

Microservice architecture, often referred to as microservices, has become a dominant paradigm for building software systems. It represents a significant shift from the traditional monolithic architecture and offers a more flexible and scalable approach to developing and maintaining applications. The history and evolution of microservice architecture are intertwined with the broader history of software development, scaling challenges, and the demands of modern applications.

## Monolithic Architecture: The Predecessor

Before microservices gained prominence, most software systems were built using a monolithic architecture. In a monolithic system, all components—whether user interfaces, business logic, or databases—are packaged together into a single, tightly-coupled application. This approach worked well in the early days of software development when applications were relatively simple and the need for scalability, agility, and deployment speed was not as urgent.

**In monolithic architectures:**

- All functionality is developed and deployed as a single unit.
- Dependencies between components are tight.
- Scaling often involves duplicating the entire system, regardless of which part of the system is under strain.
- Continuous delivery is complex, as any update requires redeploying the entire system.

Over time, as software applications grew in complexity, several challenges with monolithic architecture began to emerge:

**Scalability**: Monolithic systems are difficult to scale horizontally. If a particular component needs more resources, the entire application must be scaled, which leads to inefficiencies.

**Development Bottlenecks**: In large teams, developers working on different parts of the system can face bottlenecks because changes in one area can affect the entire system.

**Long Deployment Cycles**: Deploying new features or updates requires redeploying the whole application, increasing the risk of failures and making continuous deployment difficult.

The limitations of monolithic systems led to the search for more modular, scalable, and maintainable approaches, setting the stage for the rise of microservice architecture.

## Service-Oriented Architecture (SOA): A Precursor

The journey towards microservices began with Service-Oriented Architecture (SOA), a design principle that emerged in the early 2000s. SOA sought to address the challenges of monolithic systems by breaking down large systems into smaller, reusable services that could be combined to create a larger system. Each service in SOA was designed to perform a specific function and could communicate with other services through standard protocols like SOAP (Simple Object Access Protocol).

The key features of SOA include:
**Loose Coupling**: Services in SOA are loosely coupled, meaning changes in one service do not necessarily impact others.
**Service Reusability**: Services can be reused across different applications or business processes.
**Interoperability**: SOA emphasized using common communication protocols to allow services built on different technologies to interact.

However, while SOA introduced modularity and reusability, it still had limitations:

**Complexity**: SOA systems often involved complex governance models, with the need for centralized coordination through an Enterprise Service Bus (ESB).

**Heavyweight Protocols**: The use of SOAP and XML in SOA introduced performance overhead, making the architecture slower and harder to scale in some cases.

**Tight Governance**: SOA's focus on reusability often led to rigid governance rules that could slow down development and innovation.

Although SOA helped in breaking systems into smaller components, it was not agile enough to meet the rapidly changing demands of modern software development. This led to the development of a more granular and lightweight approach: microservices.

## The Rise of Microservices: Evolution and Core Principles

The term "microservices" was first popularized around 2011-2012 by thought leaders in the software development community, including Martin Fowler and James

Lewis. However, the architectural principles underlying microservices had been evolving for a number of years, particularly within large-scale companies like Amazon and Netflix that faced significant scaling challenges.

Microservices architecture is characterized by:

**Decentralization**: Each service is developed, deployed, and managed independently. This allows teams to build and maintain their services autonomously without relying on a central, shared database or infrastructure.

**Single Responsibility**: Microservices follow the principle of single responsibility, meaning each service is designed to do one thing and do it well. This leads to smaller, more focused codebases that are easier to maintain.

**Communication via APIs**: Microservices typically communicate over lightweight protocols such as HTTP/REST, gRPC, or messaging queues, reducing overhead compared to SOA's SOAP/XML.

**Independent Deployment**: Each service can be deployed independently, allowing for faster release cycles, continuous deployment, and better isolation of failures.

**Polyglot Programming**: Microservices allow teams to choose the best tool or programming language for the job, encouraging the use of different technologies for different services.

**Scalability**: Services can be scaled independently based on the demand of specific functionality, reducing the need for scaling the entire system.

The shift to microservices addressed many of the limitations seen in monolithic architectures:

**Faster Development Cycles**: With independent services, teams can release updates more frequently without disrupting the entire system.

**Improved Fault Isolation**: Since each service is isolated, failures in one service are less likely to impact the whole system.

**Scalable and Efficien**t: Microservices can be scaled independently, optimizing resource use.

# Adoption of Microservices in Industry

Microservices architecture has emerged as a powerful paradigm in the software development world, reshaping how applications are designed, deployed, and managed. It is a departure from traditional monolithic architectures, characterized by decomposing applications into loosely coupled, independently deployable services. Over the past decade, microservices have gained significant traction across various industries, driven by the need for agility, scalability, and resilience in rapidly evolving digital ecosystems. This essay explores the key factors driving the adoption of microservices, the benefits and challenges associated with their implementation, industry case studies, and the future trends shaping their continued use.

### Drivers of Microservices Adoption

The adoption of microservices in the industry has been motivated by several key drivers that address the limitations of traditional monolithic architectures and respond to evolving business and technological requirements.

### Scalability and Performance Needs

With the growth of digital platforms, applications often need to handle massive volumes of users and transactions. Monolithic architectures struggle to meet these demands because scaling involves duplicating the entire application, even if only a specific component (such as a payment system) requires more resources. Microservices, on the other hand, allow scaling of individual services based on demand, providing a more efficient and flexible scaling solution. This capability is especially crucial for industries such as e-commerce, finance, and entertainment, where high traffic and performance are essential.

## Rapid Feature Delivery

The competitive nature of today's markets requires companies to release new features and updates at an accelerated pace. Monolithic systems typically have long development and deployment cycles, as even small changes in one part of the system require redeploying the entire application. Microservices, by decoupling components, enable independent development and deployment of services. This allows for faster iteration cycles, continuous deployment, and a more agile response to changing business needs.

## Decentralization and Flexibility in Development

In large organizations, development teams may specialize in different areas of the application. In a monolithic architecture, coordination among teams can be challenging, with bottlenecks occurring as changes in one part of the system impact others. Microservices facilitate decentralized development by enabling teams to work autonomously on individual services. This autonomy promotes flexibility in choosing the most appropriate tools, languages, and databases for each service, leading to more innovation and tailored solutions.

## Resilience and Fault Isolation

In a monolithic system, a failure in one part of the application can potentially bring down the entire system. Microservices, with their isolated services, reduce this risk. A failure in one service (e.g., the recommendation engine of an e-commerce platform) is less likely to affect other services (e.g., payment processing), improving overall system resilience. This fault isolation is crucial for industries that require high availability and uptime, such as finance, healthcare, and telecommunications.

## Cloud-Native and Containerization Ecosystem

The rise of cloud computing and containerization technologies (such as Docker and Kubernetes) has made microservices easier to adopt. These tools provide the infrastructure for deploying, managing, and scaling microservices efficiently. Cloud platforms like AWS, Microsoft Azure, and Google Cloud offer native support for microservices architectures, including automated scaling, orchestration, and monitoring features.

## Benefits of Microservices in Industry

The shift towards microservices offers numerous benefits that align with the operational and strategic goals of businesses.

## Improved Scalability

Microservices allow organizations to scale specific components of an application independently, optimizing resource allocation. For example, in a video streaming service, the video delivery service might require more resources than the user authentication service. Microservices enable horizontal scaling, allowing organizations to scale individual services based on demand rather than scaling the entire system, thereby reducing costs and improving performance.

## Faster Time-to-Market

In industries where speed is a competitive advantage, microservices offer the agility needed to innovate and release features quickly. By allowing small, cross-functional teams to work on independent services, microservices reduce the dependencies and coordination efforts that often slow down development in monolithic systems. This faster development cycle allows companies to respond to customer feedback more rapidly, experiment with new features, and bring products to market faster.

### Resilience and High Availability

Microservices promote the concept of "design for failure," where systems are built to handle partial failures without causing a complete system outage. By isolating services, microservices ensure that the failure of one service does not necessarily affect the entire system. This resilience is particularly valuable in sectors like finance or healthcare, where system downtime can lead to significant financial losses or critical service disruptions.

### Technological Flexibility

With microservices, teams are free to use the best tools and languages suited to each service's requirements. For example, a machine learning service might be implemented in Python using specialized libraries, while another service might use Java for high-performance transaction processing. This polyglot programming approach enables organizations to leverage the most appropriate technologies for specific problems, fostering innovation and optimizing performance.

### Easier Maintenance and Upgrades

Microservices promote a modular approach to software development, where each service can be maintained and upgraded independently. This isolation makes it easier to refactor or replace outdated services without affecting the entire application. As a result, long-term maintenance becomes more manageable, and technical debt is reduced.

## Challenges in Adopting Microservices

Despite their benefits, adopting microservices comes with challenges that organizations must address to succeed.

## Increased Complexity

Microservices introduce significant operational complexity compared to monolithic systems. Managing numerous independent services, each with its own lifecycle, deployment, and dependencies, requires advanced tooling and orchestration. Organizations must invest in robust DevOps practices, automated testing, and monitoring tools to manage this complexity effectively.

## Data Management and Consistency

In a monolithic system, a single database is often used for all components, making it relatively easy to maintain data consistency. In microservices, each service typically manages its own database, leading to challenges in ensuring data consistency across services. Distributed transactions are complex and can introduce latency, and organizations must adopt strategies like eventual consistency and event-driven architectures to address this challenge.

## Latency and Network Overhead

Microservices rely on network communication between services, which introduces latency and can impact performance, particularly for real-time applications. Additionally, the increased number of network calls between services can introduce network overhead, requiring optimization strategies such as caching and efficient API design.

## Cultural and Organizational Shifts

Adopting microservices often requires not only technical changes but also organizational and cultural shifts. Traditional siloed teams need to adopt a more collaborative, cross-functional approach, with developers, operations, and QA teams working closely together. This shift to a DevOps culture can be challenging for organizations accustomed to traditional development models.

## Industry Case Studies

Several leading companies have adopted microservices to address their unique challenges, offering insights into the effectiveness of this architecture.

### Netflix

Netflix is one of the most prominent examples of successful microservices adoption. As the company transitioned from a DVD rental service to a global streaming platform, its monolithic architecture could no longer handle the scale and complexity required for millions of simultaneous users. By adopting microservices, Netflix was able to break down its monolith into hundreds of services that could be independently developed, deployed, and scaled. This allowed the company to innovate rapidly, improve reliability, and maintain high availability, even during peak usage periods.

### Amazon

Amazon's transition to microservices is another well-documented case. In the early 2000s, Amazon faced scalability challenges as its e-commerce platform grew. The company moved from a monolithic architecture to a service-oriented architecture (SOA), which eventually evolved into microservices. By breaking down its platform into small, independently managed services, Amazon improved its ability to scale, innovate, and maintain high availability. The flexibility offered by microservices has allowed Amazon to introduce new features rapidly and scale its infrastructure efficiently.

### Spotify

Spotify, the global music streaming platform, adopted microservices to handle the complexity of managing millions of songs, playlists, and user interactions. By using microservices, Spotify was able to scale its platform, ensure resilience, and support rapid feature development. The company's focus on autonomous development teams, known as "squads," enabled it to align its organizational structure with the microservices architecture, promoting faster innovation and better alignment with business goals.

## Future Trends in Microservices Adoption

As microservices continue to evolve, several trends are shaping their future adoption in the industry.

### Serverless and Function-as-a-Service (FaaS)

Serverless computing is a natural extension of microservices, allowing organizations to deploy functions without managing underlying infrastructure. Platforms like AWS Lambda and Azure Functions enable organizations to build applications as collections of functions that scale automatically. This shift toward serverless architecture simplifies operations and further reduces the overhead of managing microservices infrastructure.

### Edge Computing

As applications increasingly move closer to the user, microservices are being deployed at the edge of the network. This trend is particularly relevant in industries like IoT, where latency and real-time processing are critical. Edge computing, combined with microservices, allows organizations to process data closer to where it is generated, improving performance and reducing latency.

### Service Meshes

Service mesh technology, such as Istio and Linkerd, is gaining traction as a way to manage the communication, security, and observability of microservices. Service meshes provide a layer of infrastructure that handles service-to-service communication, making it easier to manage large-scale microservices deployments, improve security, and monitor performance.

The adoption of microservices architecture in the industry has been driven by the need for scalability, agility, and resilience in the face of increasing digital complexity. By breaking down monolithic applications into smaller, independent services, organizations can scale more efficiently, innovate faster, and improve system resilience. However, the adoption of microservices comes with challenges, including increased complexity, data consistency issues, and the need for cultural shifts within organizations. Despite these challenges, the benefits of microservices, combined with advancements in cloud-native tools, containerization, and serverless computing, make them a key architectural pattern for modern software development. As industries continue to embrace digital transformation, microservices will likely remain central to building scalable, agile, and resilient applications.

# CHAPTER 2. THE SERVICE ORIENTED ARCHITECTURE

Service-Oriented Architecture (SOA) is a software design paradigm that emphasizes the creation and use of loosely coupled services to build software systems. It emerged as a response to the growing complexity of enterprise applications and the need for greater flexibility, scalability, and reuse of components across systems. SOA represents a significant shift from traditional monolithic architectures, where software systems were often tightly coupled and difficult to change.

## The Origins and Evolution of SOA

### Pre-SOA Era: Monolithic Systems

Before the advent of SOA, most enterprise systems were built as monolithic applications. In monolithic architectures, all components of an application—such as user interfaces, business logic, and data access layers—were packaged and deployed as a single unit. While this approach worked well for small or simple applications, it became problematic as systems grew in size and complexity. Monolithic systems often exhibited several challenges:

- Tight Coupling: Components were highly dependent on each other, making it difficult to modify one part of the system without affecting others.

- Scalability Issues: Scaling monolithic systems required replicating the entire application, leading to inefficiencies in resource use.

- Slow Development Cycles: Any change required rebuilding and redeploying the entire system, which slowed down the release of new features and updates.

**The Rise of SOA**

SOA was developed in response to these limitations in the early 2000s. It aimed to decouple various parts of a software system into individual services, each performing a specific business function. These services could communicate with each other over a network using standardized protocols, such as HTTP, SOAP (Simple Object Access Protocol), or REST (Representational State Transfer). SOA represented a more modular and scalable approach to building complex applications, particularly in enterprise environments where integration across multiple systems was a common requirement.

## Core Principles of SOA

SOA is built on several key principles that define its architecture and functioning:

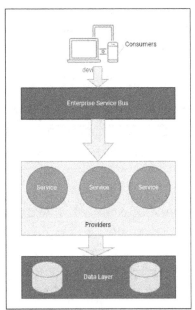

**2.1 Service oriented architecture**

## Loose Coupling

One of the primary goals of SOA is to reduce the dependencies between different services, which is known as loose coupling. Each service in an SOA system operates independently and can be developed, deployed, and maintained separately from other services. Changes to one service, such as updates or bug fixes, should have minimal impact on other services, enabling greater flexibility and easier maintenance.

## Service Abstraction

Services in SOA are treated as black boxes, meaning that their internal workings are hidden from the consumer. A service's functionality is exposed through a well-defined interface, usually via a set of publicly available operations. This abstraction allows consumers to interact with services without needing to understand their underlying implementation, which promotes flexibility and reuse.

## Service Reusability

A key benefit of SOA is that services are designed to be reusable across multiple applications. By defining services around business functions (e.g., customer management, order processing), organizations can leverage these services in different contexts without the need to rewrite code. This principle reduces duplication of effort and encourages consistent business logic across applications.

## Interoperability

SOA promotes the use of open standards for communication between services. This allows services to be built using different technologies, platforms, or programming languages, as long as they adhere to common communication protocols (e.g., SOAP, REST, XML, or JSON). Interoperability is essential for integrating systems across diverse technology stacks, making SOA particularly valuable in large enterprise environments with legacy systems.

## Standardized Service Contracts

Every service in an SOA architecture follows a formal contract that defines its capabilities, inputs, outputs, and behavior. This contract acts as an agreement between the service provider and consumers, ensuring that both parties understand how the service operates and how to interact with it. Standardized contracts also facilitate easier integration of services from different vendors or platforms.

## Discoverability

In SOA, services are designed to be easily discoverable within an organization's service registry. A service registry acts as a centralized directory where service descriptions and endpoints are stored. Consumers can search for services within the registry based on their functionality or business needs, enabling dynamic discovery and integration.

## SOA Architecture and Key Components

SOA architecture can be broken down into several key components that work together to deliver its benefits:

### Services

The core building blocks of SOA are services, which are self-contained, reusable units of functionality that perform a specific business process. Services communicate with one another over a network, typically using web protocols. These services can range from simple data retrieval operations to complex business transactions.

### Service Registry

The service registry is a critical component of SOA that stores metadata about available services, including their endpoints and descriptions. It acts as a centralized directory where services are published, making it easier for other systems to discover and consume them. Universal Description, Discovery, and Integration (UDDI) is an example of a protocol used for implementing a service registry in SOA.

### Service Consumer

A service consumer is any application or system that interacts with a service. The consumer sends requests to a service through its published interface and receives responses based on the service's functionality. Consumers could be end-user applications, other services, or even external systems.

### Service Provider

The service provider is the entity responsible for creating and maintaining the service. It defines the service's contract and publishes it to the service registry, making it available for consumption. Providers are also responsible for ensuring that services meet agreed-upon quality of service (QoS) standards.

## Enterprise Service Bus (ESB)

An ESB is often a crucial component in SOA implementations, acting as a middleware layer that facilitates communication between services. The ESB handles tasks such as routing, message transformation, protocol translation, and service orchestration. By managing these tasks centrally, the ESB simplifies service integration, particularly in large-scale, complex systems.

## Orchestration and Choreography

In SOA, services can be composed into higher-level processes through orchestration and choreography. Orchestration involves a central controller, often referred to as a workflow engine, that coordinates the interactions between multiple services to achieve a specific business outcome. Choreography, on the other hand, is a decentralized approach where each service knows its role in the interaction and operates independently, without a central controller.

# Benefits of SOA

SOA offers numerous benefits, particularly for large organizations that need to manage complex, heterogeneous IT environments.

## Improved Flexibility and Agility

One of the primary advantages of SOA is that it allows organizations to respond more quickly to changing business needs. By breaking down systems into modular services, organizations can update or replace individual components without disrupting the entire system. This flexibility is especially valuable in industries where rapid adaptation to market trends or regulatory changes is required.

## Reusability

The reuse of services is a major benefit of SOA. Services designed around common business functions (e.g., customer data management) can be reused across multiple applications or departments, reducing duplication of effort and ensuring consistency across the organization. This reusability helps organizations save time and resources by avoiding the need to create redundant services for different applications.

## Interoperability and Integration

SOA facilitates integration across diverse systems, platforms, and technologies by using standard communication protocols. This is particularly valuable for organizations with legacy systems that need to integrate with modern applications. SOA's ability to bridge the gap between different technology stacks makes it an ideal solution for large enterprises with complex IT environments.

## Scalability

SOA supports the scaling of services independently, allowing organizations to allocate resources where they are most needed. For example, if a service handling payment processing experiences high demand, it can be scaled independently of other services like inventory management. This targeted scalability helps optimize resource use and improve system performance.

## Ease of Maintenance

Since services are modular and independent in SOA, maintaining and updating them is easier compared to monolithic systems. Changes to one service do not affect others, reducing the risk of introducing bugs or system failures during updates. This modularity also makes it easier to test individual services, improving the overall quality of the system.

# Challenges in SOA Implementation

Despite its benefits, implementing SOA comes with challenges that organizations must address to succeed.

### Complexity of Governance

SOA introduces complexity in governance, particularly when it comes to managing the lifecycle of services. Organizations must implement strict governance policies to ensure that services are correctly versioned, documented, and comply with security and performance standards. Failure to manage these aspects effectively can lead to service sprawl, where too many services exist, making it difficult to manage them efficiently.

### Performance Overhead

While SOA improves flexibility and scalability, the use of multiple services communicating over a network introduces performance overhead. The need for message transformation, routing, and protocol translation can slow down system performance, particularly when dealing with large volumes of data or real-time transactions. Organizations must carefully design their SOA systems to minimize this overhead.

### Security Concerns

In an SOA environment, services are exposed to external consumers, making security a critical concern. Each service must be secured against potential threats, including unauthorized access, data breaches, and denial-of-service attacks. Implementing consistent security measures across all services and ensuring secure communication between services is a complex but necessary task.

### Cultural and Organizational Shifts

Adopting SOA often requires significant changes to an organization's culture and processes. Traditional development teams need to adapt to a more service-oriented mindset, focusing on the design, reuse, and integration of services. This shift can be challenging for organizations accustomed to working with monolithic systems, and may require retraining and restructuring of teams.

# Modern Relevance of SOA

While SOA has been a foundational architecture for enterprise applications over the past two decades, its prominence has been somewhat overshadowed by newer architectural patterns such as microservices. However, SOA remains highly relevant in many large organizations, particularly those with complex legacy systems and the need for robust integration solutions.

### SOA vs. Microservices

Microservices architecture, which emphasizes smaller, more granular services, can be seen as an evolution of SOA. While both architectures promote the use of services, microservices typically focus on finer-grained, independently deployable services, whereas SOA tends to involve larger, more comprehensive services. However, SOA's principles of loose coupling, service reusability, and interoperability remain fundamental in both architectures.

### SOA in the Cloud

The rise of cloud computing has given new life to SOA, particularly in the context of hybrid cloud and multi-cloud environments. SOA's emphasis on interoperability and standardized communication protocols makes it well-suited for integrating on-premise systems with cloud-based services. Many organizations are now leveraging SOA principles to build cloud-native applications and integrate legacy systems with cloud platforms.

Service-Oriented Architecture (SOA) represents a significant shift in how enterprise applications are designed and built. By decoupling systems into independent, reusable services, SOA offers numerous benefits, including improved flexibility, scalability, and interoperability. Despite the challenges of governance, performance, and security, SOA has proven to be an effective architecture for large organizations with complex IT environments.

As the software development landscape continues to evolve, SOA remains a foundational architecture that informs newer paradigms like microservices. In particular, SOA's emphasis on modularity, reusability, and loose coupling continues to influence the design of modern software systems, particularly in cloud and hybrid environments. While microservices may be more suited for highly granular, independently deployable services, SOA continues to provide a robust solution for large-scale enterprise applications where integration, scalability, and flexibility are key concerns.

# CHAPTER 3.
# CLOUD NATIVE

## Cloud Nativity: The Evolution of Modern Application Development

Cloud nativity is a software development approach that takes full advantage of cloud computing platforms, allowing applications to be built, deployed, and run in a way that leverages the scalability, flexibility, and resilience of the cloud. It represents a fundamental shift from traditional, on-premises infrastructure models to modern architectures designed specifically for cloud environments. The cloud-native approach has rapidly transformed the way applications are developed and deployed, enabling businesses to innovate faster, scale efficiently, and meet the ever-evolving demands of the digital landscape.

## The Origins of Cloud Nativity

### The Rise of Cloud Computing

The concept of cloud computing emerged in the mid-2000s as a response to the limitations of traditional IT infrastructure. Instead of building and maintaining costly on-premises data centers, organizations began using cloud services provided by third-party vendors like Amazon Web Services (AWS), Microsoft Azure, and Google Cloud. These cloud platforms offered on-demand access to computing resources such as storage, processing power, and networking, enabling businesses to scale their IT operations without the need for significant upfront investment.

The first wave of cloud adoption involved migrating existing applications to cloud infrastructure, a practice known as "lift and shift." While this allowed organizations to take advantage of the cloud's elasticity and cost-effectiveness, these applications were not designed to fully exploit the cloud's capabilities.

## The Birth of Cloud-Native Development

As cloud platforms matured, organizations began to recognize the limitations of simply migrating monolithic applications to the cloud. These applications, often designed for on-premises environments, were difficult to scale, lacked fault tolerance, and were challenging to update in an agile manner. To address these challenges, the concept of cloud-native development was introduced.

Cloud-native applications are built from the ground up to run in cloud environments. They embrace architectural patterns and practices that are optimized for the cloud, such as microservices, containers, serverless computing, and continuous delivery pipelines. The goal is to create applications that are scalable, resilient, and flexible, enabling organizations to innovate faster and respond more quickly to changes in the market.

## Key Principles of Cloud Nativity

Cloud-native development is guided by several core principles that differentiate it from traditional software development approaches:

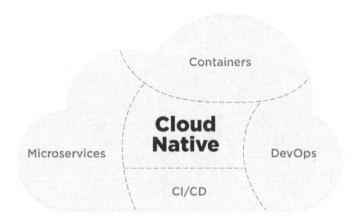

**3.1 Cloud Native**

## Microservices Architecture

At the heart of cloud-native development is the microservices architecture, where applications are broken down into smaller, independently deployable services. Each microservice performs a specific business function and communicates with other services through APIs. This decoupling of services allows for greater flexibility, as individual services can be developed, deployed, and scaled independently.

Microservices also promote agility in software development. By allowing different teams to work on separate services simultaneously, organizations can accelerate the development process and deploy new features more frequently without impacting the entire system.

## Containerization

Containers play a crucial role in cloud-native development by providing a lightweight, portable environment for running applications. A container packages an application and its dependencies into a single, self-contained unit that can run consistently across different environments. This eliminates the "it works on my machine" problem that often arises when moving applications between development, testing, and production environments.

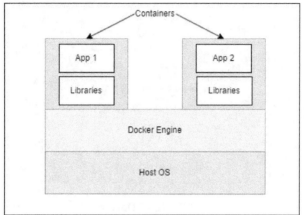

**3.2 Containerization**

Docker is the most widely used containerization platform, and Kubernetes, an open-source container orchestration platform, has become the de facto standard for managing and scaling containerized applications in cloud-native environments. Kubernetes automates tasks such as load balancing, scaling, and rolling updates, enabling organizations to manage complex microservices architectures at scale.

**DevOps and Continuous Delivery**

Cloud-native development emphasizes the integration of DevOps practices, which bridge the gap between development and operations teams. DevOps promotes collaboration, automation, and continuous feedback, allowing for faster, more reliable software delivery.

Continuous delivery (CD) is a key practice in cloud-native environments. It involves automating the process of deploying code changes to production, ensuring that applications can be updated frequently and with minimal risk. Continuous integration (CI) tools are used to automatically test and integrate code changes, enabling organizations to maintain a high level of software quality while accelerating the release cycle.

### Infrastructure as Code (IaC)

Infrastructure as Code (IaC) is a practice that allows infrastructure to be defined, managed, and provisioned through code, rather than manual processes. By using code to automate the setup and management of infrastructure, organizations can achieve consistency, repeatability, and scalability in cloud environments. IaC tools like Terraform, AWS CloudFormation, and Ansible enable developers to treat infrastructure as part of the application development process, improving collaboration between development and operations teams.

### Automation and Orchestration

Automation is a cornerstone of cloud-native development. In cloud-native environments, everything from infrastructure provisioning to application deployment is automated. This reduces human error, speeds up processes, and ensures consistency across environments.

Orchestration tools like Kubernetes manage the lifecycle of containerized applications, including deployment, scaling, and monitoring. By automating complex tasks, orchestration simplifies the management of large-scale microservices architectures, enabling organizations to focus on delivering business value rather than managing infrastructure.

### Resilience and Fault Tolerance

Cloud-native applications are designed to be resilient and capable of handling failures gracefully. By distributing services across multiple cloud instances, regions, or even providers, cloud-native applications can continue operating even in the event of hardware failures or outages. Techniques such as circuit breakers, retry mechanisms, and graceful degradation ensure that applications remain available even when individual services fail.

# Cloud-Native Architectural Patterns

Several architectural patterns are commonly associated with cloud-native development, enabling organizations to build scalable, resilient, and flexible applications:

## Microservices

As previously mentioned, microservices architecture is foundational to cloud-native development. It involves decomposing applications into smaller, autonomous services that can be developed, deployed, and scaled independently. Each microservice is responsible for a specific piece of business logic and communicates with other services via APIs or messaging systems.

## Serverless Computing

Serverless computing is a cloud-native architectural pattern that abstracts away infrastructure management, allowing developers to focus solely on writing code. In a serverless model, developers define individual functions that are executed in response to specific events (e.g., an API request or database update). Cloud providers like AWS Lambda, Google Cloud Functions, and Azure Functions automatically scale these functions and charge based on execution time, providing a cost-efficient way to build applications.

Serverless computing is particularly useful for applications with variable or unpredictable workloads, as it eliminates the need to provision and manage servers.

## Event-Driven Architecture

In an event-driven architecture, services communicate by producing and consuming events. This pattern is well-suited to cloud-native environments because it promotes loose coupling between services and supports asynchronous communication. For example, in an e-commerce application, an "order placed" event might trigger multiple downstream processes, such as updating inventory, sending a confirmation email, and initiating payment processing.

Event-driven architectures are often used in conjunction with messaging systems like Apache Kafka, RabbitMQ, or cloud-native services like AWS EventBridge.

### Service Mesh

A service mesh is a dedicated infrastructure layer that manages service-to-service communication in a microservices architecture. Service meshes provide features such as load balancing, traffic routing, security (e.g., encryption and authentication), and observability (e.g., monitoring and logging) for microservices. Tools like Istio and Linkerd are popular service mesh solutions that help manage the complexity of large-scale microservices deployments.

## Benefits of Cloud-Native Development

The adoption of cloud-native development offers numerous benefits for organizations, enabling them to innovate faster, scale efficiently, and improve resilience:

### Scalability

Cloud-native applications are designed to scale horizontally, meaning that new instances of services can be added or removed based on demand. This ensures that applications can handle large volumes of traffic without over-provisioning resources. Cloud platforms provide auto-scaling features that allow applications to automatically adjust resource allocation based on usage patterns.

### Agility and Faster Time-to-Market

By adopting cloud-native practices such as microservices,

DevOps, and continuous delivery, organizations can significantly accelerate the software development lifecycle. Cloud-native applications can be updated frequently, enabling businesses to respond quickly to changing market conditions and customer needs. This agility gives organizations a competitive edge in industries where speed to market is critical.

## Cost Efficiency

Cloud-native applications are cost-efficient because they allow organizations to pay only for the resources they use. Instead of provisioning resources for peak demand, organizations can dynamically scale resources based on actual usage, reducing wasted capacity. Serverless computing further enhances cost efficiency by charging only for the execution time of individual functions.

## Resilience and High Availability

Cloud-native applications are inherently resilient due to their distributed nature. By deploying services across multiple instances, regions, or even cloud providers, organizations can ensure high availability and fault tolerance. When one component of the system fails, others continue to operate, minimizing downtime and ensuring a seamless user experience.

## Portability

Cloud-native applications, particularly those that use containers, are highly portable. Containers encapsulate an application and its dependencies, allowing it to run consistently across different environments. This portability enables organizations to avoid vendor lock-in and deploy applications across multiple cloud providers or hybrid environments.

## Automation and Efficiency

Automation is a key enabler of cloud-native development. By automating infrastructure provisioning, testing, deployment, and scaling, organizations can achieve greater efficiency

and reduce the risk of human error. Automation also enables teams to focus on higher-value activities, such as writing code and developing new features.

## Challenges of Cloud-Native Development

Despite its many advantages, cloud-native development comes with challenges that organizations must address to be successful:

### Increased Complexity

Cloud-native architectures, particularly those based on microservices, can be more complex to manage than monolithic applications. With many independent services interacting across distributed environments, organizations need to invest in robust monitoring, logging, and observability tools to gain visibility into the system's performance and troubleshoot issues.

### Security Concerns

In cloud-native environments, security must be built into every layer of the application, from the code itself to the infrastructure it runs on. With microservices, organizations need to secure the communication between services and ensure that sensitive data is protected across distributed systems. Cloud providers offer various security tools and services, but organizations must still implement best practices such as encryption, authentication, and access control.

### Cultural and Organizational Changes

Adopting cloud-native development often requires significant cultural and organizational changes. Development and operations teams must work closely together to implement

DevOps practices and automate the software delivery process. Organizations may also need to retrain teams or hire new talent with expertise in cloud-native technologies and practices.

# The Future of Cloud Nativity

As cloud computing continues to evolve, so too will cloud-native development. Several trends are shaping the future of cloud-native computing:

### Multi-Cloud and Hybrid Cloud

Many organizations are adopting multi-cloud and hybrid cloud strategies, where applications are deployed across multiple cloud providers or a combination of on-premises and cloud environments. Cloud-native applications, with their emphasis on portability and scalability, are well-suited to these strategies, enabling organizations to avoid vendor lock-in and optimize their cloud resources.

### AI and Machine Learning Integration

As artificial intelligence (AI) and machine learning (ML) become increasingly integrated into business processes, cloud-native platforms are evolving to support these workloads. Cloud providers offer AI and ML services that can be easily integrated into cloud-native applications, allowing organizations to build intelligent applications that leverage advanced data analytics, automation, and predictive capabilities.

### Edge Computing

Edge computing is an emerging trend where data processing occurs closer to the source of data generation, such as IoT devices or local data centers, rather than in a central cloud. Cloud-native principles are being extended to edge environments, enabling organizations to build distributed, cloud-native applications that operate at the edge while maintaining the benefits of scalability and resilience.

Cloud nativity represents a transformative approach to software development that fully leverages the capabilities of modern cloud computing platforms. By embracing principles such as microservices architecture, containerization, DevOps, and automation, organizations can build applications that are scalable, resilient, and flexible. Cloud-native development enables faster innovation, cost-efficient scaling, and improved resilience, making it a key driver of digital transformation in today's fast-paced business environment.

While cloud-native development introduces new complexities and challenges, its benefits far outweigh these difficulties, particularly for organizations that are committed to adopting best practices and investing in the necessary tools and expertise. As cloud technologies continue to evolve and new trends like multi-cloud, AI integration, and edge computing emerge, cloud nativity will remain at the forefront of modern application development, shaping the future of how software is built and deployed.

# CHAPTER 4. THE MICROSERVICES ARCHITECTURE

Microservice architecture has become one of the most influential architectural styles in modern software development. It is an approach that decomposes large, monolithic applications into smaller, loosely coupled, independently deployable services, each responsible for a specific piece of functionality. This allows for greater flexibility, scalability, and resilience in software systems, making it ideal for building complex and evolving applications.

## Understanding Microservice Architecture

Microservices are a way of designing software applications as a collection of independently deployable services, where each service corresponds to a distinct business capability. Each microservice runs in its own process, has its own database (or data management system), and communicates with other microservices through lightweight protocols, often using HTTP/REST, gRPC, or messaging queues.

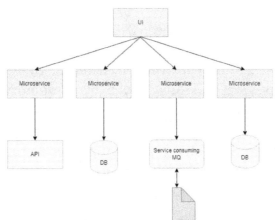

**4.1 Microservices architecture**

## Key Characteristics of Microservices

- Independently Deployable: Each microservice can be developed, tested, and deployed without affecting other services. This enables teams to release new features or bug fixes frequently and safely.

- Single Responsibility: A microservice is typically responsible for one specific business functionality, such as managing customer data, processing orders, or handling payments. Each microservice focuses on doing one thing well, making the system more modular and maintainable.

- Loose Coupling: Microservices are loosely coupled, meaning they have minimal dependencies on each other. They interact using well-defined APIs or messaging protocols, ensuring that changes in one service don't necessitate changes in others.

- Scalability: Microservices enable horizontal scaling. Individual services can be scaled independently based on their demand, ensuring that resources are efficiently utilized.

- Polyglot Persistence: Each microservice can use its own database and technology stack. This allows teams to use the best tool for the job, whether that's a relational database, NoSQL store, or even an in-memory cache.

## Monolith vs. Microservices

In a monolithic architecture, all components of an application are tightly coupled and deployed as a single unit. For example, in an e-commerce platform, the catalog, user management, payment, and inventory systems are all part of the same codebase and deployed together. This creates a few challenges:

- Lack of Flexibility: Changes to any one part of the system require redeploying the entire application.
- Scaling Limitations: Scaling a monolith often means scaling the entire application, even when only one component needs more resources.
- Tight Coupling: Since components are tightly integrated, changes in one module can affect others, leading to longer development cycles.

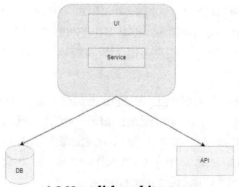

**4.2 Monolith architecture**

By contrast, in microservices, each of these components (catalog, user management, payment, etc.) would be separate services, independently developed and deployed, which leads to greater flexibility, scalability, and agility.

# Common Design Patterns in Microservices Architecture

To build effective microservice-based systems, several design patterns are used to address the common challenges that arise. These patterns provide guidance on structuring, deploying, and interacting between services.

### API Gateway Pattern

In the API Gateway pattern, a single entry point is provided for all client requests. Rather than clients interacting directly with multiple microservices, the API Gateway routes requests to the appropriate backend services, aggregates data, and returns a unified response. It can also handle cross-cutting concerns like authentication, logging, rate-limiting, and monitoring.

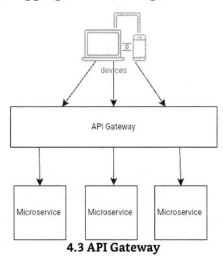

**4.3 API Gateway**

**Example** In an e-commerce platform, the API Gateway can route requests for product details to the catalog service, order processing requests to the order service, and payment requests to the payment service.

**Benefit** Simplifies client interactions, centralizes cross-cutting concerns, and provides flexibility for evolving backend services without affecting the client.

**Database per Service Pattern**

Each microservice in a microservices architecture has its own database, leading to a pattern known as Database per Service. This pattern enforces the principle of autonomy, allowing services to manage their own data independently. This avoids the tightly coupled data schema that monoliths tend to suffer from.

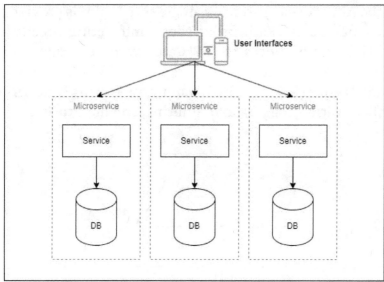

4.4 Database per service pattern

**Example** A microservices system for an online marketplace might have one database for the order management service, another for the inventory service, and a third for the user service.

**Benefit** Independent scalability and isolation, which improves fault tolerance and ensures that changes to one service's database do not impact others.

**Circuit Breaker Pattern**

The Circuit Breaker pattern helps prevent cascading failures in a microservices architecture. When one service fails, it can cause failures in other services that depend on it. The Circuit Breaker pattern prevents services from continuously making requests to a failing service by opening a "circuit" and returning a fallback response.

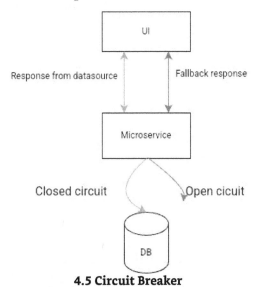

**4.5 Circuit Breaker**

**Example**: If the payment service in an e-commerce platform is unavailable, the order service can return a fallback response indicating that the payment system is down and allow the user to try again later.

**Benefit**: Improves the system's resilience by preventing failures from propagating and overwhelming the entire system.

### Service Discovery Pattern

In a microservices architecture, services are dynamic—they can be added or removed, or their locations can change. The Service Discovery pattern helps services find and communicate with each other by providing a registry where services can register themselves and look up other services dynamically.

- Example: When a user places an order, the order service can look up the address of the inventory and payment services via the service discovery registry before interacting with them.

- Benefit: Enables services to remain loosely coupled and scalable, even as new instances are added or removed.

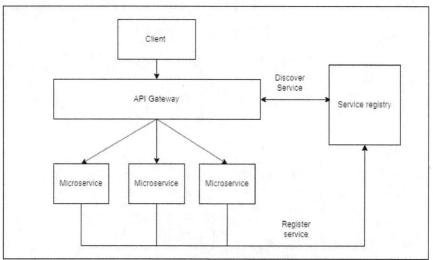

**4.6 Service discovery pattern**

**Event-Driven Pattern**

The Event-Driven pattern is often used to enable loose coupling between services. In this pattern, services communicate by publishing events that other services subscribe to. This allows services to be unaware of each other's implementation and operate asynchronously.

**Example**: In a ride-sharing application, when a user requests a ride, an event like "ride requested" is published. This event can be consumed by different services, such as the driver matching service, ride-tracking service, and payment service.

**Benefit**: Decouples services, enabling scalability and flexibility, especially when new services are added to the system without changing existing ones.

### Saga Pattern

The Saga pattern is used to manage distributed transactions in microservices. Instead of relying on a central transaction manager, each service in the transaction performs its part and sends a message to the next service. If any part of the transaction fails, compensating transactions are triggered to undo the previous work.

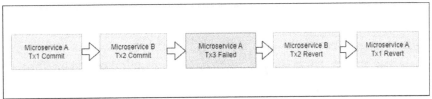

**4.7 SAGA Pattern**

**Example**: In an online booking system, a flight reservation service might need to book both a flight and a hotel. If the hotel booking fails, the flight booking is canceled via a compensating transaction.

**Benefit**: Provides a way to handle long-running business transactions in a distributed system without the need for two-phase commit protocols.

## Advantages of Microservices Architecture

### Faster Development and Deployment

Microservices enable independent development and deployment of services, allowing multiple teams to work on different components of the application simultaneously. This accelerates development cycles, enabling faster time to market for new features.

### Scalability

Each microservice can be scaled independently based on demand. For example, in an e-commerce platform, the inventory service might need to handle more traffic than the payment service, so it can be scaled accordingly without impacting other parts of the system.

### Fault Isolation

Microservices enhance fault isolation, meaning that if one service fails, the others remain unaffected. For example, if the recommendation service in a streaming platform fails, users can still stream videos without interruption.

### Technology Flexibility

Since microservices are loosely coupled, each service can use the most appropriate technology stack, whether that's a particular programming language, database, or framework. This flexibility enables teams to choose the best tools for their specific use cases.

### Easier Maintenance and Updates

By breaking down the application into smaller, independent services, it becomes easier to maintain and update individual parts of the system without needing to understand or modify the entire codebase.

## Challenges in Microservices

### Increased Complexity

While microservices offer many benefits, they also introduce complexity. Managing multiple services, each with its own database, deployment pipeline, and communication mechanisms, can be challenging.

### Network Latency

In a microservices architecture, communication between services happens over the
network, which introduces latency and the potential for network failures. Organizations must implement strategies

like caching, load balancing, and retries to minimize the impact.

## Data Consistency

Since each microservice manages its own data, ensuring data consistency across services can be challenging, particularly in distributed transactions. Patterns like Saga help, but they introduce their own complexity.

## Monitoring and Debugging

With multiple services running in production, monitoring and debugging becomes more difficult. Organizations need sophisticated monitoring, logging, and tracing tools to gain visibility into the interactions between services.

Microservice architecture has emerged as a powerful approach for building complex, scalable, and maintainable applications. By decomposing large monolithic systems into smaller, autonomous services, organizations can achieve greater agility, scalability, and fault tolerance. However, adopting microservices also introduces new challenges in terms of managing distributed systems, ensuring data consistency, and handling network communication.

The various patterns—like API Gateway, Circuit Breaker, Event-Driven, and Saga—provide valuable tools for addressing these challenges and optimizing microservice architectures. Despite the complexity, the benefits of microservices, particularly in terms of enabling fast-paced development and scalable architectures, make it a popular choice for many organizations, especially those operating at scale like Netflix, Amazon, and Spotify.

Ultimately, microservice architecture is not a one-size-fits-all solution, but when used appropriately, it can unlock significant advantages in software development, offering the flexibility, resilience, and agility needed in today's dynamic technological landscape.

# Microservices architecture using Google cloud platform (GCP)

The microservice architecture paradigm has gained immense popularity for its ability to decompose monolithic applications into smaller, independently deployable services. Organizations are increasingly adopting this approach to build scalable, flexible, and resilient systems. One of the most powerful cloud platforms to support the development, deployment, and management of microservices is Google Cloud Platform (GCP).

GCP offers a comprehensive set of tools, services, and infrastructure that are specifically designed to simplify the implementation of microservices architecture.

**Overview of Microservices and Google Cloud Platform (GCP)**

Microservices architecture involves breaking down large, monolithic applications into smaller, independent services, each focusing on a specific business function. These microservices communicate via lightweight protocols such as HTTP/REST, gRPC, or messaging systems like Pub/Sub. The benefits of microservices include independent scalability, faster deployment cycles, enhanced fault isolation, and easier maintenance.

Google Cloud Platform (GCP) is a suite of cloud computing services that runs on the same infrastructure Google uses for its own products, such as Gmail, YouTube, and Google Search. GCP provides a range of services for deploying microservices, from container orchestration to serverless computing, data storage, networking, and monitoring.

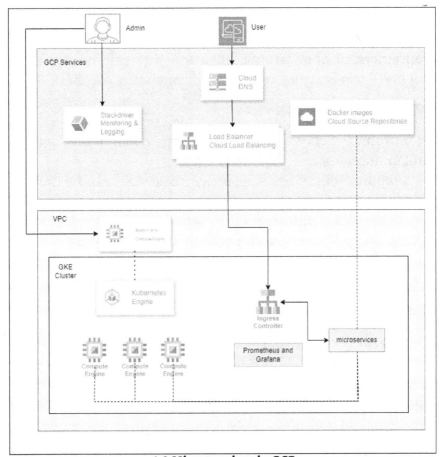

**4.8 Microservices in GCP**

## Key GCP Services for Microservices

GCP offers a variety of services that cater to different needs within a microservice architecture. These services help with deployment, orchestration, scaling, communication, storage, and monitoring of microservices.

### Google Kubernetes Engine (GKE)

Google Kubernetes Engine (GKE) is one of the most popular services for deploying and managing microservices. It is a managed Kubernetes service that automates much of the infrastructure management associated with running containers in a microservices architecture. Kubernetes, originally developed by Google, provides orchestration for containerized applications, ensuring that microservices are deployed in a scalable, reliable, and consistent manner.

## Why GKE for Microservices

 - Automates container management, deployment, scaling, and maintenance.
 - Supports rolling updates, so microservices can be updated with zero downtime.
 - Provides auto-scaling, which allows individual microservices to scale automatically based on traffic.
 - Manages service discovery, enabling microservices to dynamically locate and communicate with one another.

## Cloud Run

Cloud Run is a fully managed serverless platform that allows developers to run containers without having to manage infrastructure. It abstracts away the complexities of server and cluster management, enabling teams to focus on building and deploying their microservices.

## Why Cloud Run for Microservices:

 - Fully managed and serverless, so there is no need to manage clusters or servers.
 - Supports auto-scaling from zero to thousands of instances based on traffic.
 - Can run any container, which makes it language and framework-agnostic.
 - Provides built-in integration with other GCP services like Pub/Sub, Cloud Functions, and Cloud Storage.

## Cloud Functions

Google Cloud Functions is a serverless compute service that allows developers to run event-driven microservices in response to events. It is particularly well-suited for implementing small, isolated functions within a broader microservices architecture.

## Why Cloud Functions for Microservices:

- Event-driven, allowing microservices to be triggered by events such as Pub/Sub messages, HTTP requests, or database updates.
- Serverless, scaling automatically based on demand.
- Ideal for lightweight, stateless functions that handle specific tasks within a microservices architecture.

## Cloud Pub/Sub

Google Cloud Pub/Sub is a messaging service that enables microservices to communicate asynchronously. It decouples producers from consumers, allowing services to interact without needing to be aware of each other's presence or state.

## Why Cloud Pub/Sub for Microservices

- Asynchronous messaging ensures microservices can communicate without being tightly coupled.
- Supports real-time message delivery and scalability, handling millions of messages per second.
- Guarantees "at least once" message delivery, ensuring reliable communication between microservices.

## Google Cloud API Gateway

The Google Cloud API Gateway enables developers to create, secure, and monitor APIs for their microservices. API Gateways are critical in microservices architecture as they provide a single entry point for external consumers to interact with multiple microservices.

## Why API Gateway for Microservices:

- Manages routing, security, and versioning of APIs across multiple microservices.

- Centralizes cross-cutting concerns like rate limiting, authentication, logging, and monitoring.
- Simplifies the client-side experience by exposing a unified API for interacting with multiple backend services.

## Google Cloud SQL and Firestore

For microservices requiring persistent data storage, GCP provides several options:

Cloud SQL is a managed relational database service that supports MySQL, PostgreSQL, and SQL Server. Each microservice can have its own instance to manage its data independently, following the "Database per Service" pattern.

Firestore is a NoSQL document database that scales horizontally and offers real-time synchronization, making it ideal for event-driven and real-time applications within a microservices architecture.

## Cloud Monitoring and Logging

Google Cloud Monitoring and Cloud Logging are essential for observing, troubleshooting, and optimizing microservices in production. They provide deep insights into how services are performing and how they are interacting with one another.

## Why Cloud Monitoring and Logging for Microservices

- Provides real-time metrics and logs for monitoring microservices health and performance.
- Supports distributed tracing, making it easier to identify bottlenecks and failure points across microservices.
- Integrates with other GCP services like GKE and Cloud Run for end-to-end visibility into service performance.

## Patterns for Implementing Microservices on GCP

Several architectural patterns are commonly used when implementing microservices on GCP. These patterns help address challenges like service communication, resilience, scaling, and transaction management.

**API Gateway Pattern**

The API Gateway acts as a single entry point for clients to access multiple microservices. It handles API requests, routes them to the appropriate microservices, and aggregates responses if necessary.

**Example on GCP:** The Google Cloud API Gateway can be used to route external client requests to various backend services deployed on GKE, Cloud Run, or Cloud Functions.

**Event-Driven Pattern**

In an Event-Driven Architecture, microservices communicate through events instead of direct API calls. This pattern decouples services, improving scalability and fault tolerance.

Example on GCP: Using Cloud Pub/Sub, microservices can publish events to a topic and have other services consume those events asynchronously. For example, an e-commerce platform might publish events like "order placed" or "payment processed," which are consumed by other services like inventory and shipping.

**Circuit Breaker Pattern**

The Circuit Breaker Pattern prevents cascading failures in a microservices architecture. If a service fails, the circuit breaker "trips" and prevents subsequent calls to the failing service, returning a fallback response instead.

Example on GCP: GCP provides support for circuit breakers through third-party libraries like Hystrix or via service meshes like Istio. Istio can be integrated with GKE to manage circuit-breaking, retries, and timeouts for services.

**Saga Pattern**

The Saga Pattern is used to manage distributed transactions across multiple microservices. Instead of relying on a central transaction manager, each microservice performs its part of the transaction and triggers the next service.

Example on GCP: In an order-processing system, a sequence of services might handle order placement, payment, inventory, and shipping. If any of these services fail, compensating actions are triggered to roll back the preceding operations.

## Real-World Use Cases of Microservices on GCP

### Spotify

Spotify, the popular music streaming service, relies on microservices to manage a wide variety of functions such as playlist management, music recommendations, and user preferences. Spotify uses GCP services like GKE and Pub/Sub to ensure its services are decoupled, scalable, and resilient.

### Snapchat

Snapchat uses Google Cloud Platform to run its backend services. Snapchat's ephemeral messaging system is built on microservices that use GKE for container orchestration and Pub/Sub for real-time event streaming between services.

### Khan Academy

Khan Academy, a platform offering free educational resources, uses GCP's microservices architecture to manage large-scale deployments and ensure smooth user experience across multiple regions. Khan Academy leverages GKE to deploy microservices and Cloud SQL for persistent data storage.

## Benefits of Using GCP for Microservices

### Scalability

With services like GKE, Cloud Run, and Cloud Functions, GCP

provides automatic scaling based on demand. Microservices can scale horizontally without manual intervention.

## Cost Efficiency

GCP offers pay-as-you-go pricing, meaning organizations only pay for the resources they use. Serverless offerings like Cloud Run and Cloud Functions also scale down to zero, reducing costs during idle times.

## Developer Productivity

GCP's integration with CI/CD pipelines, managed infrastructure, and robust monitoring tools enables faster development, deployment, and debugging, allowing developers to focus on building features rather than managing infrastructure.

## Security

GCP offers robust security measures, including Identity and Access Management (IAM), Virtual Private Cloud (VPC), and Cloud Armor for protecting services from external threats. API Gateway and other security features can be used to secure communication between microservices and clients.

## Challenges and Considerations

Despite the advantages, deploying microservices on GCP comes with challenges:

1. **Complexity**: Managing multiple services, each with its own deployment, scaling, and monitoring needs, can add complexity.
2. **Service Communication**: Microservices require efficient communication mechanisms, and handling inter-service communication and data consistency can be tricky.
3. **Latency**: When services communicate over the network, latency issues may arise. It's crucial to use

caching and load balancing strategies effectively.

Google Cloud Platform provides an ideal ecosystem for building, deploying, and managing microservices at scale. With services like GKE, Cloud Run, Pub/Sub, and API Gateway, developers can easily build scalable, resilient, and cost-effective microservices architectures. Although challenges such as complexity and inter-service communication remain, the rich set of tools and patterns offered by GCP ensures that teams can overcome these obstacles effectively.

The flexibility and power of microservices on GCP make it a compelling choice for organizations looking to modernize their applications and deliver highly scalable, resilient solutions.

## Microservice architecture in Azure

In Azure, implementing a microservice architecture involves leveraging various services and features to build, deploy, and manage these distributed components efficiently.

Here's a detailed description of how microservice architecture can be implemented in Azure:

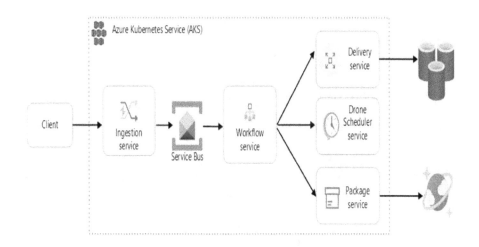

**4.9 Microservices in Azure**

# Service Design and Development

### Azure App Services

- Azure Web Apps: You can deploy your microservices as web applications using Azure App Services, which provides a fully managed platform with built-in scaling and patching.
- Azure Functions: For lightweight, event-driven microservices, Azure Functions allows you to write serverless functions that respond to triggers such as HTTP requests, queues, or timers.

### Azure Kubernetes Service (AKS)

Containerized Microservices: AKS is a managed Kubernetes service that simplifies deploying, managing, and scaling containerized applications using Docker. It's ideal for managing a microservices architecture with complex deployments.

### Azure Container Instances (ACI)

Lightweight Containers: For scenarios where you need quick, isolated environments for your microservices, ACI provides a serverless container service.

## Service Communication

### Azure API Management

API Gateway: Acts as a gateway for your microservices, handling routing, rate limiting, security, and analytics. It helps to manage and expose APIs in a secure and scalable manner.

### Azure Service Bus

Messaging: A fully managed message broker that supports asynchronous messaging between services. It ensures reliable communication, message queuing, and event handling.

### Azure Event Grid

Event-Driven Architecture: Facilitates event-based communication between microservices, allowing for scalable and decoupled event handling.

### Azure Relay

Hybrid Connectivity: Provides secure communication between cloud and on-premises services, allowing microservices to interact across different network environments.

## Service Discovery and Load Balancing

### Azure Application Gateway

Load Balancer: Provides built-in load balancing, SSL termination, and application firewall capabilities to distribute traffic among your microservices.

### Azure Traffic Manager

Global Traffic Distribution: Distributes incoming traffic across multiple Azure regions to ensure high availability and reliability.

**Azure Service Fabric**
Service Management: Offers built-in service discovery and load balancing capabilities for microservices, along with state management and resiliency features.

## Monitoring and Logging

**Azure Monitor**
Comprehensive Monitoring: Collects metrics, logs, and diagnostics data from your microservices. It includes application insights, which provide deep insights into application performance and user behavior.

**Azure Log Analytics**
Centralized Logging: Aggregates logs and provides analytics capabilities to query and analyze log data from various sources.

## Security

**Azure Active Directory (AAD)**
Authentication and Authorization: Provides identity management and access control for your microservices. It supports OAuth, OpenID Connect, and other authentication protocols.

**Azure Key Vault**
Secrets Management: Stores and manages sensitive information such as API keys, passwords, and certificates securely.

**Azure Security Center**
Threat Protection: Offers unified security management and advanced threat protection across your microservices and other Azure resources.

## Deployment and CI/CD

### Azure DevOps
Continuous Integration/Continuous Deployment (CI/CD): Provides a suite of DevOps tools for automating the build, test, and deployment processes of your microservices.

### GitHub Actions
CI/CD Pipelines: Integrates with GitHub for building and deploying microservices, enabling automated workflows and deployments.

## Data Management

### Azure Cosmos DB
Distributed Database: A globally distributed, multi-model database service that supports various data models and provides low-latency access, making it ideal for microservices.

### Azure SQL Database
Managed Relational Database: Provides a fully managed relational database with high availability and scaling capabilities.

### Azure Blob Storage
Object Storage: Stores large amounts of unstructured data, such as logs, files, and backups.

By leveraging these Azure services, you can build a robust, scalable, and resilient microservice architecture that can handle various business requirements and workloads efficiently.

# Microservice architecture in AWS

AWS provides a wide array of tools and services that help to build, deploy, and manage microservices efficiently. Here's a detailed breakdown of how microservice architecture can be implemented in AWS:

# Service Design and Development

### Amazon Elastic Container Service (ECS)

Container Orchestration: ECS is a fully managed container orchestration service that allows you to run Docker containers. It helps manage containerized microservices on either AWS Fargate (serverless) or Amazon EC2 (with control over underlying instances).

### Amazon Elastic Kubernetes Service (EKS)

Kubernetes on AWS: EKS is AWS's managed Kubernetes service, which simplifies running containerized microservices using Kubernetes, an open-source orchestration system. It helps with scaling, monitoring, and managing microservices deployed in Kubernetes clusters.

### AWS Lambda

Serverless Microservices: AWS Lambda is a serverless computing service that allows you to run functions in response to events (e.g., HTTP requests, changes in data, etc.). Each function can act as a microservice, with AWS managing the infrastructure, scaling, and security.

### AWS Fargate

Serverless Containers: Fargate allows you to run containers without managing the underlying servers or clusters. It's integrated with ECS and EKS, enabling serverless execution of containerized microservices.

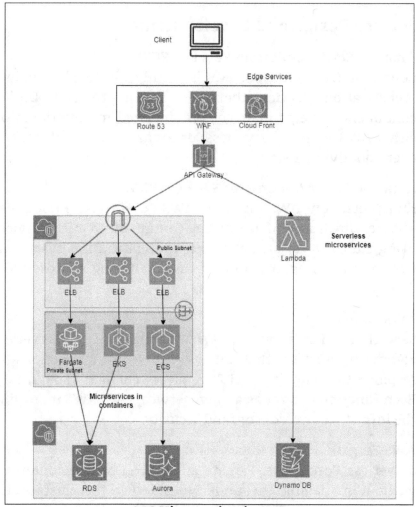

**4.10 Microservices in AWS**

# Service Communication

### Amazon API Gateway

API Management: API Gateway acts as a front door for your microservices, enabling you to create, publish, maintain, monitor, and secure APIs at scale. It provides routing, throttling, and authorization for your microservices.

### Amazon Simple Queue Service (SQS)

Asynchronous Messaging: SQS is a fully managed message queuing service that enables reliable, asynchronous communication between microservices. It's often used for decoupling and handling long-running processes.

### Amazon Simple Notification Service (SNS)

Pub/Sub Messaging: SNS provides a publish-subscribe messaging service that allows microservices to communicate asynchronously using message topics and subscribers.

### AWS App Mesh

Service Mesh: App Mesh helps microservices communicate by managing service discovery, traffic routing, and monitoring across different environments. It abstracts the networking logic so that each service can communicate reliably and securely with others.

### Amazon EventBridge

Event-Driven Communication: EventBridge provides a serverless event bus to connect microservices using events. It's used to route events from AWS services, SaaS providers, or your applications to other AWS services.

## Service Discovery and Load Balancing

### AWS Cloud Map

Service Discovery: Cloud Map provides service discovery for microservices by dynamically registering instances as they become available and enabling other services to discover them using DNS or API-based queries.

### Elastic Load Balancing (ELB)

Traffic Distribution: ELB helps distribute incoming traffic across multiple microservices running on Amazon EC2, ECS, EKS, or Lambda. It supports application load balancing (ALB) for HTTP/HTTPS traffic and network load balancing (NLB) for TCP/UDP traffic.

### AWS Route 53

DNS-Based Service Discovery: Route 53, AWS's DNS service, helps to route end-user traffic to microservices deployed across multiple regions or availability zones, ensuring high availability.

## Monitoring and Logging

### Amazon CloudWatch
Monitoring and Alerts: CloudWatch provides real-time monitoring of logs, metrics, and events generated by your microservices. It also allows for the creation of dashboards and automated alarms based on specific thresholds or metrics.

### AWS X-Ray
Distributed Tracing: X-Ray provides end-to-end tracing for microservices, giving visibility into the request flow, latency, and errors across services. This is especially useful in troubleshooting and performance optimization.

### Amazon OpenSearch Service (formerly Elasticsearch Service)
Centralized Logging: OpenSearch allows centralized logging and search capabilities for logs generated by microservices, helping to debug issues and analyze performance data.

## Security

### AWS Identity and Access Management (IAM)
Access Control: IAM manages permissions and access to AWS resources, ensuring secure interactions between microservices. You can define fine-grained access control policies to restrict permissions at the service level.

### AWS Secrets Manager
Secrets Management: Secrets Manager helps securely store and manage access credentials such as API keys, passwords, and database credentials. It also rotates secrets automatically.

### Amazon Cognito

Authentication and Authorization: Cognito provides authentication for users of microservices, supporting OAuth 2.0, OpenID Connect, and SAML for integrating with other identity providers.

### AWS WAF (Web Application Firewall)

Security Protection: WAF protects your microservices against common web exploits and vulnerabilities such as SQL injection and cross-site scripting.

# Continuous Integration and Continuous Delivery (CI/CD)

### AWS CodePipeline

CI/CD Automation: CodePipeline automates the build, test, and deployment processes for microservices. It integrates with various services like CodeBuild, CodeDeploy, and third-party tools like Jenkins.

### AWS CodeBuild

Build Automation: CodeBuild is a fully managed service that compiles your code, runs tests, and produces software packages that are ready for deployment.

### AWS CodeDeploy

Automated Deployments: CodeDeploy automates the deployment of applications (including microservices) to Amazon EC2, ECS, and Lambda, ensuring zero-downtime or blue/green deployments.

### AWS CodeCommit

Version Control: CodeCommit is a fully managed source control service that hosts Git repositories for storing your code and versioning changes.

## Data Management

### Amazon RDS

Relational Database: RDS provides fully managed relational

databases such as MySQL, PostgreSQL, and Oracle. It's often used when microservices need transactional data management.

### Amazon DynamoDB

NoSQL Database: DynamoDB is a fully managed, serverless NoSQL database that is scalable, offering low-latency and high throughput, making it suitable for event-driven microservices.

### Amazon S3

Object Storage: S3 is a highly durable and scalable object storage service for storing unstructured data, such as images, logs, backups, and large datasets.

## Resilience and Scaling

### Auto Scaling

Dynamic Scaling: Auto Scaling adjusts the number of instances of microservices based on demand, ensuring optimal resource utilization and cost-efficiency.

### Amazon EC2 Auto Scaling

Compute Auto Scaling: Automatically adjusts the number of Amazon EC2 instances in response to incoming traffic, ensuring that the microservices run efficiently during high or low demand periods.

### Amazon Aurora

Highly Scalable Database: Aurora is a managed relational database that automatically scales its storage and read capacity to accommodate your microservice needs without manual intervention.

By leveraging these AWS services, you can build a robust and scalable microservice architecture that is adaptable to changes in load, easy to manage, and resilient to failures. This architecture also supports flexibility in service development, deployment, and operations.

# CHAPTER 5. DOMAIN DRIVEN DESIGN AND DECOMPOSITION PATTERN

Domain-Driven Design (DDD) is a software design approach that focuses on modeling software systems based on the complex, real-world domains they represent. In the context of microservices architecture. DDD plays a critical role in determining how to decompose a large, complex system into smaller, well-structured services. DDD ensures that the boundaries between microservices are aligned with the core business concepts and processes, resulting in services that are more maintainable, scalable, and aligned with the business needs.

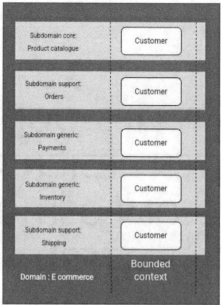

**5.1 Domain driven design**

# Key Concepts of Domain-Driven Design in Microservices

### 1. Domain

A domain refers to the business problem that your software is trying to solve. In microservices, each service focuses on a specific area of the domain, handling a particular business capability.

Example: In an e-commerce system, domains could include "Order Management," "Inventory," "Customer Support," etc.

### 2. Subdomains

A large domain is often divided into smaller, more manageable subdomains, each handling a distinct part of the business logic.

Subdomains are categorized into:

- **Core Subdomain:** The part of the domain that provides the most business value and is usually the differentiator for the business. Example: In an e-commerce system, the "Order Management" system could be a core subdomain.

- **Supporting Subdomain:** These subdomains support the core domain but are not as critical. Example: "Customer Support" in the same e-commerce system could be a supporting subdomain.
- **Generic Subdomain:** These are common across many systems and can often be off-the-shelf solutions. Example: "Billing" or "Authentication."

## 3. Bounded Contexts:

- Bounded contexts are one of the core principles of DDD, and they refer to distinct boundaries within the domain where a particular model is defined and used.
- In microservices, each bounded context can be mapped to one or more services. The model (and its rules) within a bounded context should not "leak" into another context, which enforces loose coupling between services.

**Example:** The "Customer" concept in a "Billing" service might mean something different than in a "Customer Relationship Management (CRM)" service. Each service operates in its own bounded context with its own data model, which avoids conflicts or confusion.

## 4. Entities and Value Objects:

- Entities: Objects in the domain that have a unique identity and life cycle. In microservices, entities are often persisted in the data storage of a service.

Example: In an "Order Service," the "Order" entity would be uniquely identified by an order ID and have a lifecycle that could include states like "Created," "Shipped," and "Completed."

- Value Objects: Objects that don't have a distinct identity but represent descriptive aspects of the domain.

In microservices, value objects are often passed between services.

Example: In an "Order Service," an "Address" could be a value object that is part of an order but doesn't have an identity on its own.

## 5. Aggregates and Aggregate Roots:

- Aggregates: These are clusters of related entities and value objects that are treated as a single unit within a bounded context. Aggregates encapsulate the domain logic and help maintain consistency within the microservice.
- Aggregate Root: The single entry point to an aggregate. In microservices, the aggregate root manages the lifecycle of the aggregate and ensures that the aggregate remains in a consistent state.

Example: In an "Order Service," an "Order" might be the aggregate root, with related entities like "Order Line Items" and value objects like "Shipping Address" being part of the aggregate.

## 6. Repositories:

A repository is responsible for persisting and retrieving aggregate roots. In microservices, each service typically has its own repository or database. The repository pattern abstracts the data storage, allowing the microservice to operate without knowledge of the underlying data infrastructure.

Example: In an "Order Service," a repository would handle storing and retrieving order data.

## 7. Domain Events:

- Domain events represent significant occurrences within a domain that other parts of the system may need to react to. In microservices, domain events are often used for decoupled communication between services.

- Domain events are emitted when something important happens, such as an "Order Placed" event in an e-commerce system.

Example: The "Order Service" may emit an "OrderCreated" event when a new order is placed, and other microservices like the "Payment Service" or "Shipping Service" may listen for this event to trigger their own processes.

## 8. Command Query Responsibility Segregation (CQRS):

CQRS is a pattern that splits the responsibilities of reading and writing data into separate models. In a microservices architecture, it helps handle complex domain logic by separating the command model (responsible for modifying state) from the query model (responsible for reading state).

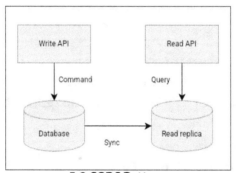

**5.2 CQRS Pattern**

Example: In an e-commerce application, an "Order Service" might have a command model for processing orders and a separate query model optimized for retrieving order details.

## 9. Event Sourcing:

In event sourcing, the state of an entity is stored as a sequence of events rather than as the current state in a database. This is often used in microservices to ensure that all state changes are traceable and replayable.

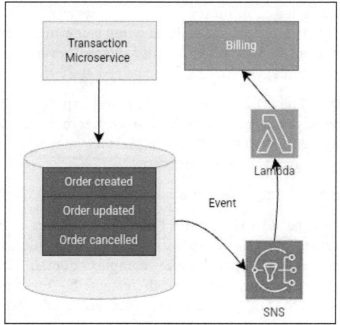

**5.3 Event sourcing**

Example: Instead of saving the current state of an order in a database, the system stores every event that has occurred for that order ("Order Created," "Payment Received," "Order Shipped"), and the current state can be rebuilt by replaying the events.

## How DDD Maps to Microservices:

### 1. Service Boundaries via Bounded Contexts:

One of the key contributions of DDD to microservices is the concept of bounded contexts. Each microservice is designed to operate within its own bounded context, meaning it owns its own data, logic, and model. By clearly defining bounded contexts, services avoid overlapping responsibilities, thus minimizing complexity.

Example: In an e-commerce platform, the "Order Service" would manage everything related to orders (e.g., creation, modification, cancellation) within its bounded context. The "Inventory Service" would manage stock levels independently, even though they interact during an order placement.

## 2. Clear Ownership of Data:

DDD encourages each microservice to have full control and ownership over its data, reducing dependencies and ensuring loose coupling. Data duplication may occur, but this is a common practice in microservice architectures to ensure autonomy.

Example: The "Order Service" might store customer shipping addresses independently from the "CRM Service," even though both are dealing with customer-related data.

## 3. Event-Driven Architecture with Domain Events:

- Domain events are a natural fit for communication between microservices. Instead of direct calls, services can publish events when something significant happens, and other services that are interested in those events can react accordingly.
- This approach ensures that services remain decoupled while still communicating in a reliable and scalable way.

Example: When an order is created, the "Order Service" publishes an "OrderCreated" event. The "Inventory Service" listens to the event and reserves items, and the "Shipping Service" may start processing shipment.

## 4. Microservices Representing Aggregates:

In DDD, aggregates represent clusters of related objects. Microservices often map to aggregates, encapsulating all related entities and value objects within a bounded context.

Example: The "Order Service" could be responsible for the "Order" aggregate, which includes related entities like "Order Line Items," "Shipping Address," and "Payment Details." The aggregate root (Order) ensures the consistency of all these objects.

## 5. Handling Complexity with CQRS and Event Sourcing:

- CQRS and event sourcing can help manage the complexity of a distributed system by decoupling the read and write models and by providing a complete history of changes to an entity.
- Event sourcing ensures that all microservices have access to a reliable event log, which can be used for auditing or re-building the current state of an entity.

Example: The "Order Service" might use CQRS to split the process of updating order status (writing) from retrieving order history (reading). It could also implement event sourcing to record all changes to an order for future auditing.

## 6. Isolation of Business Logic:

Each microservice in DDD encapsulates its own business logic. This helps ensure that changes in one area of the system do not impact other parts.

Example: The "Payment Service" encapsulates all payment-related logic, including refunds, fraud checks, and payment processing. Changes to this logic do not affect the "Order Service" or the "Shipping Service."

## Benefits of Using DDD in Microservices

## 1. Alignment with Business:

DDD ensures that microservices are designed around business capabilities, making the system more intuitive and aligned with real-world processes.

## 2. Clear Service Boundaries:

DDD's concept of bounded contexts helps define clear boundaries between services, reducing the risk of overlap or tightly coupled services.

### 3. Scalability:

By breaking down the system into smaller, well-defined services, DDD allows for independent scaling. Each service can be scaled based on its specific performance needs.

### 4. Flexibility:

With services being decoupled and designed around bounded contexts, changes to one service do not have cascading effects on others, making the system more flexible to evolve.

### 5. Resilience:

Since services are independent and communicate through events, failures in one service are less likely to impact the entire system.

## Challenges of DDD in Microservices:

**1. Complexity in Understanding the Domain:** The success of DDD depends on a deep understanding of the business domain, which requires close collaboration between developers and domain experts.

**2. Distributed Data Management:** DDD encourages data ownership within microservices, which can lead to challenges in maintaining consistency across services.

**3. Overhead of Event-Driven Communication:** While domain events provide decoupling, they can add complexity in terms of event handling, eventual consistency, and error handling in distributed systems.

**4. Over-Engineering Risks:** Without careful planning, DDD concepts can lead to over-complication, especially if too many domain events or aggregates are introduced without a clear need.

Domain-Driven Design provides a valuable framework for building microservices that are aligned with business needs, maintainable, and scalable. By leveraging concepts like bounded contexts, aggregates, domain events, and CQRS, microservices can be designed to handle complex business logic while remaining loosely coupled and autonomous. However, DDD requires careful implementation and a deep understanding of the business domain to ensure that the architecture does not become overly complex or fragmented.

# Decomposition pattern

The decomposition pattern of microservices involves breaking down a monolithic application into smaller, independent services, where each microservice is responsible for a specific, well-defined business capability. Decomposition is crucial in a microservice architecture as it defines how to split an application into smaller units that can be developed, deployed, and scaled independently. This process must be well-planned to ensure that each service has clear boundaries, communicates effectively with other services, and adheres to principles such as loose coupling and high cohesion.

Two Major Decomposition Patterns for Microservices:

1. Decomposition by Business Capability (Domain-Driven Design)
2. Decomposition by Subdomain (Bounded Contexts)

Let's dive deeper into each.

### 1. Decomposition by Business Capability

In this pattern, the decomposition is driven by the core

business capabilities of the organization. The idea is to organize microservices around the key functional areas or modules of the business. Each microservice is responsible for a specific capability and contains all necessary logic to perform tasks related to that capability.

**Key Concepts:**

- Business Capabilities: A business capability is a specific function that an organization performs, such as customer management, billing, inventory, or order processing. Each capability becomes a candidate for a separate microservice.

- Self-Contained Services: Each microservice encapsulates all the functionality and data required for its business function. For example, the "Order Service" might handle all aspects of order creation, modification, and deletion.

**Benefits:**

- Alignment with Business: This pattern aligns the technical architecture with the structure of the business, making it easier to evolve and scale over time.
- Autonomy: Each microservice is independent and can evolve separately. Teams responsible for different business capabilities can work autonomously.
- Flexibility in Technology: Since microservices are independent, each service can use the most appropriate technology stack, programming language, or database based on its specific requirements.

**Example:**

Consider an e-commerce application. It can be decomposed into microservices based on the following business capabilities:

- ➤ Order Service: Responsible for processing orders.
- ➤ Payment Service: Manages payment processing and

refunds.

➤ Inventory Service: Tracks inventory levels and restocking.

➤ Shipping Service: Handles shipment and delivery tracking.

Each service corresponds to a business capability and operates independently, handling the data and logic for its domain.

## 2. Decomposition by Subdomain (Bounded Contexts)

This pattern is closely related to Domain-Driven Design (DDD), where the domain (business area) is divided into multiple subdomains. The main idea here is to decompose the system into smaller, domain-specific microservices based on bounded contexts, which encapsulate different parts of the domain.

**Key Concepts:**
Subdomains: A subdomain is a specific part of the overall domain. In DDD, the domain is broken into core, supporting, and generic subdomains.

- **Core Subdomain:** The primary business area that differentiates the company (e.g., order processing in an e-commerce company).
- **Supporting Subdomain:** A domain that supports the core domain but is not as critical (e.g., reporting or analytics).
- **Generic Subdomain:** A domain common to many companies and can often be handled with off-the-shelf solutions (e.g., billing or user management).
- **Bounded Context:** A bounded context defines a clear boundary around a subdomain where a specific domain model applies. Each bounded context translates into one or more microservices.

**Benefits:**

- **Consistency within Boundaries:** Each bounded

context has its own model and ensures that concepts and business rules are consistent within the context.

- **Isolated Models:** Different microservices can use different models for the same concept, depending on their bounded context. For example, "Customer" in an ordering system may have different attributes than "Customer" in a CRM system.
- **Encapsulation of Complexity:** Complex subdomains can be encapsulated in their own bounded context, simplifying integration and communication with other services.

**Example:**

Consider a retail system with various subdomains:

- Order Management: Responsible for processing orders, cancellations, and returns.
- Customer Relationship Management (CRM): Manages customer profiles, loyalty points, and communications.
- Billing: Manages invoices and payments.

Each of these subdomains operates within its own bounded context and can be decomposed into separate microservices. The "Order Service" may focus on the core domain of the system, while "Billing Service" and "CRM Service" are supporting subdomains.

## Considerations in Decomposition

When decomposing a monolithic system into microservices, several critical factors need to be considered:

### 1. Service Boundaries

- **High Cohesion, Low Coupling:** Each microservice should encapsulate related functionality (high cohesion) and communicate with other services through well-defined APIs (low coupling). This ensures that changes in one service have minimal impact on others.

- **Data Ownership:** Each service should own its data store, preventing direct access to another service's database. All communication between services should happen via APIs or events.

## 2. Database Decomposition

- **Decentralized Data Management:** Each microservice manages its own database (polyglot persistence). For instance, the "Order Service" might use a relational database, while the "Inventory Service" might use NoSQL.
- **Data Consistency:** Achieving consistency across distributed services is challenging. Event-driven architectures or distributed transaction techniques (e.g., Saga Pattern) may be used to ensure eventual consistency.

## 3. Communication between Services

- Synchronous Communication: RESTful APIs are commonly used for synchronous communication. However, over-reliance on synchronous calls can lead to bottlenecks.
- Asynchronous Communication: Messaging services such as Kafka, RabbitMQ, or AWS SQS are used for decoupling services through asynchronous communication.
- Event-Driven: An event-driven approach, where services publish events to notify other services of changes (e.g., a "Order Created" event), is often employed to decouple services further.

## 4. Cross-Cutting Concerns

- **Authentication and Authorization:** Implement centralized security mechanisms (e.g., OAuth, JWT) using API gateways or service meshes to manage authentication and authorization across services.
- **Monitoring and Logging:** Distributed systems require

centralized logging (e.g., ELK Stack or AWS CloudWatch) and monitoring (e.g., Prometheus, Grafana) to track the behavior of individual services.

- **Service Discovery:** Service discovery tools (e.g., Consul, Eureka, or AWS Cloud Map) help microservices find each other dynamically.

## 5. Performance and Scalability

- Scalability: Microservices can be scaled independently based on their specific workload, ensuring that each service has the right amount of resources.

- Performance Optimization: Different services may require different performance tuning techniques based on their role in the system (e.g., cache for read-heavy services, optimized database queries for transaction-heavy services).

### Common Decomposition Challenges:

1. Over-Decomposition: Breaking down the system into too many small services can lead to complex orchestration, increased communication overhead, and management challenges.
2. Coupling through Shared Data: If multiple services access the same database tables or shared state, it introduces tight coupling, which negates the benefits of microservices.
3. Complexity in Coordination: Managing distributed transactions, consistency, and retries across multiple microservices can increase complexity, especially in scenarios where data consistency is critical.

The decomposition of microservices can be done using different patterns, mainly focusing on business capabilities or subdomains. A successful decomposition ensures that services are small, cohesive, and loosely coupled, while promoting independent development, deployment, and scaling. The key to microservice decomposition is identifying the right boundaries, ensuring effective communication, and managing cross-cutting concerns such as security and monitoring effectively. By aligning microservices with business domains and focusing on bounded contexts, organizations can achieve both agility and scalability.

# CHAPTER 6. API GATEWAY

An API Gateway is a crucial component in modern software architecture, particularly in microservices and cloud-native applications. It acts as a single entry point that handles requests, routing them to appropriate backend services, transforming data if needed, and managing concerns such as security, load balancing, and caching. Here's a detailed breakdown:

## Core Functionality

1. Routing: The API Gateway receives incoming requests and forwards them to the appropriate backend service. It routes based on the request's path, headers, or other criteria.
2. Protocol Translation: It can handle various communication protocols such as HTTP, WebSockets, gRPC, and more, converting between them as necessary. For example, an API Gateway can translate REST requests into gRPC calls or SOAP messages.
3. Load Balancing: API Gateways can distribute incoming traffic across multiple instances of a service, ensuring efficient use of resources and high availability.

## Routing

Routing is one of the core functionalities of an API Gateway, enabling the gateway to direct incoming client requests to the appropriate backend services. Routing via an API Gateway is crucial for managing traffic in distributed systems, especially in microservices architectures, where a single client request may need to interact with multiple services. Below is a detailed explanation of how routing works within an API Gateway.

## Basic Concept of Routing

In the context of an API Gateway, routing refers to the mechanism by which the gateway directs client requests to the correct backend service based on predefined rules. These rules can be based on various factors such as:

- **URL path**: The API Gateway inspects the URL path (e.g., `/api/orders`) and forwards the request to the corresponding service (e.g., the Orders Service).

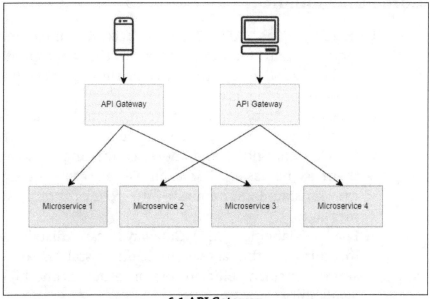

**6.1 API Gateway**

- **HTTP method**: Routing can also depend on the HTTP method (e.g., `GET`, `POST`, `PUT`, `DELETE`), so different actions can be taken for the same URL path depending on the method used.

- **Headers and Query Parameters**: Routing rules can inspect HTTP headers or query parameters to determine which service to forward the request to.

- **Body Content**: In some cases, the body of the request (such as JSON or XML) might influence routing decisions, such as when different services handle different content types.

## Routing Mechanisms and Strategies

Different routing mechanisms are implemented by API Gateways, depending on the complexity of the application. Some of the key routing strategies are:

a. **Path-based Routing**
- Definition: Requests are routed based on the URL path specified by the client.
    - Example:
        - `GET /api/users` → routed to the User Service.
        - `GET /api/orders` → routed to the Order Service.
- Use case: This is the most common routing mechanism for microservices where different URL paths correspond to different services.

b. **Host-based Routing**
- Definition: Routing decisions are made based on the hostname in the request. For instance, different domains or subdomains may map to different services.
    - Example:
        - `api.example.com` → routed to the Main API Service.
        - `billing.example.com` → routed to the Billing Service.

- Use case: Useful in scenarios where multiple services are exposed on different domains or subdomains, such as multi-tenant architectures or services with distinct subdomains.

## c. **HTTP Method-based Routing**

- Definition: Requests are routed based on the HTTP method used (e.g., `GET`, `POST`, `PUT`, `DELETE`).
- Example:
  - `GET /api/products` → routed to the Product Read Service.
  - `POST /api/products` → routed to the Product Write Service.
- Use case: This is commonly used when the same resource (e.g., `/api/products`) can perform different operations handled by different backend services.

## d. **Header-based Routing**

- Definition: Specific HTTP headers, such as `Authorization`, `User-Agent`, or custom headers, are used to decide the destination service.
- Example:
  - Requests with the header `X-API-Version: v1` → routed to API Version 1 Service.
  - Requests with the header `X-API-Version: v2` → routed to API Version 2 Service.
- Use case: This is useful for versioning APIs or managing different versions of the same service without changing the URL.

## e. **Query Parameter-based Routing**

- Definition: The API Gateway inspects query parameters in the URL and routes the request accordingly.
- Example:
  - `GET /api/search?q=books` → routed to the Books Search Service.
  - `GET /api/search?q=movies` → routed to the Movies Search Service.

- Use case: Ideal for services that perform similar operations but based on different query parameters, like search services or multi-category operations.

### f. **Content-based Routing**
- Definition: The API Gateway inspects the body or content of the request (e.g., a JSON payload) to make routing decisions.
- Example:
  - If the request body contains `"type": "order"`, route to the Order Service.
  - If the request body contains `"type": "invoice"`, route to the Billing Service.
- Use case: Useful in scenarios where the type of request or operation is embedded within the request body itself.

### g. **Weighted Routing (A/B Testing, Canary Releases)**
- Definition: Routing can be weighted across multiple versions of the same service, which is helpful in progressive rollouts or A/B testing.
- Example:
  - 80% of traffic routed to Service Version 1.
  - 20% of traffic routed to Service Version 2.
- Use case: Canary releases and A/B testing where a small percentage of traffic is directed to a new version of the service.

### h. **Geolocation-based Routing**
- Definition: The API Gateway routes requests based on the geographical location of the client, determined by IP address or headers.
- Example:
  - Requests from Europe are routed to a European Data Center.
  - Requests from the US are routed to a US Data Center.
- Use case: This is used to optimize latency and comply with data sovereignty laws.

## Routing to Microservices

In a microservices architecture, each service typically handles a specific domain or functionality. The API Gateway acts as a front door, routing requests to individual microservices behind it. Since microservices often interact with each other, the gateway can also implement service discovery, helping to dynamically route requests as services are scaled, updated, or added.

- Service Discovery Integration: API Gateways can dynamically route to services by integrating with service discovery tools like Consul, Eureka, or Kubernetes. These tools help the gateway identify the current instances of the service and route requests accordingly.

## Health Checks and Failover

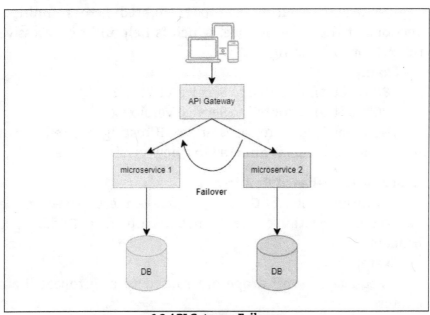

**6.2 API Gateway Failover**

- API Gateways often perform health checks on backend services to ensure they are available and functioning properly. If a service is unhealthy, the gateway can automatically route requests to a failover service or an alternate instance of the same service.

- Circuit Breaker Pattern: If a service is consistently failing, the gateway can stop sending requests to that service temporarily (tripping the circuit breaker) and instead return a predefined error or route to a fallback service.

## Error Handling and Retries

API Gateways can be configured to retry failed requests, route around failures, or return custom error messages to the client. For example, if a service times out, the gateway can retry the request to another instance or provide a custom error page to the user.

## API Gateway Configuration

API Gateways usually define routing rules through configuration files, administrative consoles, or APIs. Configuration can be static (written in a config file) or dynamic (using APIs or management consoles to update routing rules in real-time). In some cases, routing rules are stored in a database or service registry that the gateway consults.

## Examples of API Gateways Handling Routing

- **AWS API** Gateway: AWS API Gateway uses method-based routing and path-based routing. For example, you can set up API resources with HTTP methods like `GET /users` and `POST /users`, and map them to AWS Lambda functions or EC2 instances.

- **Kong API** Gateway: Kong supports a variety of plugins for path-based, header-based, and JWT-based routing, allowing flexible routing rules for modern API-driven applications.

- **NGINX as an API Gateway**: NGINX is often used as a reverse proxy and API Gateway, providing routing based on URL paths, headers, or methods. It also handles load balancing, SSL termination, and caching.

- **Istio Service Mesh**: Although not strictly an API Gateway,

Istio provides routing capabilities through its sidecar proxies, allowing for service-to-service routing, load balancing, and traffic shaping.

Routing via an API Gateway is essential for controlling and managing how client requests are distributed among backend services. The gateway acts as an intelligent traffic controller, leveraging a wide range of strategies such as path-based, method-based, and content-based routing. This functionality ensures that services are isolated, scalable, and can be upgraded or replaced without affecting the client-facing API.

# Protocol Translation

Protocol translation is a critical feature of an API Gateway that allows the gateway to act as an intermediary between clients and backend services that use different communication protocols. It essentially translates requests and responses from one protocol to another, enabling seamless interaction between systems that may not natively communicate in the same way.

In modern applications, especially those involving microservices, different services may use different protocols depending on their specific needs. An API Gateway that supports protocol translation can handle requests from clients in one protocol (e.g., HTTP) and convert them to another protocol (e.g., gRPC, WebSockets) that the backend services use, and vice versa.

Detailed Breakdown of Protocol Translation in API Gateways:

### 1. Common Protocols in Use
   - **HTTP/HTTPS:** The most common protocol for web APIs, especially in REST-based architectures.
   - **WebSockets:** A protocol providing full-duplex communication over a single TCP connection, useful for real-time applications like chat, gaming, and financial data

streaming.

- **gRPC:** A high-performance, open-source RPC (Remote Procedure Call) framework, often used in microservices because of its efficiency, use of protocol buffers, and native support for streaming.

- **SOAP (Simple Object Access Protocol):** A protocol based on XML used for web services, commonly found in older, enterprise environments.

- **MQTT (Message Queuing Telemetry Transport):** A lightweight messaging protocol, commonly used in IoT (Internet of Things) devices for low-bandwidth, high-latency networks.

## 2. How Protocol Translation Works

Protocol translation involves two main steps:

- **Request Translation:** The API Gateway receives a request from the client in one protocol, translates it into the protocol understood by the target backend service, and forwards the translated request.

- **Response Translation:** When the backend service responds, the API Gateway translates the response from the service protocol back into the client protocol and sends it to the client.

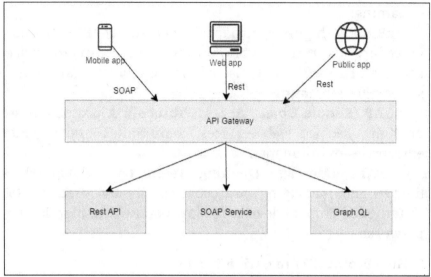

**6.3 API Gateway Protocol Translation**

## 3. Use Cases of Protocol Translation

### a. HTTP to gRPC Translation

- Scenario: A client sends a RESTful HTTP request to the API Gateway, but the backend microservices communicate using gRPC for better performance and lower overhead.

- Translation Process:

1. The API Gateway accepts the HTTP request.

2. It converts the HTTP payload (typically JSON) into a gRPC request, which may involve translating the JSON to Protocol Buffers (the data serialization format used by gRPC).

3. It forwards the gRPC request to the appropriate microservice.

4. The service processes the gRPC request and sends a gRPC response.

5. The gateway translates the gRPC response (typically serialized as Protocol Buffers) back into JSON and sends it to the client as an HTTP response.

- Example:
  - Client: `GET /users/123` (HTTP request)
  - Gateway translates this to a gRPC call to

`GetUser(user_id: 123)`.

## b. WebSockets to HTTP Translation

- Scenario: A real-time application (e.g., a stock trading app) requires constant data updates via WebSockets, but the backend service operates over RESTful HTTP APIs.

- Translation Process:

1. The API Gateway establishes a WebSocket connection with the client.

2. The client sends data or requests over the WebSocket connection.

3. The gateway translates these messages into standard HTTP requests to the backend service.

4. When the backend sends an HTTP response, the API Gateway translates it back into WebSocket messages and sends them to the client.

- Example: A real-time chat application where the frontend uses WebSockets for fast bi-directional communication, but the backend services are exposed via HTTP.

## c. HTTP to SOAP Translation

- Scenario: A modern application using RESTful HTTP APIs needs to interact with legacy systems that expose SOAP-based web services.

- Translation Process:

1. The API Gateway receives a RESTful HTTP request.

2. It generates a corresponding SOAP request with the appropriate XML format and required SOAP envelope headers.

3. The translated SOAP request is sent to the backend SOAP service.

4. The SOAP response (in XML format) is received by the gateway, translated back into JSON (or whatever format the client expects), and sent to the client as an HTTP response.

- Example: A customer information system that has an HTTP API on the frontend but needs to query a SOAP-based backend system to retrieve customer data.

### d. MQTT to HTTP Translation

- Scenario: An IoT device (such as a sensor) communicates with the API Gateway using MQTT, but the backend service supports only HTTP.
- Translation Process:

    1. The API Gateway receives an MQTT message.

    2. It converts the MQTT message (which may contain telemetry data, such as temperature readings) into an HTTP request.

    3. It forwards the translated HTTP request to the backend service, which processes it.

    4. The backend service returns an HTTP response, which the gateway translates back into an MQTT message to send to the IoT device.

- Example: Smart home devices that use MQTT to communicate with an API Gateway, which then routes the data to an HTTP-based backend that stores and processes the sensor data.

### 4. Key Components Involved in Protocol Translation

- Payload Conversion: Translating data between protocols often involves converting between different data formats. For example:

    - Converting JSON (commonly used in RESTful APIs) into Protocol Buffers (used in gRPC).

    - Converting XML (used in SOAP) into JSON (used in modern REST APIs).

- Header Management: Different protocols have different header formats and requirements. The API Gateway manages these headers, converting them appropriately. For example:

    - In HTTP, headers like `Authorization` may be passed differently compared to gRPC metadata.

    - SOAP headers need to be added in the envelope for legacy systems.

- Request/Response Structure Mapping: Different protocols

have different structures. For instance, REST APIs are resource-based, while gRPC uses remote procedure calls. The gateway must map REST API operations (e.g., `GET`, `POST`) to corresponding gRPC methods or SOAP actions.

## 5. Advantages of Protocol Translation in API Gateways

- Interoperability: Enables different parts of an architecture to communicate even if they use different protocols, allowing newer systems to work with legacy systems.

- Simplified Client Interaction: Clients only need to interact with one protocol (e.g., HTTP) while the gateway handles the complexity of communicating with multiple services using different protocols.

- Flexibility in Backend Systems: Backend services can use the most suitable protocol for their needs (e.g., gRPC for high-performance microservices), while clients remain unaffected by the changes.

- Decoupling: Protocol translation helps decouple clients from backend services, meaning services can evolve independently of how clients communicate.

## 6. Challenges of Protocol Translation

- Performance Overhead: Translation between protocols adds latency, especially when converting between complex formats like XML (used in SOAP) and JSON.

- Complex Configuration: Managing multiple protocols and ensuring correct mappings between requests, responses, and headers can be complex and error-prone.

- Data Integrity: There's a risk of losing data during translation, especially when converting between formats with different capabilities (e.g., converting rich SOAP XML responses into simpler JSON structures).

- Error Handling: Different protocols have different error formats, so the gateway must appropriately translate error messages and status codes. For example, translating gRPC status codes to HTTP status codes.

**7. Popular API Gateways with Protocol Translation Support**

- AWS API Gateway: Supports HTTP to WebSocket, HTTP to gRPC, and HTTP to Lambda (which can use different protocols internally).
- Kong: Can handle HTTP to gRPC and other protocol translations via plugins.
- NGINX: Functions as an API Gateway and can be configured for protocol translation between HTTP, gRPC, WebSocket, and other protocols.
- Apigee: Supports protocol translation between HTTP, SOAP, and gRPC, commonly used in large enterprises needing hybrid solutions.
- Envoy: A popular service mesh that supports translating between HTTP, gRPC, and WebSocket, and is often used in microservice environments.

Protocol translation in an API Gateway is crucial for ensuring interoperability between diverse systems and services that use different communication protocols. It allows modern applications to interact with legacy systems, provides flexibility in service design, and ensures that clients can use a uniform protocol (e.g., HTTP) without needing to worry about how backend services communicate. While it adds complexity and potential performance overhead, its benefits in terms of flexibility, decoupling, and interoperability make it a powerful tool in distributed systems and microservice architectures.

# Load Balancing

Load balancing in an API Gateway is the process of distributing incoming client requests across multiple backend services or instances to ensure high availability, reliability, and optimal resource utilization. API Gateways typically serve as the first point of contact for external clients and route requests to backend services. By incorporating load balancing, the API Gateway ensures that no single backend instance is overwhelmed, which helps in maintaining system performance and preventing downtime.

# Key Concepts of Load Balancing in API Gateway

## Purpose
- Distribute traffic evenly across multiple backend servers or instances.

- Improve fault tolerance and reliability by redirecting traffic when a server fails.

- Scale horizontally by adding more instances of services as traffic increases.

- Provide higher availability by preventing overload of individual service instances.

## Types of Load Balancing Algorithms:

API Gateways employ various load-balancing strategies or algorithms to distribute traffic efficiently. Here are some common methods:

### a. Round-Robin Load Balancing
- Definition: Requests are distributed in a circular manner to each available instance in sequence.

- How It Works: If there are three instances (A, B, and C), the first request goes to A, the second to B, the third to C, and the process repeats.

- Use Case: Simple, effective when all instances are equal in terms of performance and capacity.

- Example:
  - Request 1 → Server A
  - Request 2 → Server B
  - Request 3 → Server C
  - Request 4 → Server A (and so on).

### b. Least Connections
- Definition: The API Gateway directs the request to the instance that has the fewest active connections.

- How It Works: This algorithm ensures that no instance is overwhelmed by too many concurrent requests and is particularly useful for long-running requests.

- Use Case: Ideal when request loads can vary significantly or when some instances are handling more resource-intensive tasks than others.

- Example: If Server A has 5 connections, Server B has 2 connections, and Server C has 3 connections, the next request will go to Server B.

### c. IP Hashing (Client IP Hashing)

- Definition: Requests from the same client IP are routed to the same server instance.

- How It Works: The gateway uses a hash of the client's IP address to consistently route requests from that client to the same backend server.

- Use Case: Useful when maintaining session consistency is essential, such as in cases where backend services are stateful and store session-specific data.

- Example: All requests from client IP `192.168.1.1` always go to Server A.

### d. Weighted Round Robin

- Definition: Similar to round-robin, but each backend instance is assigned a weight based on its capacity or performance. Requests are distributed proportionally to the weight.

- How It Works: Instances with higher weights receive more traffic, ensuring that more powerful servers handle more requests.

- Use Case: Useful when backend services have different resource capacities or are running on different hardware.

- Example: If Server A has a weight of 3 and Server B has a weight of 1, Server A will receive three times as many requests as Server B.

### e. Geolocation-based Load Balancing

- Definition: Requests are routed to the closest data center or server based on the geographical location of the client.

- How It Works: The API Gateway analyzes the client's IP address to determine its geographical location and forwards the request to the closest or most suitable backend server.

- Use Case: Ideal for global applications where latency can be reduced by routing requests to geographically closer servers.

- Example: Clients from Europe are routed to servers in a European data center, while clients from North America are routed to servers in a US data center.

### f. Random Load Balancing

- Definition: The API Gateway randomly selects a backend server to forward each request to.

- How It Works: Each request is assigned to a randomly selected instance.

- Use Case: Simple approach, though not optimal for high-performance or resource-intensive environments, as it doesn't consider server load or capacity.

### g. Request Queueing

- Definition: Requests are queued when all backend services are busy and processed as soon as a server becomes available.

- How It Works: The API Gateway maintains a queue of requests if no backend instances are available to process them, improving reliability during traffic spikes.

- Use Case: Useful during traffic bursts or when backend capacity is temporarily limited.

## Session Persistence (Sticky Sessions):

- Definition: Ensures that a client's requests are routed to the same backend server during a session, useful for applications where user-specific state is stored on the backend server (e.g., shopping carts, login sessions).

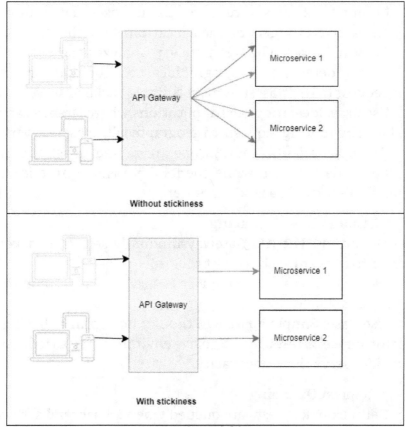

**6.4 Session stickiness**

- How It Works: The API Gateway uses cookies, session IDs, or IP hashing to maintain client-server affinity.

- Use Case: Ideal for stateful services or when session-specific data is stored locally on a backend instance.

- Example: In an e-commerce application, once a user's session starts, all subsequent requests from that user are routed to the same server until the session ends.

## Auto-scaling and Load Balancing:

- Integration with Auto-scaling: API Gateways can integrate with auto-scaling mechanisms to automatically add or remove backend instances based on current traffic demand. As new instances are added, the gateway dynamically includes them in the load-balancing pool.

- Elastic Load Balancing: This ensures that the system scales up to handle more traffic during peak times and scales down during low traffic periods to conserve resources.

**Load Balancing in Cloud Environments:**

- Cloud-native Load Balancing: Most cloud providers, such as AWS, Azure, and Google Cloud, offer API Gateway services with integrated load balancing (e.g., AWS Elastic Load Balancer with AWS API Gateway).

- Auto-discovery of Instances: In cloud environments, the API Gateway can automatically discover new backend instances as they are added or removed, using service registries or orchestration systems like Kubernetes.

**Examples of Load Balancing in API Gateways**

- AWS API Gateway: AWS API Gateway integrates with Elastic Load Balancer (ELB) to route requests to multiple EC2 instances or Lambda functions. It uses health checks, session stickiness, and weighted round-robin for efficient load distribution.

- Kong API Gateway: Kong allows multiple upstream services to be load-balanced across, with strategies like round-robin, least connections, and hash-based routing.

- NGINX: NGINX can act as both an API Gateway and a load balancer, supporting various algorithms like round-robin, least connections, and IP hashing. It is commonly used for HTTP load balancing in high-traffic web applications.

- Istio: Istio is a service mesh that includes load balancing as part of its traffic management features, typically used for inter-service communication in a microservices architecture.

**Benefits of Load Balancing in API Gateways:**
- Improved Availability: Load balancing helps ensure that services remain available even if individual instances fail.

- Scalability: Traffic can be distributed across multiple instances, allowing the system to scale horizontally by adding more instances as needed.
- Optimized Resource Usage: By distributing traffic evenly, the system avoids overloading specific instances, maximizing the performance of the entire architecture.
- Fault Tolerance: If a backend service goes down, traffic is rerouted to healthy instances, ensuring continuity of service.
- Latency Reduction: With techniques like geolocation-based routing, requests are routed to the nearest or most optimal instance, reducing response times.

Load balancing in an API Gateway is a fundamental aspect of managing traffic in distributed, cloud-based, or microservices architectures. By intelligently distributing client requests across multiple backend instances, API Gateways improve system reliability, scalability, and performance. With various load-balancing strategies such as round-robin, least connections, IP hashing, and more, gateways ensure efficient traffic management and enable applications to handle high traffic volumes without downtime.

## Security Features

### Authentication and Authorization in API Gateways

API gateways are crucial components of modern application architectures, acting as a single entry point for all API requests. To ensure secure access and control over API usage, they implement robust authentication and authorization mechanisms.

### Authentication

Authentication is the process of verifying the identity of a user or client making an API request. It ensures that only authorized entities can access the API. Common authentication methods used in API gateways include:

- API keys: A simple method where clients provide a unique key to identify themselves.
- OAuth 2.0: A widely used authorization framework that allows users to grant third-party applications access to their data on behalf of the resource owner.
- Basic authentication: A straightforward method where clients send a base64-encoded username and password in the HTTP Authorization header.
- JWT (JSON Web Token): A self-contained token that can be used to securely transmit information between parties.
- OpenID Connect: A single sign-on (SSO) protocol built on top of OAuth 2.0, providing additional features like user profile information.

**Authorization**

Authorization determines what actions a user or client is permitted to perform once their identity has been verified. It involves granting or denying access to specific resources or functionalities within the API. Common authorization mechanisms include:

- Role-based access control (RBAC): Assigns users to roles and grants permissions based on those roles.
- Attribute-based access control (ABAC): Evaluates policies based on attributes associated with users, resources, and environments.
- Fine-grained access control: Allows for precise control over access to individual resources or operations within the API.
- Token-based authorization: Uses tokens (e.g., JWT) to represent permissions and privileges.

**Implementation**

API gateways can implement authentication and authorization in various ways:

- Middleware: Adding middleware components to the gateway to handle authentication and authorization logic.
- Plugins: Using plugins or extensions provided by the gateway platform to implement specific authentication and authorization methods.
- Custom code: Developing custom code within the gateway to implement complex authentication and authorization rules.

**Best Practices**

- Choose appropriate methods: Select authentication and authorization methods that align with your security requirements and application architecture.
- Implement strong security measures: Use encryption, hashing, and other security techniques to protect sensitive data.
- Regularly review and update policies: Keep your authentication and authorization policies up-to-date to address evolving security threats.
- Monitor and audit access: Track API usage and audit logs to identify unauthorized access attempts or security breaches.

By effectively implementing authentication and authorization mechanisms in API gateways, you can protect your APIs from unauthorized access, ensure data privacy, and maintain the integrity of your applications.

# Rate Limiting & Throttling:

Rate limiting and throttling are essential mechanisms in API gateways to manage the traffic load and prevent abuse. They help ensure that the API remains responsive and available for all users by controlling the rate at which requests are processed.

**Rate Limiting**

Rate limiting involves setting a maximum number of requests that a client can make within a specific time period. This helps prevent excessive load on the API and ensures fair distribution of resources among all users.

**Common rate limiting strategies:**

- Fixed window: Sets a fixed time window (e.g., 1 minute) and limits the number of requests within that window.
- Sliding window: Uses a sliding window that moves over time, allowing for more flexibility in handling burst traffic.
- Token bucket: Maintains a bucket of tokens that can be used to represent requests. Tokens are replenished at a fixed rate, limiting the overall request rate.

**Throttling**

Throttling is a more granular approach to controlling API traffic, allowing for different rate limits based on various factors such as client identity, API endpoint, or request type. It helps prevent abuse from specific clients or endpoints while maintaining a reasonable level of service for others.

**Throttling factors:**

- Client-based throttling: Limits the rate of requests from individual clients or IP addresses.
- Endpoint-based throttling: Sets different rate limits for different API endpoints.
- Request type-based throttling: Controls the rate of specific request types (e.g., GET, POST).

**Implementation in API Gateways**

API gateways typically provide built-in features or plugins for implementing rate limiting and throttling. These mechanisms can be configured to meet the specific needs of an API, such as:

- Configurable rate limits: Setting different rate limits for different clients, endpoints, or request types.
- Burst handling: Allowing for short bursts of traffic beyond the normal rate limit.
- Customization: Tailoring the rate limiting and throttling behavior to match the application's requirements.

**Best Practices**

- Monitor and adjust: Continuously monitor API usage and adjust rate limits as needed to maintain optimal performance.
- Provide clear error messages: Inform clients when rate limits are exceeded with informative error messages.
- Consider tiered pricing: Offer different pricing plans based on usage levels to incentivize responsible API consumption.
- Implement fallback mechanisms: Provide alternative options or downgrade services when rate limits are reached to avoid complete outages.

By effectively implementing rate limiting and throttling in API gateways, you can ensure that your APIs remain responsive, scalable, and resilient to abuse, providing a positive experience for your users.

# Request Handling and Transformation

## Request/Response Transformation

API gateways often act as intermediaries between clients and backend services, allowing for flexible transformations of requests and responses. This capability is crucial for:

- Adapting to different protocols: Translating between different protocols (e.g., HTTP, REST, GraphQL) to accommodate diverse clients.
- Enriching data: Adding or modifying data elements in requests or responses to meet specific requirements.
- Validating data: Ensuring that requests adhere to predefined schemas and formats.
- Caching responses: Storing frequently accessed responses to improve performance.

## Request Transformation

- Protocol conversion: Transforming requests from one protocol (e.g., REST) to another (e.g., SOAP) or from a custom format to a standardized one.
- Data validation: Checking requests against predefined schemas or rules to ensure they are valid and complete.
- Query parameter manipulation: Modifying or adding query parameters to requests based on specific criteria.
- Request routing: Directing requests to the appropriate backend service based on URL paths, headers, or other criteria.
- Security measures: Applying security measures like encryption, authentication, and authorization to requests.

## Response Transformation

- Data filtering: Selecting specific data elements from responses to be returned to the client.
- Data formatting: Transforming responses into a desired format (e.g., JSON, XML, CSV).
- Data enrichment: Adding or modifying data elements in responses based on specific requirements.
- Error handling: Handling errors from backend services and returning appropriate error messages to the client.
- Caching: Storing frequently accessed responses to

improve performance.

## Implementation Techniques

API gateways can implement request and response transformation using various techniques:

- Middleware: Adding middleware components to the gateway to handle transformation logic.
- Plugins: Using plugins or extensions provided by the gateway platform to implement specific transformation rules.
- Custom code: Developing custom code within the gateway to implement complex transformation logic.

## Best Practices

Keep transformations simple: Avoid overly complex transformations that can introduce performance overhead or errors.

- Use declarative configuration: Define transformation rules using declarative syntax to improve maintainability.
- Test thoroughly: Test transformations carefully to ensure they are working as expected and do not introduce security vulnerabilities.
- Consider performance implications: Be mindful of the performance impact of transformations, especially for high-traffic APIs.

By effectively implementing request and response transformation in API gateways, you can enhance the flexibility, security, and performance of your API, providing a better experience for your users.

# Aggregation

Aggregation in API gateways involves combining data from multiple backend services into a single response. This is useful when a client needs a unified view of information that is dispersed across different systems.

## Common Aggregation Scenarios

- Joining data from multiple services: Combining data from different services into a single response, such as joining customer information with order history.
- Creating summary reports: Aggregating data to generate summary reports or statistics, like calculating total sales or average order value.
- Implementing composite APIs: Combining data from multiple endpoints into a single API to simplify client interactions.

## Implementation Techniques

**6.5 Aggregation via API Gateway**

API gateways can implement aggregation using various techniques:

**Data transformation**: Transforming data from multiple services into a common format and combining it into a single response.

**Data enrichment**: Adding additional data to responses from different services to create a more comprehensive view.

**Data filtering**: Filtering data from different services based on specific criteria to include only relevant information.

**Data caching**: Caching aggregated data to improve performance and reduce load on backend services.

### Challenges and Considerations

- Performance: Aggregation can be computationally intensive, especially when dealing with large datasets or complex transformations.
- Consistency: Ensuring data consistency across different services can be challenging, especially when dealing with real-time updates.
- Complexity: Implementing aggregation logic can be complex, especially for large-scale systems with many interconnected services.

By effectively implementing aggregation in API gateways, you can provide clients with a more unified and informative view of your data, while also improving the overall performance and scalability of your API.

# Performance Optimization

## Caching

Caching in an API Gateway is a performance-enhancing feature that stores copies of frequently requested responses to reduce the load on backend services, decrease response times, and improve scalability. When a client sends a request, the API Gateway can return a cached response instead of forwarding the request to the backend service, provided the response is still valid. This reduces the need for repeated processing of identical requests by the backend and improves the overall performance of the system.

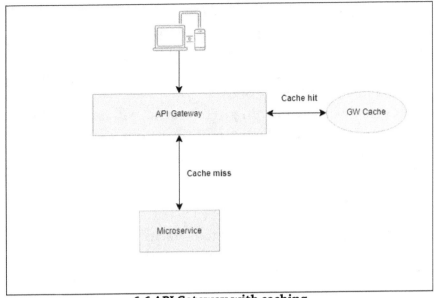

**6.6 API Gateway with caching**

Key Concepts of Caching in an API Gateway

## 1. Purpose:

- Reduce Load on Backend Services: By serving cached responses, the gateway can reduce the number of requests sent to backend services, freeing up resources and improving the performance of the entire system.

- Decrease Latency: Cached responses are served faster since they don't require backend processing, resulting in lower response times and a better user experience.

- Handle Traffic Spikes: During high-traffic periods, the API Gateway can serve cached responses without overwhelming the backend services, improving system resilience.

- Improve Scalability: By handling a large volume of requests using cached data, the system can scale more easily without requiring additional backend resources.

## 2. Types of Caching:

- Response Caching: The API Gateway stores the full response (e.g., HTML, JSON, XML, etc.) to serve future requests that match the cached request criteria.

- Partial Caching (Fragment Caching): Some responses may have dynamic and static parts. The API Gateway caches only the static parts of the response, while the dynamic parts are still fetched from the backend.

- Content-based Caching: The cache can store different versions of the response based on varying content, such as different user preferences or languages (often based on request headers like `Accept-Language`).

## 3. Cache Control Mechanisms:

The API Gateway uses various techniques to determine when and how long to cache responses, and when to invalidate them. These mechanisms are often based on HTTP caching standards:

### a. HTTP Cache Headers:

- Cache-Control: Directives in the `Cache-Control` header instruct the gateway on how to cache the response. For example:
    - `Cache-Control: max-age=60`: The response can be cached for 60 seconds.
    - `Cache-Control: no-cache`: The response must always be validated with the backend before serving the cached version.
    - `Cache-Control: public`: The response can be cached by any intermediate cache (e.g., gateway, browser).
    - `Cache-Control: private`: Only the client (browser) and API Gateway can cache the response, not other proxies.
- ETag (Entity Tag): A unique identifier assigned to a specific version of a resource. The API Gateway can use `ETag` to determine if the cached version is still valid by comparing it with the current version from the backend.
- Expires: Specifies the date and time after which the response is considered stale. After this time, the gateway will either fetch a fresh response from the backend or revalidate

the cache.

### b. Time-to-Live (TTL):

- Definition: TTL defines how long a response remains in the cache before being considered stale. TTL values are often configured at the gateway level, but they can also be derived from the `Cache-Control` headers provided by the backend service.
- How It Works: When the TTL expires, the API Gateway will either remove the cached item or revalidate it by fetching a fresh response from the backend.

c. Stale-While-Revalidate:
- Definition: This is a caching strategy where the API Gateway can serve a stale (expired) cache entry to a client while it asynchronously fetches and updates the cache with a fresh response from the backend.
- Use Case: Useful in scenarios where a slightly outdated response is acceptable, but fresh data is still fetched in the background.

### 4. Cache Invalidation:

- Automatic Invalidation: Caches are automatically invalidated based on TTL or `Expires` headers. Once expired, a fresh response is fetched from the backend.
- Manual Invalidation: In some cases, the cache must be invalidated manually when data is updated on the backend. For instance, when a new product is added to an inventory, the cache related to that product list must be cleared.
- Cache Purging: Administrators can explicitly purge specific cached items (e.g., via API commands or triggers) when certain conditions are met (e.g., database updates).

### 5. Cache Key Management:

The API Gateway uses cache keys to store and retrieve cached responses. The key is typically derived from a combination of:

- Request URL: The path and query parameters.

- Request Headers: Some headers, like `Accept-Language`, `Authorization`, or `Content-Type`, may influence the response and are included in the cache key.

- Request Method: GET requests are often cached, while POST requests are typically not cached as they usually involve data changes.

## 6. Caching Strategies:

Different caching strategies can be implemented in an API Gateway, depending on the nature of the application and the type of data being served.

### a. Full-page Caching:
- Definition: The entire response is cached. This is common for static content, such as documentation, homepages, or product listings that don't change frequently.
- Use Case: Useful for public-facing APIs where responses do not change often, such as fetching static assets or infrequently updated data.

### b. Per-resource Caching:
- Definition: Only specific resources or endpoints are cached. For example, a `GET /products` API might be cached, but a `POST /orders` API will not be cached.
- Use Case: Useful in RESTful APIs where different endpoints have different caching needs (e.g., frequently requested resources like product catalogs).

### c. Layered Caching (Multi-tier Caching):
- Definition: Responses are cached at multiple layers (e.g., client-side, API Gateway, CDN). Each layer reduces the load on the lower layers.
- Use Case: Common in global applications where a CDN caches responses close to the client, and the API Gateway caches responses to reduce load on the backend.

### d. Read-through Caching:

- Definition: The API Gateway checks the cache first, and if the requested data is not found, it fetches the data from the backend, stores it in the cache, and serves it to the client.

- Use Case: Ensures that only fresh data is cached when it's first requested, reducing the chance of stale data being served.

### e. Write-through Caching:

- Definition: When data is updated or written to the backend service, the API Gateway immediately writes the new data to the cache as well.

- Use Case: Ensures that the cache is always in sync with the latest state of the data.

## 7. Cache Hit vs. Cache Miss:

- Cache Hit: When the API Gateway successfully finds a valid response in the cache, it serves it directly without involving the backend service.

- Cache Miss: When the requested data is not found in the cache or has expired, the gateway fetches it from the backend service and then stores it in the cache for future requests.

## 8. Benefits of Caching in an API Gateway:

- Improved Performance: Cached responses can be served more quickly than those that need to be processed by the backend, leading to lower latency and faster response times.

- Reduced Backend Load: Caching reduces the number of requests that need to reach the backend services, which can lead to lower infrastructure costs and better utilization of resources.

- Scalability: By offloading traffic from backend services, caching helps the system handle larger volumes of traffic without needing to scale backend services as aggressively.

- Cost Efficiency: Fewer backend requests mean reduced resource consumption (e.g., server processing, database queries), which can lower operational costs.

- Enhanced User Experience: Faster response times lead to a smoother and more responsive user experience, especially for data-heavy applications.

## 9. Challenges and Considerations:

- Stale Data: If not managed carefully, the API Gateway may serve outdated responses from the cache, leading to a poor user experience. Proper cache invalidation is crucial to avoid this.

- Dynamic Data: Caching is less effective for APIs that serve highly dynamic data or personalized responses (e.g., user-specific dashboards), as each request may require a fresh backend response.

- Cache Consistency: In distributed systems, maintaining consistency between the cache and the backend can be challenging, especially in scenarios where data is updated frequently.

- Security: Sensitive data should not be cached (e.g., personal information, financial data), as it could be served to unintended clients. Proper cache key management and encryption can mitigate this risk.

## 10. Popular API Gateways with Caching Support:

- AWS API Gateway: AWS API Gateway provides built-in caching mechanisms. You can configure cache size, TTL, and cache keys as well as invalidate cache entries.

- Kong API Gateway: Kong supports caching via plugins that allow for response caching with custom TTLs and cache keys.

- NGINX: NGINX is often used as an API Gateway and provides powerful caching mechanisms, including cache keys, TTLs, and cache purging features.

- Apigee: Apigee's API Gateway includes a caching layer that supports response caching, cache keys, TTLs, and more.

Caching in an API Gateway is a powerful optimization technique that reduces backend load, improves response times, and enhances the scalability of your system. By intelligently caching responses based on HTTP headers, TTLs, and caching strategies, API Gateways can serve requests more efficiently while ensuring that data remains consistent and up to date. Implementing the right caching policies can greatly improve the performance of API-driven applications, especially in high-traffic environments.

## Compression

Compression in an API Gateway is the process of reducing the size of data transmitted between clients and backend services by encoding it in a more efficient format. Compression is particularly useful for reducing bandwidth usage and speeding up data transfer, especially for large payloads such as JSON, XML, or HTML responses. By compressing the data, the API Gateway can improve performance, lower network costs, and enhance the overall user experience, particularly in scenarios where clients have limited bandwidth or when APIs handle high volumes of data.

Key Concepts of Compression in an API Gateway

**1. Purpose:**

 - Reduce Bandwidth Usage: Compressed data requires less bandwidth, making it faster to transfer over the network, particularly in environments with limited network capacity.
 - Decrease Latency: Since smaller payloads take less time to travel across the network, compression reduces the overall response time, improving the speed of API calls.
 - Enhance Scalability: By reducing the amount of data being transferred, the API Gateway can handle more concurrent requests, improving the scalability of the system.

## 2. Types of Compression:

The most commonly used compression algorithms in API Gateways are:

- Gzip: One of the most widely supported and used compression algorithms. It is efficient for text-based payloads like JSON, HTML, XML, and CSS.
- Brotli: A newer and more efficient compression algorithm than Gzip, offering better compression ratios, particularly for large payloads and text-based content.
- Deflate: A compression method similar to Gzip but slightly less common. It combines the LZ77 algorithm and Huffman coding.
- Zstd: A newer compression algorithm with better compression ratios and faster decompression speeds compared to both Gzip and Brotli.

## 3. How Compression Works in an API Gateway:

- Request from Client: The client sends a request to the API Gateway, and it may indicate its support for compression by including the `Accept-Encoding` header, specifying the compression algorithms it supports (e.g., `Accept-Encoding: gzip, deflate, br`).

- Compression by Gateway: The API Gateway checks the client's `Accept-Encoding` header and chooses an appropriate compression algorithm (e.g., Gzip or Brotli). If the client supports compression and the response data is compressible, the API Gateway compresses the response before sending it to the client.

- Decompression at Client: Once the client receives the compressed response, it decompresses the payload using the corresponding algorithm. For example, if the response was compressed with Gzip, the client decompresses it using Gzip before processing the data.

## 4. Use Cases for Compression in API Gateway:

- Large Payloads: When API responses contain large amounts of data (e.g., large JSON arrays, XML documents, file downloads), compression can significantly reduce the size of the payload.
- Text-based Responses: APIs that serve text-heavy data, such as JSON, XML, HTML, or CSV, benefit greatly from compression as text data is highly compressible.
- Mobile Applications: Mobile clients often operate on limited bandwidth connections, so compressing API responses can improve the performance and responsiveness of mobile apps.
- High-latency Networks: In environments where network latency is high, compressing the response data reduces the time required to transmit the data across the network.

## 5. Compression Headers:

- Request Headers:
- `Accept-Encoding`: Specifies the types of compression algorithms supported by the client (e.g., `Accept-Encoding: gzip, deflate, br`). The API Gateway selects one of the algorithms supported by the client to compress the response.

- Response Headers:
- `Content-Encoding`: Indicates the compression algorithm used by the API Gateway in the response (e.g., `Content-Encoding: gzip`).
- `Vary: Accept-Encoding`: This header informs caches (e.g., CDNs, browsers) to store different versions of the response based on the `Accept-Encoding` header. This ensures that both compressed and uncompressed versions are cached and served appropriately.

## 6. Compression Techniques:

- On-the-Fly Compression: The API Gateway dynamically compresses responses before sending them to the client. This method is commonly used for compressing frequently requested content that changes often (e.g., JSON responses from a REST API).

- Pre-compression: Some static content, like HTML pages, CSS files, or JavaScript assets, can be pre-compressed and stored on the server. When a request is made, the pre-compressed version is served by the API Gateway if supported by the client.

- Conditional Compression: The API Gateway may apply compression based on certain conditions, such as:
- Response Size: Compression is only applied if the response exceeds a certain size threshold (e.g., responses larger than 1KB).
- Content Type: Only specific content types are compressed (e.g., `application/json`, `text/html`, but not binary files like images or PDFs).
- Client Capability: Compression is only applied if the client explicitly supports it via the `Accept-Encoding` header.

## 7. Compression for Different Content Types:

- Compressible Content:
- Text-based formats: JSON, XML, HTML, CSS, JavaScript, CSV
- Static assets: Web page resources such as HTML and CSS files are highly compressible.

- Non-compressible or Less Compressible Content:
- Binary formats: Files like images (JPEG, PNG), videos (MP4), and PDFs are already compressed in their native formats and generally do not benefit from additional compression.
- Encrypted Content: Compressed encrypted data does not

offer much advantage, as encryption algorithms often result in randomness that is difficult to compress.

## 8. Benefits of Compression in API Gateway:

- Reduced Bandwidth Consumption: Compression minimizes the amount of data sent over the network, which is particularly important for bandwidth-constrained environments such as mobile networks or cloud-based APIs.

- Faster API Responses: Since smaller payloads are faster to transmit, compression decreases the time it takes for clients to receive the API response, improving the overall performance.

- Cost Savings: Reducing bandwidth usage can lead to cost savings, especially for services that charge based on data transfer, such as cloud platforms (e.g., AWS, Google Cloud, Azure).

- Improved User Experience: Compression reduces the time needed to load responses, especially for large datasets, improving the user experience, particularly for mobile users or users with slower connections.

## 9. Challenges and Considerations:

- Processing Overhead: Compression and decompression require CPU resources. Although the performance benefits of reduced network transfer often outweigh the CPU overhead, compression should be used judiciously, particularly in high-load systems.

- Not All Data Is Compressible: Compressing already compressed files (e.g., images, videos, PDFs) is ineffective and can even increase file sizes in some cases. Therefore, it's essential to apply compression only to compressible data (like text-based formats).

- Latency in Small Payloads: For very small payloads, the time taken to compress and decompress data may introduce additional latency. Therefore, it's essential to set appropriate thresholds for when compression should be applied (e.g., payloads larger than 1KB).

- Client Support: Not all clients may support certain compression algorithms. While Gzip is almost universally supported, newer algorithms like Brotli may not be supported by older browsers or systems.

- Content Type Awareness: API Gateways must be aware of the content type they are compressing to ensure that compression is only applied to suitable data types.

## 10. Examples of API Gateways with Compression Support:

- AWS API Gateway: AWS API Gateway supports both request and response compression using Gzip. You can configure settings for minimum compression size and content types to be compressed.

- Kong API Gateway: Kong has plugins that allow for on-the-fly compression of responses. You can configure the compression algorithm (e.g., Gzip, Brotli) and define thresholds for when to compress.

- NGINX API Gateway: NGINX supports Gzip and Brotli compression natively. Compression can be configured based on request headers, response content types, and minimum response sizes.

- Apigee API Gateway: Apigee provides compression support based on `Accept-Encoding` headers. Administrators can define policies for when and how to apply compression to API responses.

Compression in an API Gateway is a vital technique to optimize the performance and efficiency of API communication. By reducing the size of data being transmitted between clients and servers, compression improves response times, reduces bandwidth usage, and enhances the scalability of the system. While compression offers significant benefits, it's important to configure it properly, applying it to suitable data types and payload sizes to ensure the best balance between performance gains and resource usage.

# Service Discovery

API Gateways often integrate with service discovery mechanisms to dynamically route requests to services as they scale or change. This is crucial in environments where services are added or removed dynamically (such as in containerized environments with Kubernetes).

Service discovery is a critical component of modern microservices architectures. It allows API gateways to dynamically locate and interact with backend services, ensuring that the system remains resilient and scalable.

### Types of Service Discovery

- Client-side discovery: Clients are responsible for discovering the addresses of backend services using techniques like DNS or a service registry.
- Server-side discovery: The API gateway handles service discovery, using a service registry or configuration management tool to locate backend services.

### Service Registry

A service registry is a centralized repository that stores information about available services, including their addresses, health status, and metadata. API gateways can use service registries to dynamically discover and route requests to the appropriate backend services.

### Popular service registries:

- Consul: A distributed, highly available service discovery

and configuration management system.

- ZooKeeper: A distributed coordination service used for managing large-scale distributed systems.
- Eureka: A service discovery tool developed by Netflix.

API gateways typically use server-side discovery to locate backend services. This approach offers several benefits, including:

- Centralized management: Service discovery is managed centrally, simplifying configuration and maintenance.
- Load balancing: API gateways can use service discovery to distribute traffic across multiple instances of a service.
- Fault tolerance: If a backend service becomes unavailable, the API gateway can automatically reroute requests to a healthy instance.
- Dynamic scaling: API gateways can dynamically adjust the number of backend service instances based on load.

## Implementation Techniques

API gateways can implement service discovery using various techniques:

- Integration with service registries: Directly integrating with popular service registries like Consul, ZooKeeper, or Eureka.
- Custom discovery mechanisms: Implementing custom discovery mechanisms based on specific requirements.
- Configuration management: Using configuration management tools to store service discovery information.

## Best Practices

- Choose a suitable service registry: Select a service registry that aligns with your infrastructure and requirements.
- Implement health checks: Regularly monitor the health

of backend services to ensure they are available and functioning correctly.

- Use load balancing: Distribute traffic across multiple instances of a service to improve performance and fault tolerance.

- Consider service mesh: Explore using a service mesh for advanced service discovery and traffic management capabilities.

By effectively implementing service discovery in API gateways, you can create a more resilient, scalable, and flexible microservices architecture.

API Gateways play a pivotal role in managing communication, security, and performance in distributed systems, especially in microservices architectures. They offer a wide range of functionalities, from simple routing and load balancing to complex transformations, security, and monitoring, making them indispensable for modern applications.

# API Gateway pattern in Google Cloud Platform (GCP)

On Google Cloud Platform (GCP), the API Gateway pattern can be implemented using several tools and services, including Google Cloud API Gateway, Cloud Load Balancing, Cloud Run, Google Kubernetes Engine (GKE), and Cloud Functions.

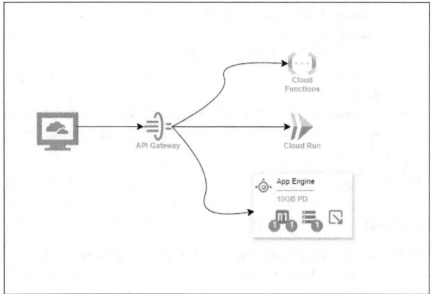

**6.7 API Gateway in Google cloud platform**

## Key Components in GCP for API Gateway with Microservices

1. Google Cloud API Gateway: Manages and secures APIs, acting as the single entry point for all client requests.

2. Cloud Run / GKE / Cloud Functions: These services host your microservices, allowing you to deploy containerized applications or serverless functions.

3. Cloud Endpoints / Apigee: Additional API management options for advanced use cases, offering features like developer portals, API monetization, and more.

4. Cloud Load Balancing: Distributes incoming traffic to backend services, ensuring availability and scalability.

5. IAM (Identity and Access Management): Manages authentication and authorization for API Gateway access.

6. Pub/Sub / Cloud Tasks: For async communication and decoupled service interaction within the microservices architecture.

## Example of an API Gateway Pattern with Microservices on GCP

Let's consider an example where you have a microservices-based e-commerce platform hosted on GCP. The platform is composed of the following microservices:

1. Product Service: Manages product details (deployed on Cloud Run).
2. Order Service: Handles orders (deployed on GKE).
3. Payment Service: Processes payments (deployed on Cloud Functions).
4. User Service: Manages user accounts and authentication (deployed on Cloud Run).

These microservices are decoupled, and clients (web, mobile, etc.) need to access them through a single entry point, which is managed by the Google Cloud API Gateway.

**Step-by-Step Implementation**

1. Create and Deploy Microservices
Each microservice is deployed separately using appropriate GCP services like Cloud Run, GKE, or Cloud Functions.

- Product Service: Deployed as a containerized application using Cloud Run.
- Order Service: Deployed on a Kubernetes cluster using GKE.
- Payment Service: Deployed as serverless functions using Cloud Functions.
- User Service: Deployed on Cloud Run as a containerized service.

Each microservice has its own unique URL once deployed, such as:

- `https://product-service-xyz.run.app`
- `https://order-service-gke.example.com`
- `https://payment-service.cloudfunctions.net`
- `https://user-service-abc.run.app`

2. Configure Google Cloud API Gateway

The API Gateway is configured to act as the single entry point for all these services. It routes client requests to the appropriate backend services, handles authentication, and applies security policies.

- Create an API Configuration: You define an OpenAPI specification or a gRPC service definition that describes the API, including the paths for each service (e.g., `/products`, `/orders`, `/payments`, `/users`).

Example of OpenAPI specification for routing:

**Yaml:**

```yaml
swagger: '2.0'
info:
  title: E-commerce API
  version: 1.0.0
paths:
  /products:
    get:
      x-google-backend:
        address: https://product-service-xyz.run.app
      description: Get product details
      responses:
        '200':
          description: A list of products
  /orders:
    post:
      x-google-backend:
        address: https://order-service-gke.example.com
      description: Place an order
      responses:
        '200':
          description: Order placed successfully
  /payments:
    post:
```

```
x-google-backend:
  address:                        https://payment-
service.cloudfunctions.net
  description: Process a payment
  responses:
    '200':
      description: Payment processed
/users:
  get:
    x-google-backend:
      address: https://user-service-abc.run.app
    description: Get user details
    responses:
      '200':
        description: User details
```

Deploy API Gateway: After defining the OpenAPI spec, you deploy the API Gateway and configure it to handle requests coming from clients to the different microservices.

3. Implement Authentication and Authorization

To secure the microservices, the API Gateway can be configured to handle authentication using Google Cloud Identity and Access Management (IAM) and OAuth 2.0. For example, only authorized users can access the `/payments` endpoint.

- IAM Roles: Assign appropriate IAM roles to the API Gateway to control access to different resources.
- OAuth 2.0: Configure the API Gateway to require OAuth tokens for specific endpoints (e.g., `/payments` or `/orders`).

4. Set Up Rate Limiting and Quotas

To ensure fair usage and prevent abuse, you can define rate-limiting and quota policies within the API Gateway. This helps to protect backend services from being overwhelmed.

Example configuration for rate limiting:

**Yaml**

```yaml
x-google-quota:
  limits:
    - name: product_requests_per_minute
      metric: requests
      unit: minute
      values:
        STANDARD: 100
```

This policy limits requests to the `/products` endpoint to 100 requests per minute.

5. Monitoring and Logging with Cloud Monitoring

Google Cloud's built-in monitoring tools, such as Cloud Monitoring and Cloud Logging, provide real-time insights into API Gateway usage, request/response metrics, and the performance of backend services.

- Cloud Logging: Logs API requests, responses, errors, and latencies.
- Cloud Monitoring: Tracks performance metrics like API response times, number of requests, error rates, and CPU utilization for each microservice.

6. Caching Responses

For frequently accessed endpoints like `/products`, you can enable caching at the API Gateway layer. This reduces the load on the backend services by serving cached responses for repeated requests.

Example configuration for caching:

**Yaml**

```yaml
x-google-backend:
  address: https://product-service-xyz.run.app
```

```
protocol: https
path_translation: APPEND_PATH_TO_ADDRESS
timeout_sec: 30
caching:
  enabled: true
  cache_ttl_sec: 60
```

## 7. Handling Asynchronous Requests with Pub/Sub

For operations like order processing, where immediate feedback is not required, you can implement asynchronous communication between the API Gateway and microservices using Pub/Sub. For example, the Order Service can publish messages to a Pub/Sub topic, which the Payment Service consumes to complete the payment processing.

**Example Flow of API Requests**

1. Client Request: A client (e.g., a web or mobile app) sends a request to the API Gateway to fetch product details:
   - `GET https://api-gateway-url/products`

2. API Gateway Routing: The API Gateway receives the request and forwards it to the Product Service hosted on Cloud Run:
   - `GET https://product-service-xyz.run.app`

3. Response: The Product Service processes the request and sends the response (e.g., a list of products) back to the API Gateway, which then forwards it to the client.

4. Order and Payment: For an order, the client sends a request to the `/orders` endpoint, and the API Gateway routes it to the Order Service hosted on GKE. Once the order is placed, a request is sent to the Payment Service to process the payment via Cloud Functions.

5. Logging and Monitoring: All the API traffic, including request and response times, is logged and monitored using Cloud Logging and Cloud Monitoring.

**Benefits of Using API Gateway with Microservices in GCP**

- Simplified Client Interaction: Clients interact with a single API Gateway, simplifying communication with multiple microservices.
- Security: API Gateway manages authentication, authorization, and security policies, centralizing these concerns.
- Scalability: With GCP services like Cloud Run, GKE, and Cloud Functions, the microservices can scale independently based on demand.
- Load Balancing: Traffic is automatically load-balanced across multiple instances of each microservice, ensuring high availability.
- Observability: GCP's built-in monitoring and logging tools provide deep insights into API performance and microservice health.

The API Gateway pattern on Google Cloud Platform helps streamline the management of microservices by acting as a single point of entry, handling concerns like routing, security, and monitoring. By combining services like Google Cloud API Gateway, Cloud Run, GKE, and Cloud Functions, you can build a scalable, secure, and efficient microservices architecture tailored to your application needs.

# API Gateway pattern in Azure

The API Gateway pattern in Microsoft Azure is used to provide a centralized entry point for client applications to interact with a set of microservices. In an Azure-based microservices architecture, an API Gateway can manage various concerns such as routing, security, rate limiting, protocol translation, and authentication, which simplifies client interaction with backend services. Azure provides a robust set of tools for implementing the API Gateway pattern, such as Azure API Management, Azure Application Gateway, Azure Kubernetes Service (AKS), Azure Functions, and Azure Logic Apps.

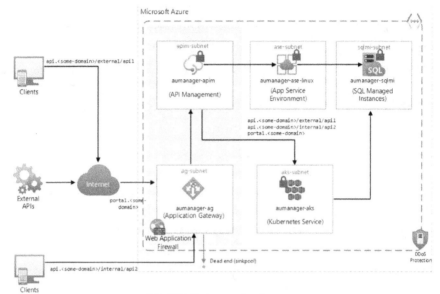

**6.8 API Gateway in Azure**

## Key Azure Services for API Gateway with Microservices

1. Azure API Management (APIM): Provides a fully managed service for publishing APIs, acting as the API Gateway. It offers features like routing, security, rate limiting, caching, and analytics.

2. Azure Kubernetes Service (AKS): Manages containerized microservices in a Kubernetes cluster.

3. Azure App Service: Hosts microservices in a fully managed platform as a service (PaaS).

4. Azure Functions: Supports serverless microservices for event-driven or lightweight operations.

5. Azure Logic Apps: Provides workflows for integrating various microservices and systems.

6. Azure Front Door: Used for global load balancing and traffic routing.

## Example of API Gateway Pattern with Microservices on Azure

Consider an e-commerce application where different microservices handle product management, order processing, user authentication, and payment processing. These microservices are deployed on various Azure services like Azure Kubernetes Service (AKS), Azure Functions, and Azure App Service. The client interacts with these microservices through Azure API Management.

### Microservices Breakdown:

1. Product Service: Manages product catalog (hosted on Azure App Service).
2. Order Service: Processes customer orders (hosted on AKS).
3. Payment Service: Handles payments (hosted on Azure Functions).
4. User Service: Manages user accounts (hosted on AKS).

Each service is exposed via its own endpoint, such as:
- `https://product-service.azurewebsites.net`
- `https://orders-service.aks.contoso.com`
- `https://payment-service.azurewebsites.net`
- `https://user-service.aks.contoso.com`

### Step-by-Step Implementation

1. Create and Deploy Microservices
Each microservice is deployed to its respective Azure service. For example:
- Product Service: Deployed using Azure App Service as a web app or REST API.
- Order Service: Deployed in a Kubernetes cluster using Azure Kubernetes Service (AKS).
- Payment Service: Deployed using Azure Functions for serverless processing.
- User Service: Deployed as a containerized microservice in

AKS.

Each microservice is independently scalable and operates with its own URL.

2. Set Up Azure API Management
Azure API Management (APIM) is used as the API Gateway. It acts as the entry point for client applications and provides a unified endpoint for accessing all backend services.

- Create an API Management Instance: You can create a new instance of Azure API Management via the Azure Portal.

- Define API Configuration: You create a set of APIs in APIM that route requests to the respective microservices.

Example OpenAPI definition for routing requests in Azure API Management:

**Yaml**

```yaml
swagger: "2.0"
info:
  title: E-commerce API Gateway
  version: 1.0.0
paths:
  /products:
    get:
      operationId: getProducts
      description: Retrieve product information
      responses:
        '200':
          description: A list of products
      x-azure-backend:           https://product-service.azurewebsites.net/products
  /orders:
    post:
      operationId: placeOrder
      description: Place an order
```

```
      responses:
       '200':
         description: Order placed successfully
       x-azure-backend:              https://orders-
    service.aks.contoso.com/orders
     /payments:
      post:
       operationId: processPayment
       description: Process a payment
       responses:
        '200':
          description: Payment processed
       x-azure-backend:              https://payment-
    service.azurewebsites.net/payments
     /users:
      get:
       operationId: getUser
       description: Retrieve user details
       responses:
        '200':
          description: User details
       x-azure-backend:                    https://user-
    service.aks.contoso.com/users
```

- Routing: APIM handles routing requests based on the endpoint paths (e.g., `/products`, `/orders`) to the correct backend service.

3. Authentication and Authorization
Azure API Management integrates with Azure Active Directory (AAD) and supports OAuth 2.0 and JWT token validation to manage authentication.

- OAuth 2.0: Configure APIM to enforce OAuth 2.0 authentication, ensuring that only authenticated clients can access sensitive endpoints like `/orders` and `/payments`.

- Azure AD Integration: You can configure the API Gateway to authenticate requests using Azure AD. For example, clients must provide a valid Azure AD token to access APIs.

Example security policy in Azure API Management:

**Xml**

```
<policies>
  <inbound>
    <validate-jwt       header-name="Authorization"
failed-validation-httpcode="401"    failed-validation-
error-message="Unauthorized">
      <openid-config                        url="https://
login.microsoftonline.com/{tenant-id}/v2.0/.well-
known/openid-configuration" />
      <audiences>
        <audience>{api-app-id-uri}</audience>
      </audiences>
    </validate-jwt>
  </inbound>
</policies>
```

4. Rate Limiting and Throttling
To protect backend services from being overwhelmed, APIM can implement rate limiting and throttling policies.

Example rate limiting policy:

**Xml**

```
<inbound>
  <rate-limit calls="100" renewal-period="60" />
</inbound>
```

This policy limits the API to 100 calls per minute, ensuring backend services are not overwhelmed by traffic spikes.

## 5. Caching API Responses

To reduce load on the backend services and improve performance, you can enable caching in Azure API Management. For example, caching responses from the Product Service for commonly requested product data.

Example caching policy in APIM:

### Xml

```xml
<inbound>
    <cache-lookup vary-by-developer="false" vary-by-developer-groups="false" />
</inbound>
<backend>
    <forward-request />
</backend>
<outbound>
    <cache-store duration="300" />
</outbound>
```

This policy caches the API response for 5 minutes (`300` seconds), reducing the number of calls to the Product Service.

## 6. Monitoring and Logging with Azure Monitor

Azure API Management integrates with Azure Monitor to provide detailed analytics and monitoring for API traffic, errors, and performance.

- Application Insights: Each microservice can also be monitored using Azure Application Insights, which tracks metrics like response time, error rates, and request rates.
- Azure Monitor Dashboards: Set up dashboards to visualize API performance, request rates, and traffic patterns.

## 7. Global Load Balancing with Azure Front Door

For global distribution and low-latency access, Azure Front Door can be used in conjunction with API Management to provide load balancing and traffic routing across geographically distributed instances of microservices.

- Azure Front Door ensures that requests are routed to the nearest available API Gateway instance based on the client's location, providing faster response times.

8. Event-Driven Architecture with Azure Functions
For asynchronous tasks like payment processing, Azure Functions can be used. For example, the Payment Service is triggered asynchronously when an order is placed, allowing the system to decouple the payment process from the order placement process.

**Example Workflow for API Requests**

1. Client Request: A client (web or mobile) sends a request to the API Gateway to get product details:
   - `GET https://apim-contoso.azure-api.net/products`

2. Routing via API Management: The API Gateway routes the request to the appropriate microservice, in this case, the Product Service hosted on Azure App Service:
   - `GET https://product-service.azurewebsites.net/products`

3. Authentication: If required, Azure API Management verifies the client's OAuth token using Azure AD before routing the request to the backend.

4. Response: The Product Service sends the response back to the API Gateway, which forwards it to the client.

5. Order Placement: A user places an order by sending a POST request to the `/orders` endpoint. API Management forwards this request to the Order Service running in AKS.

6. Payment Processing: Once the order is placed, the Payment Service (hosted on Azure Functions) processes the payment. This is triggered asynchronously by the order placement

event.

7. Monitoring: Azure Monitor and Application Insights track the API performance, logging request rates, errors, and response times for each microservice.

**Benefits of Using API Gateway with Microservices in Azure**

- Centralized Management: Azure API Management acts as a central hub for managing multiple microservices, providing a unified API for clients.
- Security: API Management handles OAuth, Azure AD, and JWT token validation, simplifying security across microservices.
- Scalability: Azure's cloud services (App Service, AKS, Functions) enable individual microservices to scale independently.

- Global Reach: With Azure Front Door, the API Gateway can handle global traffic and ensure low-latency access for users across different regions.
- Monitoring: Detailed logs and metrics are available through Azure Monitor, allowing for easy tracking and troubleshooting.

The API Gateway pattern on Azure simplifies client interaction with microservices by providing a single point of access, enabling features like authentication, rate limiting, caching, and logging. By using Azure API Management alongside AKS, Azure Functions, and other Azure services, you can create a scalable, secure, and flexible microservices architecture tailored to your business needs.

# API Gateway pattern in AWS

In Amazon Web Services (AWS), the API Gateway pattern is commonly used with microservices to provide a single entry point for clients to interact with multiple backend services. The API Gateway abstracts the complexity of communication between clients and microservices by handling concerns like routing, security, rate limiting, throttling, and protocol translation. AWS offers Amazon API Gateway, along with services like AWS Lambda, Amazon ECS (Elastic Container Service), Amazon EKS (Elastic Kubernetes Service), and AWS Fargate, which help manage microservices architectures.

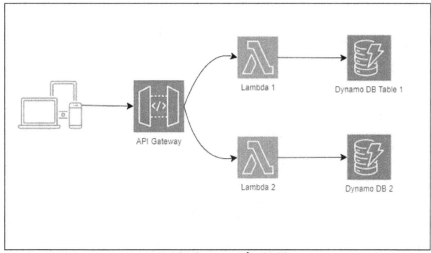

**6.9 API Gateway in AWS**

## Key AWS Services for API Gateway with Microservices

1. Amazon API Gateway: The main service for creating, publishing, maintaining, and securing APIs. It provides features like routing, request validation, throttling, security, and caching.

2. AWS Lambda: A serverless compute service that runs code in response to API Gateway requests.

3. Amazon ECS / Amazon EKS: Container orchestration services for deploying and managing microservices.

4. AWS Fargate: Serverless compute engine for containers, working with ECS and EKS to deploy microservices without managing servers.

5. AWS IAM (Identity and Access Management): Manages

authentication and authorization for API Gateway access.

6. Amazon Cognito: Used for user authentication and access control in APIs.

7. AWS CloudWatch: Monitoring and logging service used to observe API Gateway and microservices performance.

## Example of API Gateway Pattern with Microservices on AWS

Consider a scenario where an e-commerce platform is built using microservices hosted on AWS. The system includes services for managing products, processing orders, handling payments, and managing users. These services are independently deployed across Amazon ECS, AWS Lambda, and Amazon RDS (Relational Database Service).

## Microservices Breakdown:

1. Product Service: Manages product details (deployed on Amazon ECS).

2. Order Service: Processes orders (deployed on Amazon EKS).

3. Payment Service: Processes payments (deployed using AWS Lambda).

4. User Service: Manages user accounts (deployed on AWS Lambda).

Each service exposes its functionality as a set of APIs or functions, but the clients do not interact with these directly. Instead, all client requests are routed through Amazon API Gateway, which directs the requests to the correct microservice.

## Step-by-Step Implementation

### 1. Create and Deploy Microservices
Each microservice is deployed independently using AWS services:

- Product Service: Deployed as a containerized service using Amazon ECS or EKS.

- Order Service: Deployed in Amazon EKS, managing order data and coordinating other services.
- Payment Service: Implemented as serverless functions using AWS Lambda.
- User Service: Deployed using AWS Lambda for user management tasks such as registration, login, and profile management.

Each microservice is assigned its own unique endpoint, such as:
- `https://product-service.mydomain.com`
- `https://order-service.mydomain.com`
- `https://payment-service.mydomain.com`
- `https://user-service.mydomain.com`

## 2. Set Up Amazon API Gateway

Amazon API Gateway is configured to route incoming client requests to the appropriate backend services. It acts as the centralized entry point for the application, handling routing, security, and transformation of requests.

- Create an API in API Gateway: In the AWS Management Console, you can create a new REST API or HTTP API, which serves as the frontend for the microservices.

- Define API Resources and Methods: For each microservice, define the resource paths (e.g., `/products`, `/orders`, `/payments`, `/users`) and HTTP methods (e.g., GET, POST).

## Example of API Gateway routing configuration:

- Products Endpoint (`/products`) routes to Product Service (ECS/EKS).
- Orders Endpoint (`/orders`) routes to Order Service (EKS).
- Payments Endpoint (`/payments`) routes to Payment Service (Lambda).
- Users Endpoint (`/users`) routes to User Service (Lambda).

## 3. Routing Requests

The API Gateway routes incoming requests to the appropriate backend service based on the configured resource paths.

- For example, a request to `https://api.mydomain.com/products` is routed to the Product Service hosted in Amazon ECS.
- A request to `https://api.mydomain.com/orders` is routed to the Order Service hosted in Amazon EKS.
- A request to `https://api.mydomain.com/payments` triggers the Payment Service function in AWS Lambda.

**Example API Gateway OpenAPI definition for routing:**

**Yaml**

```yaml
openapi: 3.0.1
info:
  title: E-commerce API Gateway
  version: 1.0.0
paths:
  /products:
    get:
      x-amazon-apigateway-integration:
        uri: arn:aws:apigateway:region:ecs:path/services/ProductService
        httpMethod: GET
        type: http_proxy
  /orders:
    post:
      x-amazon-apigateway-integration:
        uri: arn:aws:apigateway:region:eks:path/services/OrderService
        httpMethod: POST
        type: http_proxy
  /payments:
    post:
      x-amazon-apigateway-integration:
```

```
uri:      arn:aws:apigateway:region:lambda:path/
functions/PaymentService
    httpMethod: POST
    type: aws_proxy
/users:
  get:
    x-amazon-apigateway-integration:
      uri:      arn:aws:apigateway:region:lambda:path/
functions/UserService
    httpMethod: GET
    type: aws_proxy
```

## 4. Authentication and Authorization

Amazon API Gateway integrates with AWS IAM and Amazon Cognito for managing authentication and authorization.

- IAM Roles and Policies: Set up IAM roles to control access to the API. For example, certain endpoints like `/orders` and `/payments` may require elevated permissions.
- Amazon Cognito: Used for user authentication. Clients are required to authenticate via Cognito, which issues JWT tokens to be included in the requests.

**Example of a security policy in API Gateway using Cognito:**

**Yaml**

```
security:
 - cognitoAuth: []
components:
  securitySchemes:
   cognitoAuth:
    type: oauth2
    flows:
     authorizationCode:
      authorizationUrl:      https://myapp.auth.us-west-2.amazoncognito.com/login
```

> tokenUrl:                   https://myapp.auth.us-
> west-2.amazoncognito.com/oauth2/token
> scopes:
> read: Allows reading resources

## 5. Throttling and Rate Limiting

API Gateway can limit the number of requests a client can make to prevent the backend services from being overwhelmed. You can define request throttling limits and quotas for each API stage.

Example rate limiting policy:

- Burst Limit: 500 requests per second.
- Rate Limit: 1,000 requests per minute.

These limits ensure that traffic spikes do not overload your microservices.

## 6. Caching Responses

To reduce the load on backend services and improve response times, API Gateway supports caching. For example, responses from the Product Service can be cached for a certain duration (e.g., 60 seconds) to reduce the need for repetitive database queries.

**Example caching configuration in API Gateway:**

**Yaml**

```yaml
x-amazon-apigateway-integration:
  type: http_proxy
  httpMethod: GET
  uri:       arn:aws:apigateway:region:ecs:path/services/
ProductService
  cacheKeyParameters:
    - name: "method.request.querystring.category"
  cachingEnabled: true
```

## 7. Monitoring and Logging with CloudWatch

AWS CloudWatch is used to monitor API Gateway metrics, including request counts, error rates, and latencies. CloudWatch Logs provides detailed logs for each API request, helping to troubleshoot issues.

- CloudWatch Metrics: Track performance metrics for the API, such as average latency, request counts, and 4xx/5xx error rates.
- CloudWatch Alarms: Set up alarms for critical conditions, such as high error rates or excessive response latencies.

## 8. Global Load Balancing with AWS CloudFront

Amazon CloudFront can be used with API Gateway to provide a global content delivery network (CDN) and caching layer, improving performance for users worldwide.

- CloudFront caches API responses closer to the clients and reduces latency, providing faster access to frequently requested resources.

## Example Workflow for API Requests

1. Client Request: A client (web or mobile) sends a request to the API Gateway to get product details:
   - `GET https://api.mydomain.com/products`

2. API Gateway Routing: The API Gateway routes the request to the Product Service running in Amazon ECS.

3. Authentication: If the request is to a secure endpoint (e.g., `/orders`), API Gateway verifies the client's authentication using Amazon Cognito and checks the IAM role permissions.

4. Response: The Product Service sends the response back to the API Gateway, which forwards it to the client.

5. Order Processing: When a user places an order, the API Gateway forwards the request to the Order Service in EKS,

which processes the order and coordinates with the

**Payment Service (AWS Lambda).**

6. Payment Service: The Payment Service (Lambda function) is invoked to process the payment asynchronously after the order is placed.

7. Monitoring: AWS CloudWatch monitors API requests and logs performance metrics like latency and error rates.

**Benefits of Using API Gateway with Microservices on AWS**

- Unified API Management: Amazon API Gateway provides a single point of access for multiple microservices, simplifying client interactions.
- Security: API Gateway integrates with AWS IAM and Amazon Cognito to secure API access and handle authentication.
- Scalability: Microservices can scale independently using AWS services like Lambda, ECS, and EKS.
- Monitoring and Analytics: CloudWatch offers comprehensive monitoring and logging, providing visibility into API usage and performance.
- Global Reach: Amazon CloudFront enables low-latency access to APIs across different geographic regions.

The API Gateway pattern in AWS, powered by Amazon API Gateway, simplifies interactions with microservices by providing a unified and secure entry point. With features like routing, authentication, rate limiting, caching, and monitoring, it effectively handles the complexities of managing multiple microservices across services like AWS Lambda, Amazon ECS, and Amazon EKS. This architecture is scalable, flexible, and well-suited for distributed microservice-based applications.

# CHAPTER 7. SERVICE DISCOVERY

In a microservices architecture, applications are broken down into multiple independent services that perform specific business functions. These services are typically distributed across different servers or containers, and they communicate over a network using APIs. One of the key challenges in such an architecture is how each service discovers the other services it needs to interact with, especially since services can scale dynamically, move between different nodes, or even fail and be restarted.

Service Discovery solves this challenge by automating the process of finding and connecting services within a microservices architecture. It ensures that services can find each other reliably, regardless of their dynamic nature.

## Key Concepts of Service Discovery

**1. Service Registration:** This involves registering services with a central registry (or service discovery mechanism) when they start. The service sends metadata like its network location (IP address, port number, etc.) to the registry.

**2. Service Lookup (Service Resolution):** When one service needs to communicate with another, it queries the service registry to find the location (IP and port) of the desired service.

**3. Heartbeat and Health Checks:** Service registries often include mechanisms to check the health of services. Services periodically send "heartbeat" signals to indicate they're still active, or health checks are performed to remove failed or unresponsive services from the registry.

**4. Dynamic Scalability:** As services are scaled up or down, instances register and deregister automatically, allowing service discovery to handle dynamic environments efficiently.

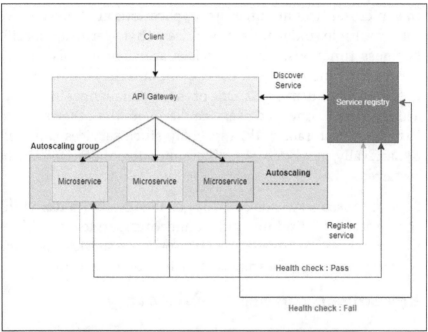

**7.1 Service discovery with autoscaling and health check**

# Types of Service Discovery

1. Client-Side Service Discovery
2. Server-Side Service Discovery

## 1. Client-Side Service Discovery

In client-side discovery, the client (or calling service) is responsible for determining the location of the target service. The client directly queries a Service Registry to find the available instances of a service and then communicates with one of the instances.

**Service Registry:** A database that holds a list of available services and their network locations.

**Load Balancing:** The client chooses a service instance from the registry based on some strategy (round-robin, least connections, etc.).

**Example of Client-Side Discovery in Practice:**

**Netflix Eureka:** A widely-used open-source service registry for client-side service discovery. Clients query Eureka to find available services.

**Consul:** Another popular service discovery tool that provides service registry and health checking capabilities.

**Workflow:**

**1. The service** (e.g., `Order Service`) registers itself with the Service Registry (Eureka/Consul).
**2. The client** (e.g., `Payment Service`) queries the service registry for available instances of the `Order Service`.
**3.** The client selects one instance based on load balancing strategies and directly communicates with that service.

**Advantages:**

- Less load on the network since the client queries the registry directly.
- The client can implement advanced load-balancing strategies (round-robin, least connections).

**Challenges:**

- Each client must implement the discovery logic.
- Tight coupling between services and service registry, as

the client needs to be aware of the registry's location.

# 2. Server-Side Service Discovery

In server-side service discovery, the client does not query the service registry directly. Instead, it makes a request to a load balancer (or reverse proxy), which is responsible for querying the service registry to locate available service instances. The load balancer handles routing and forwards the client request to the correct service instance.

**Service Registry:** The load balancer or proxy queries the service registry to find service locations.
**Load Balancer:** Manages load balancing between instances, ensuring requests are routed to healthy services.

### Example of Server-Side Discovery in Practice:

- **AWS Elastic Load Balancer (ELB):** Automatically integrates with Amazon's internal service discovery for dynamic service scaling.
- **NGINX or HAProxy:** Often used in Kubernetes or Docker environments, where these proxies dynamically update based on service discovery data.

### Workflow:

1. Services register themselves with a service registry.
2. The client sends a request to a load balancer (e.g., NGINX, AWS ELB).
3. The load balancer queries the service registry, retrieves the address of an available service instance, and forwards the request.

### Advantages:

- Simplifies the client logic since discovery is handled by the load balancer.
- Easy to scale and manage, especially in large environments with many services.

**Challenges:**

- The load balancer could become a bottleneck if not configured properly.
- More components are required, potentially adding complexity to the infrastructure.

# Service Discovery Mechanisms

### 2.1 DNS-Based Service Discovery

In DNS-based service discovery, services register themselves with a DNS server, and clients use domain names to locate services. The DNS server dynamically maps service names to available instances' IP addresses.

Example: AWS ECS with Route 53 uses DNS to resolve service instances by providing service names.

**Workflow:**

- ❖ Services register with a DNS-based service discovery tool (e.g., AWS Route 53, CoreDNS).
- ❖ Clients make requests to the DNS resolver using the service name (e.g., `orders.mydomain.com`).
- ❖ The DNS service resolves the domain to the IP address of an available service instance.

**Advantages:**

- Simplifies service discovery as DNS is widely understood and supported.
- Works well with existing networking infrastructure.

**Challenges:**

- DNS caching can lead to stale IP addresses if service instances change frequently.
- Less flexibility for advanced load balancing strategies.

## 2.2 Service Mesh

A service mesh is a dedicated infrastructure layer built into the microservices architecture to handle service-to-service communication. In a service mesh, discovery, routing, security, and load balancing are abstracted away from individual services and managed by sidecar proxies.

Example: Istio is a popular service mesh that handles service discovery, load balancing, security, and more in a Kubernetes environment.

**Workflow:**
- ❖ Each microservice has a sidecar proxy (such as Envoy) that manages traffic to and from the service.
- ❖ When a service needs to communicate with another, the sidecar proxy queries the control plane for available instances.
- ❖ The sidecar proxy forwards the request to the appropriate service instance.

**Advantages:**
- Centralized control over traffic routing, security, and load balancing.
- Transparent to services—discovery, retries, and monitoring are all handled by the mesh.

**Challenges:**
- Adds complexity to the infrastructure.
- Can introduce overhead in terms of network latency and resource usage.

**Service Discovery in Practice: Tools and Technologies**

**1. Consul**

- Consul provides a distributed service mesh, service discovery, and configuration system.

- It can manage service discovery for microservices running across multiple environments (on-prem, cloud, etc.).

## 2. Netflix Eureka

- Open-source service registry for resilient and scalable service discovery.
- Part of the Netflix OSS stack and often used in Spring Cloud-based microservices architectures.

## 3. Etcd

- A distributed key-value store used primarily for service discovery and configuration in Kubernetes.
- Kubernetes uses `etcd` to store service configurations, allowing services to dynamically discover and communicate with each other.

## 4. Kubernetes Service Discovery

- Kubernetes includes built-in service discovery using DNS. Services in Kubernetes are registered as DNS entries, and pods can discover other services via the internal DNS system.

### Service Discovery Example: Kubernetes with Consul

Let's consider a scenario where a set of microservices (Order Service, Product Service, Payment Service) are running in a Kubernetes cluster, and Consul is used for service discovery.

**1. Service Registration:** Each service (deployed as a Kubernetes pod) registers itself with Consul upon startup. It provides its metadata (IP address, port number, health check URL, etc.) to Consul.

**2. Service Lookup:** When the Payment Service needs to communicate with the Order Service, it queries Consul to find the active instances of the Order Service.

**3. Routing:** The Payment Service selects an instance of the Order Service (e.g., using round-robin or least-connection strategy) and sends the request.

**4. Health Checks:** Consul continuously performs health checks on registered services. If an instance of the Order Service fails, it is removed from the registry, ensuring that the Payment Service will not attempt to communicate with it.

## Benefits of Service Discovery in Microservices

**1. Dynamic Scalability:** Service discovery enables automatic scaling of microservices. As instances are added or removed, the service registry updates dynamically, allowing other services to connect to the new instances without manual configuration.

**2. Fault Tolerance:** By using health checks and removing unresponsive services from the registry, service discovery ensures that failed services are not called, improving system reliability.

**3. Load Balancing:** Service discovery enables efficient load distribution across multiple instances of a microservice, improving the overall performance of the system.

**4. Simplified Network Configuration:** With service discovery, services do not need to hard-code the IP addresses or URLs of other services, simplifying the configuration and deployment process.

## Challenges of Service Discovery

**1. Latency:** Introducing a service discovery mechanism can add latency, particularly when the registry is queried frequently.

**2. Complexity:** Setting up and maintaining a service discovery system, especially in large microservices architectures, can introduce operational complexity.

**3. Single Point of Failure:** The service registry itself can become a single point of failure. Proper redundancy and fault tolerance mechanisms (like replication) need to be in place to mitigate this risk.

Service discovery is a critical component in microservices architectures that enables services to find and communicate with each other efficiently in dynamic, distributed environments. Whether using client-side discovery, server-side discovery, DNS, or service meshes, proper service discovery ensures reliability, scalability, and seamless interaction between microservices.

# Service discovery in Google cloud platform (GCP)

In Google Cloud Platform (GCP), service discovery is crucial for enabling microservices to dynamically locate and communicate with each other without hardcoding service locations. GCP provides several tools and services to implement service discovery, particularly in environments where services are deployed on Google Kubernetes Engine (GKE), Google Cloud Run, Google Compute Engine (GCE), or Google App Engine.

### Service Discovery Pattern in GCP

The typical service discovery pattern in GCP is based on a combination of DNS-based service discovery and Load Balancing. With GKE, you can leverage Kubernetes Service and Kubernetes DNS, while other compute options like Cloud Run or Compute Engine can use Internal DNS, Cloud Load Balancer, and Service Directory for service registration and discovery.

### Key Components for Service Discovery in GCP:

**1. Kubernetes DNS in GKE**: Automatic DNS resolution for services within the GKE cluster.

**2. Service Directory:** A fully managed service registry that enables service discovery across various environments in GCP.

**3. Cloud Load Balancer:** Handles traffic distribution across microservices running on different instances.

**4. Internal DNS (Compute Engine):** DNS-based service discovery for virtual machine instances and other services.

**5. Health Checks and Monitoring:** Services like Cloud Monitoring and Health Checks ensure only healthy services are discoverable.

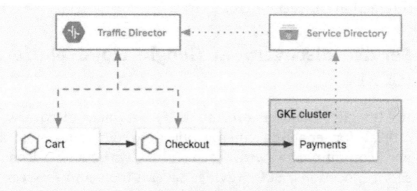

**7.2 Service discovery in GCP**

## Example: Service Discovery in GCP Using GKE and Service Directory

**Scenario:**

Let's consider a microservices architecture for an e-commerce application deployed in GCP. The system includes the following microservices:

- Product Service: Manages product catalog.
- Order Service: Handles customer orders.
- Payment Service: Processes payments.
- User Service: Manages user authentication and profiles.

These services are deployed across Google Kubernetes Engine (GKE) and Google Cloud Run. Service discovery is essential for dynamic interaction between these microservices.

# Step-by-Step Service Discovery in GCP

### 1. Using Kubernetes DNS for Service Discovery in GKE

Kubernetes DNS in GKE provides service discovery within the cluster automatically. Each service deployed in the cluster is assigned a DNS name, and pods can communicate with other services using their DNS name.

**For example:**

- Product Service is deployed in GKE and exposed as a Kubernetes service with the name `product-service`.
- Order Service is deployed similarly in GKE and exposed as `order-service`.

Kubernetes automatically registers these services in the cluster's DNS, allowing other services to discover them by querying their DNS names.

**Kubernetes DNS Workflow:**

- The Product Service is deployed in GKE and exposed as a Kubernetes service.
- The Order Service needs to communicate with the Product Service.
- Instead of hardcoding the IP address, the Order Service uses the DNS name `product-service.default.svc.cluster.local` to discover the Product Service.
- Kubernetes resolves this DNS name to the current IP address of the Product Service, ensuring that the Order Service can reach it.

## Yaml

```
apiVersion: v1
kind: Service
metadata:
```

```
          name: product-service
      spec:
        selector:
          app: product
        ports:
          - protocol: TCP
            port: 80
            targetPort: 8080
```

In this example, the Order Service simply communicates with the Product Service via `http://product-service` (within the same Kubernetes namespace).

**Benefits:**

- Automatic DNS Registration: Kubernetes services are automatically assigned a DNS name.
- Service Discovery Across Pods: Services within the same cluster can easily discover and communicate with each other without manual configuration.

## 2. Using Service Directory for Cross-Environment Discovery

For services deployed across different environments (e.g., some services in GKE, others in Cloud Run or Compute Engine), you can use Google Cloud's Service Directory to handle cross-environment service discovery.

### What is a Service Directory?

Google Cloud Service Directory is a fully managed service that allows you to register and discover services across multiple environments. It supports both VMs, serverless services, and containerized services.

### Example Workflow:

1. Product Service and Order Service are running in GKE.
2. Payment Service is deployed using Cloud Run.

3. User Service is deployed on Compute Engine as a VM.

Each of these services registers itself with Service Directory so that other services can discover them, regardless of their deployment environment.

**Step-by-Step Process:**

**1. Register Services in Service Directory:** Each service (Product, Order, Payment, and User) registers with the Service Directory using the GCP SDK, specifying its network endpoint (IP address, port, or Cloud Run URL).

**Example of service registration:**

**Bash**

```
gcloud service-directory services create product-service \
    --namespace=ecommerce-namespace \
    --service-endpoint=product-service.default.svc.cluster.local
```

**2. Service Lookup:** When the Order Service needs to call the Payment Service, it queries the Service Directory to get the endpoint of the Payment Service.

**Example of querying a service:**

**Bash**

```
gcloud service-directory endpoints lookup \
    --namespace=ecommerce-namespace \
    --service=payment-service
```

This command retrieves the current network location (IP or URL) of the Payment Service.

Example: Registering the Payment Service in Service Directory (Cloud Run Service):

## Bash

```
gcloud service-directory endpoints create payment-service \
  --namespace=ecommerce-namespace \
  --address=payment-service.run.app \
  --port=443
```

**3. Cross-Service Communication:** Once the Order Service resolves the Payment Services address via Service Directory, it can communicate with it directly over HTTP.

## Benefits of Using Service Directory:

- Cross-Environment Discovery: Supports service discovery across GKE, Cloud Run, Compute Engine, and other environments.
- Managed Service: No need to manage a service registry yourself; GCP handles it for you.
- Fine-Grained Control: Service Directory allows you to manage service visibility, set permissions, and configure health checks.

## 4. Combining Service Directory with Cloud Load Balancer

In more complex setups, where services span multiple regions or need high availability, Google Cloud Load Balancer can be used in conjunction with Service Directory. This allows service discovery to scale globally and ensures load is balanced across multiple service instances.

## Example Workflow:

A. User Service is running on multiple VMs in different regions.
B. These VMs register themselves in the Service Directory.

C. Cloud Load Balancer is configured to route traffic to the appropriate region, depending on the user's location or service availability.

D. Service Directory keeps track of service instances, and the Load Balancer dynamically routes requests to healthy service instances.

**Service Health Monitoring and Discovery in GCP**

To ensure that only healthy services are discoverable, Cloud Monitoring and Health Checks are used. GKE, Cloud Run, and Compute Engine all integrate with Cloud Monitoring, providing detailed metrics about service health and performance.

- **Health Checks:** Periodically test whether the service instances are functioning correctly. Unhealthy instances are automatically removed from the service registry (Service Directory or Load Balancer).

- **Cloud Monitoring:** Provides insights into service performance, latency, and uptime, ensuring high availability.

**Service Discovery in GCP Example Summary**

1. GKE with Kubernetes DNS: Microservices deployed within a GKE cluster automatically discover each other using Kubernetes' internal DNS system. This allows services like Order Service to communicate with Product Service using service names.

2. Service Directory for Cross-Environment Discovery: For services running in different environments (e.g., Cloud Run, Compute Engine, or across multiple GKE clusters), Service Directory enables seamless service discovery. This is especially useful in hybrid environments where services are not limited to one type of compute.

3. Cloud Load Balancer and Service Directory: Combine global

load balancing with Service Directory for service discovery in multi-region and multi-environment setups. This provides high availability, health checking, and low-latency service access.

Service discovery in GCP can be efficiently handled using a combination of tools like Kubernetes DNS, Service Directory, and Cloud Load Balancer. Depending on the environment (GKE, Cloud Run, or Compute Engine), you can implement service discovery patterns that ensure scalability, reliability, and seamless communication between microservices. By leveraging GCP's fully managed services, you can simplify the complexities of service registration, lookup, and health monitoring in a microservices architecture.

# Service discovery in Azure

In Microsoft Azure, service discovery is a key aspect of managing microservices architectures, enabling services to locate and communicate with each other dynamically. Azure provides several tools and services to implement service discovery, especially within environments like Azure Kubernetes Service (AKS), Azure App Service, and Azure Functions.

### Service Discovery Pattern in Azure

In Azure, service discovery typically involves leveraging Azure Kubernetes Service (AKS), Azure Service Fabric, or Azure App Service along with Azure DNS, Azure Front Door, and Azure Traffic Manager for effective service management and routing.

### Key Components for Service Discovery in Azure:

1. Azure Kubernetes Service (AKS): Uses Kubernetes DNS for internal service discovery within the cluster.

2. Azure Service Fabric: Provides built-in service discovery and naming services.

3. Azure DNS: Provides DNS-based service discovery for services with public and private endpoints.

4. Azure Front Door and Traffic Manager: For global load balancing and routing.

**Example: Service Discovery in Azure Using AKS and Azure Service Fabric**

Scenario:

Let's consider a microservices architecture for an online booking application deployed in Azure. The architecture includes:

- Booking Service: Manages booking operations.

- Payment Service: Processes payments.

- User Service: Handles user profiles and authentication.

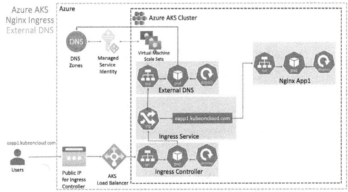

**7.3 Service Discovery in Azure**

The services are deployed using Azure Kubernetes Service (AKS) and Azure Service Fabric. Service discovery is crucial to allow these services to interact dynamically.

# Step-by-Step Service Discovery in Azure

## 1. Using Kubernetes DNS for Service Discovery in AKS

Kubernetes DNS within Azure Kubernetes Service (AKS) automatically handles service discovery inside the cluster. Each service is assigned a DNS name, making it easy for other services to communicate with it.

Example Workflow in AKS:
1. Service Deployment: Deploy the Booking Service, Payment Service, and User Service to AKS, each exposed as a Kubernetes Service.

2. DNS Registration: Kubernetes automatically registers these services with DNS. Each service gets a DNS name that follows the format: `service-name.namespace.svc.cluster.local`.

**Example Kubernetes Service manifest for the Booking Service:**
**Yaml**

```yaml
apiVersion: v1
kind: Service
metadata:
  name: booking-service
spec:
  selector:
    app: booking
  ports:
    - protocol: TCP
      port: 80
      targetPort: 8080
```

3. Service Communication: If the User Service needs to call the Booking Service, it uses the DNS name `booking-service.default.svc.cluster.local`.

**User Service making a request:**
**Python**

```python
import requests
```

*response = requests.get('http://booking-service.default.svc.cluster.local/bookings')*

Kubernetes resolves `booking-service.default.svc.cluster.local` to the current IP address of the Booking Service.

Benefits:
- Automatic DNS Registration: No need for manual configuration.
- Internal Communication: Easy service discovery within the Kubernetes cluster.

## 2. Service Discovery with Azure Service Fabric

Azure Service Fabric provides built-in service discovery through its Naming Service, which helps services discover and communicate with each other.

Example Workflow in Service Fabric:

1. Service Deployment: Deploy microservices as Stateless or Stateful Services in Azure Service Fabric.

2. Service Registration: Services register with the Service Fabric Naming Service upon startup.

Example Service Fabric code snippet to resolve a service endpoint:

### Csharp

```
var servicePartitionResolver = ServicePartitionResolver.GetDefault();
var serviceUri = new Uri("fabric:/MyApp/BookingService");
var servicePartition = await servicePartitionResolver.ResolveAsync(serviceUri);
```

3. Service Communication: Once resolved, services use the endpoint to communicate.

Example of calling the Payment Service from Booking Service:

**Csharp**

```
var client = new HttpClient();
var response = await client.GetAsync("http://
payment-service/api/payments");
```

Benefits:
- Built-in Discovery: Service Fabric handles service registration and discovery.
- Cluster-Aware: Services are aware of each other's locations within the Service Fabric cluster.

## 3. Using Azure DNS for Public and Private Service Discovery

Azure DNS provides both public and private DNS solutions, which can be used for service discovery for services with public endpoints or within Azure Virtual Networks.

Example Workflow with Azure DNS:
1. Service Deployment: Deploy services with public endpoints or within a virtual network.

2. DNS Registration: Register services with Azure DNS.

Example for a public service:

**Bash**

```
az network dns record-set a add-record --resource-group
myResourceGroup --zone-name mydomain.com --record-set-name
booking-service --ipv4-address 52.178.123.45
```

3. Service Discovery: Access services using the registered domain name.

Example of accessing the Booking Service:

## Python

```
import requests

response        =        requests.get('http://booking-
service.mydomain.com/bookings')
```

Benefits:
- Public and Private DNS: Flexibility to handle both public and private service discovery needs.
- Easy Management: Centralized DNS management in Azure.

# 4. Global Load Balancing and Routing with Azure Front Door and Traffic Manager

Azure Front Door and Azure Traffic Manager are used for global service load balancing and routing, ensuring high availability and low latency.

**Example Workflow:**

1. Deploy Services Globally: Deploy services across multiple regions.

2. Configure Azure Front Door: Set up Front Door to distribute traffic based on routing rules.

**Example configuration:**

## Bash

```
az        frontdoor        create        --resource-group
myResourceGroup      --name      myFrontDoor      --backend-
addresses  booking-service1.region1.azurewebsites.net  booking-
```

*service2.region2.azurewebsites.net*

3. Service Discovery and Routing: Azure Front Door routes user requests to the nearest or most available service instance.

Example of traffic routing:
- User requests are routed to `booking-service1.region1.azurewebsites.net` if they are in Region 1.
- Users in Region 2 are routed to `booking-service2.region2.azurewebsites.net`.

Benefits:
- Global Reach: Distributes traffic across multiple regions.
- High Availability: Ensures services are reachable and responsive from anywhere in the world.

**Service Discovery in Azure Example Summary**

1. AKS with Kubernetes DNS: Provides internal DNS-based service discovery within the AKS cluster, allowing services like Booking Service to be discovered by their DNS names.

2. Azure Service Fabric: Uses its Naming Service for built-in service registration and discovery, simplifying communication between services within a Service Fabric cluster.

3. Azure DNS: Offers both public and private DNS solutions for service discovery, suitable for services with public endpoints or within virtual networks.

4. Azure Front Door and Traffic Manager: Facilitate global load balancing and routing, ensuring efficient traffic distribution and high availability across multiple regions.

Service discovery in Azure is streamlined with a combination of built-in Kubernetes DNS, Azure Service Fabric's Naming Service, Azure DNS, and global load balancers like Azure Front Door and Traffic Manager. These tools provide robust solutions for managing dynamic microservices environments, ensuring seamless communication and scalability while simplifying infrastructure management.

# Service discovery in AWS

In Amazon Web Services (AWS), service discovery is essential for managing interactions between microservices deployed in a distributed architecture. AWS provides several services and mechanisms to facilitate service discovery, particularly in environments like Amazon ECS (Elastic Container Service), Amazon EKS (Elastic Kubernetes Service), and AWS Lambda.

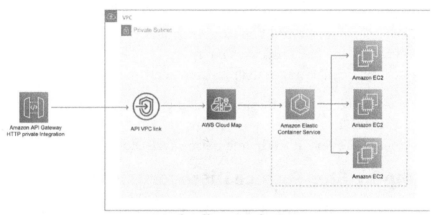

**7.4 Service discovery in AWS**

### Service Discovery Pattern in AWS

The typical service discovery pattern in AWS involves using AWS Cloud Map, Amazon Route 53, and AWS Service Discovery within ECS and EKS environments. Each of these tools helps services locate and interact with each other dynamically.

Key Components for Service Discovery in AWS:
1. AWS Cloud Map: A service registry that provides service discovery and health checking.
2. Amazon Route 53: DNS-based service discovery for both internal and external services.
3. AWS ECS Service Discovery: Built-in service discovery for

ECS services using AWS Cloud Map.

4. Amazon EKS Service Discovery: Kubernetes-native service discovery using Kubernetes DNS.

5. AWS Lambda: For serverless applications, service discovery is managed through API Gateway or service integration with AWS Cloud Map.

### Example: Service Discovery in AWS Using ECS and AWS Cloud Map

Scenario:

Consider a microservices architecture for an e-commerce application deployed in AWS. The architecture includes:

- Product Service: Manages product catalog.
- Order Service: Handles customer orders.
- Payment Service: Processes payments.
- User Service: Manages user authentication and profiles.

These services are deployed using Amazon ECS (Elastic Container Service) with AWS Fargate or EC2 instances, and service discovery is managed using AWS Cloud Map.

# Step-by-Step Service Discovery in AWS

## 1. Using AWS Cloud Map for Service Discovery

AWS Cloud Map provides a centralized service registry for discovering services. It allows you to register services with Cloud Map, which maintains a list of service instances and their health status.

### Example Workflow with ECS and AWS Cloud Map:

1. Create a Namespace in AWS Cloud Map:
   - A namespace is a container for service instances. It can be either public or private.

   Example AWS CLI command to create a private namespace:

**Bash**

*aws servicediscovery create-private-dns-namespace \*
*--name my-namespace \*
*--vpc vpc-0abcd1234efgh5678*

2. Register Services:
 - Register each service with AWS Cloud Map. For ECS, this can be done automatically when defining the service.

Example ECS Task Definition for the Product Service:

**Json**

```json
{
  "family": "product-service",
  "containerDefinitions": [
    {
      "name": "product-container",
      "image": "my-product-image",
      "essential": true,
      "portMappings": [
        {
          "containerPort": 80
        }
      ]
    }
  ],
  "networkMode": "awsvpc",
  "requiresCompatibilities": [
    "FARGATE"
  ]
}
```

Example ECS Service Definition with Cloud Map Integration:

**Json**

```json
{
```

```
    "serviceName": "product-service",
    "taskDefinition": "product-service",
    "desiredCount": 2,
    "serviceRegistries": [
      {
        "registryArn":
"arn:aws:servicediscovery:region:account-id:service/
srv-xxxxxx"
      }
    ]
}
```

3. Service Communication:
   - Services like Order Service query AWS Cloud Map to resolve the endpoint of the Product Service.

Example of querying AWS Cloud Map for the Product Service:

**Python**

```python
import boto3

client = boto3.client('servicediscovery')

response = client.discover_instances(
  NamespaceName='my-namespace',
  ServiceName='product-service'
)
instances = response['Instances']
```

The `discover_instances` call retrieves the network address of the Product Service. The Order Service then uses this address to communicate with the Product Service.

Benefits:
- Centralized Service Registry: AWS Cloud Map maintains a single source of truth for service endpoints and health status.

- Automatic Integration: ECS services can automatically register and deregister with AWS Cloud Map, simplifying management.

# 2. Using Amazon Route 53 for DNS-Based Service Discovery

Amazon Route 53 can be used for DNS-based service discovery for both internal and external services.

**Example Workflow with Route 53:**

1. Create a Hosted Zone:
   - Create a private hosted zone in Route 53 for internal service discovery.

Example AWS CLI command to create a private hosted zone:

**Bash**

```
aws route53 create-hosted-zone \
  --name myinternal.example.com \
  --vpc                          VPCRegion=us-east-1,VPCId=vpc-0abcd1234efgh5678 \
  --caller-reference my-reference
```

2. Register Service Records:
   - Create DNS records for services that are registered with Route 53.

Example AWS CLI command to create an A record:

**Bash**

```
aws route53 change-resource-record-sets \
  --hosted-zone-id Z1234567890 \
  --change-batch '{
    "Changes": [
      {
        "Action": "UPSERT",
```

```
    "ResourceRecordSet": {
    "Name": "product-service.myinternal.example.com",
    "Type": "A",
    "TTL": 60,
    "ResourceRecords": [
      {
        "Value": "10.0.0.1"
      }
    ]
   }
  }
 ]
}'
```

3. Service Communication:
   - Services can use the DNS names registered in Route 53 to locate other services.

Example of querying Route 53 from a service:

**Python**

```
import socket

address       =       socket.gethostbyname('product-service.myinternal.example.com')
```

The Order Service uses the DNS name `product-service.myinternal.example.com` to find the Product Service.

Benefits:
- DNS-Based Discovery: Leverages standard DNS protocols, simplifying service discovery for applications.
- Public and Private DNS: Supports both public-facing and internal DNS needs.

## 3. Using Amazon EKS for Kubernetes Native Service Discovery

In Amazon EKS, service discovery is handled by Kubernetes DNS, which provides built-in service discovery within the cluster.

**Example Workflow in EKS:**

1. Deploy Services:
  - Deploy services in EKS, exposing them using Kubernetes services.

Example Kubernetes Service manifest for Product Service:

## Yaml

```yaml
apiVersion: v1
kind: Service
metadata:
  name: product-service
spec:
  selector:
    app: product
  ports:
    - protocol: TCP
      port: 80
      targetPort: 8080
```

2. DNS Registration:
  - Kubernetes automatically assigns a DNS name to each service, following the format: `service-name.namespace.svc.cluster.local`.

3. Service Communication:
  - Services use the DNS names provided by Kubernetes to locate each other.

Example of service communication:

## Python

```
import requests

response            =            requests.get('http://product-
service.default.svc.cluster.local/bookings')
```

Benefits:
- Automatic DNS Management: Kubernetes handles DNS resolution automatically.
- Internal Cluster Communication: Simplifies service discovery within the Kubernetes cluster.

## Service Discovery in AWS Example Summary

1. AWS Cloud Map with ECS: Provides centralized service registration and discovery. ECS services register themselves with Cloud Map, allowing other services to discover them dynamically.

2. Amazon Route 53: Offers DNS-based service discovery for internal and public services. Services are registered with Route 53, and other services use DNS queries to discover them.

3. Amazon EKS: Uses Kubernetes DNS for internal service discovery within an EKS cluster. Services communicate using DNS names assigned by Kubernetes.

Service discovery in AWS can be efficiently managed using AWS Cloud Map, Amazon Route 53, and Amazon EKS DNS. AWS Cloud Map offers a centralized service registry for dynamic service registration and discovery, Route 53 provides DNS-based service discovery, and Kubernetes DNS in EKS simplifies internal service discovery within Kubernetes clusters. These tools ensure that microservices can seamlessly discover and communicate with each other in a distributed environment.

# CHAPTER 8. DATA PATTERNS

In microservices architecture, data management and data patterns are crucial due to the decentralized nature of the system. Each microservice typically manages its own data, leading to various challenges and patterns in data handling. Here's a detailed overview of key data patterns used in microservices architectures:

## 1. Data Ownership and Decentralization

### Pattern: Data Ownership

The Data Ownership pattern in microservices architecture is a fundamental principle that dictates how data is managed and accessed across different microservices. In this pattern, each microservice is responsible for its own data and is the sole owner of the data it processes. This approach aligns with the decentralized nature of microservices and promotes service autonomy, scalability, and maintainability.

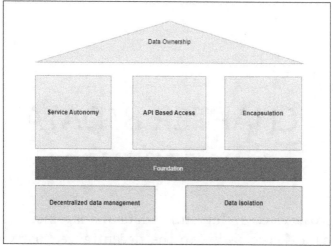

**8.1 Data Ownership**

## Key Concepts of Data Ownership Pattern

### 1. Service Autonomy:

- Each microservice is responsible for its own data store, which means it can manage and evolve its schema independently without affecting other services.

- This autonomy reduces coupling between services and allows each service to scale its data storage and processing needs according to its specific requirements.

### 2. Encapsulation:

- Data ownership implies that a service encapsulates its data and provides controlled access through well-defined APIs. This encapsulation ensures that other services interact with the data only through these APIs, maintaining a clear boundary of responsibility.

### 3. Decentralized Data Management:

- Instead of a centralized database, each service has its own database or data store. This decentralization aligns with the microservices principle of decentralization and avoids a single point of failure.

### 4. API-Based Access:

- Services expose their data through APIs, and other services must use these APIs to read or modify the data. This approach ensures that data access is controlled and consistent.

**5. Data Isolation:**

- Services are isolated from each other in terms of data management. Changes to one service's data model do not impact other services, which enhances the flexibility and maintainability of the system.

**Advantages of Data Ownership Pattern**

1. Service Autonomy:
- Each service can evolve its data model independently, leading to better maintainability and agility in development.

2. Scalability:
- Services can scale their data storage and processing capabilities based on their individual needs without affecting other services.

3. Decoupling:
- Reduces coupling between services by avoiding shared databases, which enhances the overall flexibility and resilience of the system.

4. Improved Data Security:
- Services can implement their own security and access control mechanisms, providing more granular control over data access.

**Challenges of Data Ownership Pattern**

1. Data Consistency:
- Ensuring consistency across multiple data stores can be challenging. Changes in one service may need to be propagated to others, which can be complex to manage.

2. Data Duplication:
- Some data might be duplicated across services, leading

to potential synchronization issues and increased storage requirements.

3. Integration Complexity:
   - Services need to interact through APIs to access each other's data, which can introduce additional complexity and latency in data retrieval.

4. Distributed Transactions:
   - Managing transactions that span multiple services can be complex, requiring patterns like Sagas or Two-Phase Commit to handle distributed transactions effectively.

# Examples of Data Ownership Pattern

### Example 1: E-commerce Application

In an e-commerce application, different microservices manage different aspects of the system:

- Product Service: Manages product information, such as product details, pricing, and inventory.
- Order Service: Handles customer orders, including order creation, status updates, and order history.
- User Service: Manages user profiles, authentication, and user preferences.

**Data Ownership:**
- The Product Service owns the product data and provides APIs for retrieving and updating product details.
- The Order Service owns the order data and provides APIs for managing orders.
- The User Service owns user profile data and provides APIs for user authentication and profile management.

**Data Access:**
- The Order Service might need to retrieve product details to include in an order. It accesses this information through the Product Service's API, rather than directly querying a shared

database.

## Example 2: Financial System

In a financial system, different microservices handle various financial operations:

- Account Service: Manages user accounts, including account balances and transaction history.
- Transaction Service: Handles financial transactions, such as deposits and withdrawals.
- Audit Service: Tracks and audits all financial transactions for compliance and reporting.

Data Ownership:
- The Account Service owns account data and provides APIs to query and update account information.
- The Transaction Service owns transaction data and provides APIs to process and query transactions.
- The Audit Service owns audit data and provides APIs to retrieve audit logs and reports.

Data Access:
- The Transaction Service needs to update account balances when processing transactions. It calls the Account Service's API to update account information and retrieve current balances.

## Data Ownership Pattern Implementation Strategies

1. API Design:
   - Design APIs to expose the necessary data and operations while ensuring that data access is controlled and consistent. Use RESTful APIs or GraphQL based on the requirements of the microservices.

2. Data Model Design:
   - Design each microservice's data model to reflect its specific responsibilities. Avoid tight coupling between data models of

different services.

3. Data Synchronization:
- Implement strategies for synchronizing data across services if needed. Use asynchronous communication, event-driven architectures, or data replication to handle data synchronization.

4. Service Communication:
- Use service-to-service communication patterns such as synchronous HTTP calls, asynchronous messaging, or event streaming to facilitate interactions between services.

5. Security and Access Control:
- Implement security measures such as authentication and authorization to control access to each service's data. Use mechanisms like OAuth, API keys, or JWT tokens to secure API access.

The Data Ownership pattern is a core principle in microservices architecture that promotes service autonomy, encapsulation, and decentralized data management. While it offers significant benefits in terms of flexibility, scalability, and maintainability, it also introduces challenges related to data consistency, duplication, and integration complexity. By adopting appropriate strategies for API design, data synchronization, and security, organizations can effectively implement the Data Ownership pattern and build robust microservices-based systems.

# 2. Data Synchronization and Consistency

## Pattern: Event Sourcing

Event Sourcing is a data management pattern used in microservices architecture that focuses on capturing and storing the state changes of a system as a sequence of events. Rather than persisting the current state of an entity directly, event sourcing involves recording each change or event that affects the entity. The current state of the entity can then be reconstructed by replaying these events.

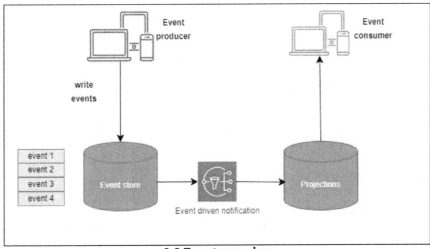

**8.2 Event sourcing**

## Key Concepts of Event Sourcing

1. Event Store:
   - An event store is a specialized database or storage system where events are recorded. Each event represents a state change and is stored in the order in which it occurred.

2. Events:
   - Events are immutable records of state changes. Each event contains the data necessary to describe the change and any relevant metadata.

3. Event Sourcing Model:
   - The model consists of three main components:
     - Event Producer: The component that generates and publishes events (e.g., a service that processes commands and creates events).
     - Event Store: The database or storage where events are persisted.
     - Event Consumer: The component that processes and

reacts to events (e.g., a service that updates projections or read models).

4. Projections:
   - Projections, or read models, are views that represent the current state of entities based on the events. They are updated by replaying events from the event store.

5. Command-Query Responsibility Segregation (CQRS):
   - Event sourcing is often used in conjunction with CQRS, where commands modify the state and generate events, while queries are handled by reading projections or read models.

## Advantages of Event Sourcing

1. Auditability:
   - Full history of changes is maintained, allowing for easy auditing and tracking of all state changes.

2. Flexibility:
   - The current state can be reconstructed at any point in time by replaying events, making it possible to handle complex state transitions and historical analysis.

3. Debugging and Recovery:
   - Errors or bugs can be identified and fixed by replaying events to recreate the state at a specific point in time.

4. Scalability:
   - Event sourcing can help in scaling read and write operations independently, as the write operations (events) are separated from the read operations (projections).

5. Event Replay:
   - Allows for easy changes to projections or read models without affecting the underlying events.

## Challenges of Event Sourcing

1. Complexity:

- Managing and implementing an event store, handling event versioning, and ensuring data consistency can add complexity to the system.

2. Event Storage:
- Event stores can grow large over time, requiring efficient storage and indexing strategies to handle high volumes of events.

3. Event Versioning:
- Changes to event schemas may require versioning and compatibility management to ensure that old events can still be processed by new versions of the system.

4. Eventual Consistency:
- Projections may not always reflect the most recent state immediately, leading to eventual consistency challenges.

# Example Implementation of Event Sourcing in Microservices

### Scenario: E-commerce Order Management System

In an e-commerce system, consider the following services and components:

1. Order Service:
- Responsible for processing orders and managing order state.

2. Inventory Service:
- Manages product inventory and stock levels.

3. Shipping Service:
- Handles shipping and delivery of orders.

### Event Sourcing Workflow

1. Event Creation:
- When an order is placed, the Order Service processes the

command and creates an event like `OrderPlaced`. This event includes details such as the order ID, customer ID, product IDs, quantities, and timestamps.

Example Event:

**Json**

```json
{
  "eventType": "OrderPlaced",
  "orderId": "12345",
  "customerId": "67890",
  "products": [
    { "productId": "prod1", "quantity": 2 },
    { "productId": "prod2", "quantity": 1 }
  ],
  "timestamp": "2024-09-16T14:00:00Z"
}
```

2. Event Storage:

- The `OrderPlaced` event is persisted in the event store. Each event is stored with a unique identifier and timestamp.

3. Event Processing:

- Inventory Service subscribes to `OrderPlaced` events to update its inventory. When it receives an `OrderPlaced` event, it decrements the stock levels based on the ordered products.

4. Projections:

- Order Service creates a projection or read model for orders. This projection maintains the current state of each order by replaying events. For example, an order projection might include the order details, current status, and shipping information.

5. Read Model:

- Queries for order details are served by the projection. When a user requests order information, the query is answered by the read model, which has been updated by replaying the relevant events.

6. Handling Changes:
  - If the order system needs to handle additional fields or different data structures, the projection can be updated to accommodate these changes. The event store remains unchanged, and only the projections need to be updated.

**Eventual Consistency and Recovery**

- Eventual Consistency: The system may need to handle eventual consistency, where the order status may not be immediately reflected in all projections or services.

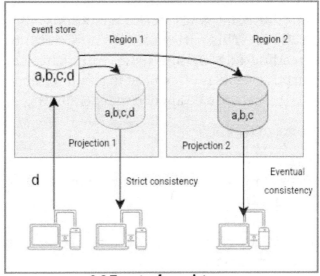

**8.3 Eventual consistency**

- Recovery: If an error occurs, such as an incorrect inventory update, the system can replay events to correct the state or rebuild projections.

The Event Sourcing pattern is a powerful approach to managing data in microservices architecture by focusing on capturing and storing state changes as events. It provides benefits such as auditability, flexibility, and scalability, but also introduces challenges like complexity, event storage management, and eventual consistency. By carefully implementing event sourcing and leveraging patterns like CQRS, organizations can build robust, scalable, and maintainable microservices systems that effectively manage and utilize their data.

# Pattern: CQRS (Command Query Responsibility Segregation)

Command Query Responsibility Segregation (CQRS) is a design pattern in microservices architecture that separates the handling of commands (write operations) from queries (read operations). This pattern allows different models to be used for reading and writing data, optimizing each for its specific purpose. CQRS is often used in conjunction with Event Sourcing, but it can also be applied independently.

**Key Concepts of CQRS**

1. Commands:
   - Commands represent requests to change the state of an entity. They are imperative, meaning they perform an action or request a change.
   - Example: A command to create a new order or update an existing product's price.

2. Queries:
   - Queries represent requests to retrieve data without altering the state. They are declarative, meaning they return information based on the current state.
   - Example: A query to fetch the details of a specific order or retrieve a list of products.

3. Command Model:

- The command model handles the write operations and typically consists of a domain model that represents the business logic and state changes. It processes commands and may generate events or update the state.

4. Query Model:
- The query model handles the read operations and consists of one or more projections or read models. These models are optimized for querying and provide a denormalized view of the data.

5. Eventual Consistency:
- Since the command and query models are separate, they may not always reflect the most recent changes immediately. The system is eventually consistent, meaning that after a write operation, the query model will eventually be updated to reflect the new state.

**Advantages of CQRS**

1. Optimized Read and Write Models:
- Different models can be optimized separately for read and write operations. This can improve performance and scalability.

2. Separation of Concerns:
- Separates the business logic (commands) from the read operations (queries), leading to cleaner and more maintainable code.

3. Scalability:
- Read and write operations can be scaled independently. For instance, read-heavy applications can scale query models separately from write models.

4. Enhanced Security:
- By separating commands and queries, you can enforce different security and validation rules for each, providing more granular control over data access and manipulation.

## 5. Flexibility:

- Allows for the use of different storage technologies or architectures for reading and writing data, based on specific requirements.

### Challenges of CQRS

## 1. Complexity:

- Implementing and maintaining separate models for reading and writing can add complexity to the system. It requires careful management of synchronization and consistency.

## 2. Eventual Consistency:

- Users may see stale data because the query model may not be updated immediately after a write operation. This requires handling eventual consistency in the application logic.

## 3. Data Duplication:

- The query model often involves data duplication or denormalization, which can lead to increased storage requirements and synchronization challenges.

## 4. Consistency Management:

- Ensuring that the read and write models remain consistent can be challenging, especially in distributed systems.

# Example Implementation of CQRS in Microservices

### Scenario: E-commerce Application

In an e-commerce application, you have the following services:

1. Order Service: Manages orders and processes commands related to orders.
2. Product Service: Manages product information and processes commands related to products.
3. Order Query Service: Handles queries related to orders and

provides read access to order data.

## CQRS Workflow

1. Command Handling:
   - A user places an order, which triggers a command to the Order Service.
   - The Order Service processes the command and performs the necessary business logic (e.g., validating stock, calculating total amount).
   - The service updates its domain model and generates events (e.g., `OrderPlaced`, `OrderShipped`).

Example Command:

### Json

```json
{
  "commandType": "PlaceOrder",
  "orderId": "12345",
  "customerId": "67890",
  "items": [
    { "productId": "prod1", "quantity": 2 },
    { "productId": "prod2", "quantity": 1 }
  ]
}
```

2. Event Generation:
   - The Order Service generates events based on the command processing. These events are stored in the event store.

Example Event:

### Json

```json
{
  "eventType": "OrderPlaced",
  "orderId": "12345",
  "customerId": "67890",
```

```json
  "items": [
    { "productId": "prod1", "quantity": 2 },
    { "productId": "prod2", "quantity": 1 }
  ],
  "timestamp": "2024-09-16T14:00:00Z"
}
```

## 3. Query Model Updates:

- The Order Query Service subscribes to events from the event store to update its read model or projection. This projection represents the current state of orders and is optimized for querying.

## 4. Read Operations:

- When a user queries for order details, the Order Query Service provides the requested information from its read model. The read model is designed to handle high-performance queries and may include denormalized or aggregated data.

Example Query:

**Json**

```json
{
  "queryType": "GetOrderDetails",
  "orderId": "12345"
}
```

Example Response:

**Json**

```json
{
  "orderId": "12345",
  "customerId": "67890",
  "items": [
    { "productId": "prod1", "quantity": 2 },
```

```
    { "productId": "prod2", "quantity": 1 }
  ],
  "status": "Shipped",
  "totalAmount": 100.00
}
```

5. Handling Updates:

- If the order status changes (e.g., it is shipped), the Order Service generates an `OrderShipped` event. The Order Query Service updates its read model to reflect this change.

### CQRS and Event Sourcing

CQRS is often used in conjunction with Event Sourcing, where events are used to update the read model. In this combination:

- Commands create or modify events, which are stored in the event store.
- Queries access the read model, which is built from replaying events.

The CQRS pattern is a powerful approach in microservices architecture that separates the concerns of reading and writing data. It allows for optimized models tailored to specific tasks, enhances scalability, and improves maintainability by separating business logic from query logic. However, it also introduces complexity and requires careful management of consistency and synchronization between the command and query models. By effectively implementing CQRS and handling associated challenges, organizations can build flexible and scalable systems that address diverse data access needs.

# 3. Data Integration

## Pattern: API Composition

The API Composition pattern is a data management and

integration approach used in microservices architecture to aggregate data from multiple microservices into a single response. This pattern is particularly useful when a client needs data that spans multiple services or when complex queries involve combining information from different sources.

## Key Concepts of API Composition

1. Aggregation of Data:
    - API Composition involves aggregating responses from multiple microservices into a single, cohesive response for the client. This approach allows clients to retrieve data from various services through a single API endpoint.

2. API Gateway:
    - An API Gateway or an API Composition Service often implements the API Composition pattern. It acts as a central point that orchestrates the retrieval of data from different services and composes the final response.

3. Backend for Frontend (BFF):
    - A Backend for Frontend (BFF) is a specific implementation of API Composition where a service is tailored to meet the needs of a specific client or user interface. The BFF composes data from various microservices to provide a custom response for that client.

4. Service Orchestration:
    - API Composition involves orchestrating multiple service calls to gather the required data. This orchestration can be synchronous (making multiple calls and combining results) or asynchronous (using messaging or event-driven approaches).

## Advantages of API Composition

1. Single Endpoint for Complex Queries:
    - Clients can obtain a comprehensive set of data through a single API endpoint, simplifying client-side logic and reducing

the number of network calls.

2. Reduced Client Complexity:
- Clients do not need to manage multiple service interactions. The composition service handles data aggregation and formatting, providing a simplified interface.

3. Flexibility:
- Allows for dynamic composition of responses based on client needs. Changes in the backend services can be abstracted from clients, allowing for more flexibility in service evolution.

4. Custom Responses:
- A composition layer can tailor responses to different client needs, optimizing data retrieval and presentation for specific use cases or user interfaces.

### Challenges of API Composition

1. Performance:
- Aggregating data from multiple services can introduce latency. The composition service must handle the performance implications of making multiple network calls and combining responses.

2. Error Handling:
- Managing errors and failures in service calls can be complex. The composition service needs to handle partial failures and provide meaningful responses to clients.

3. Data Consistency:
- Ensuring consistency across data from multiple services can be challenging. The composition service must manage synchronization issues and handle eventual consistency where necessary.

4. Complexity:
- Implementing a composition layer adds complexity to the system architecture. It requires careful design to manage

orchestration, caching, and performance optimization.

# Example Implementation of API Composition in Microservices

### Scenario: E-commerce Application

Consider an e-commerce application with the following microservices:

1. Product Service: Manages product information.
2. Order Service: Handles order processing.
3. User Service: Manages user profiles and authentication.

### API Composition Workflow

1. Client Request:
   - A client requests detailed information about a specific order, including product details and user information.

   Example Request:

   GET /orders/12345/details

2. API Composition Service:
   - The API Composition Service (or API Gateway) handles the request and orchestrates the retrieval of data from multiple services.

   Steps:
   - Retrieve Order Details: The composition service calls the Order Service to get the details of order `12345`.
   - Retrieve Product Information: The service extracts product IDs from the order details and calls the Product Service to fetch information about each product.
   - Retrieve User Information: The service calls the User Service to get details about the user who placed the order.

3. Data Aggregation:
   - The composition service aggregates the responses from

each service:

 - Combines order details with product information.

 - Includes user profile information in the final response.

4. Response:

 - The API Composition Service formats and returns a unified response to the client.

Example Response:

**Json**

```json
{
  "orderId": "12345",
  "orderDate": "2024-09-16",
  "user": {
    "userId": "67890",
    "name": "John Doe",
    "email": "john.doe@example.com"
  },
  "products": [
    {
      "productId": "prod1",
      "name": "Product 1",
      "price": 25.00,
      "quantity": 2
    },
    {
      "productId": "prod2",
      "name": "Product 2",
      "price": 15.00,
      "quantity": 1
    }
  ],
  "totalAmount": 65.00
}
```

## Handling Errors and Failures

- If one of the service calls fails (e.g., Product Service is down), the composition service must handle the error gracefully. It might return a partial response or an error message indicating the issue.

Example Error Handling Response:

**Json**

```
{
  "orderId": "12345",
  "error": "Unable to retrieve product details. Please try again later."
}
```

## Optimizations

1. Caching:
   - To improve performance, the composition service can implement caching for frequently accessed data, such as product information or user profiles.

2. Asynchronous Processing:
   - For non-critical data, the composition service can use asynchronous processing or messaging to gather and aggregate data, reducing the impact on response times.

3. Data Transformation:
   - The composition service can perform data transformation and formatting to meet the client's requirements, ensuring that the response is tailored to specific use cases.

The API Composition pattern is a valuable approach for aggregating data from multiple microservices into a single, unified response. It simplifies client interactions by providing a single endpoint for complex queries, reduces client-side complexity, and offers flexibility in response composition. However, it also introduces challenges related to performance, error handling, and data consistency. By implementing effective strategies for orchestration, caching, and error management, organizations can leverage API Composition to build efficient and user-friendly microservices architectures.

# Pattern: Data Replication

The Data Replication pattern in microservices architecture involves duplicating data across multiple microservices to ensure consistency, availability, and scalability. By replicating data, services can maintain their own local copies of data, reducing dependency on a centralized data store and improving performance for read operations.

### Key Concepts of Data Replication Pattern

1. Data Replication:

   - Data replication involves copying data from one microservice's database or data store to another. This can be done in real-time or in periodic intervals, depending on the needs of the application.

2. Data Consistency:

   - Ensuring that replicated data remains consistent across different services is crucial. Different consistency models can be applied, such as eventual consistency or strong consistency, based on the requirements of the system.

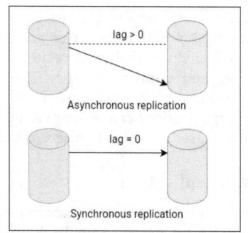

**8.4 Synchronous and asynchronous data replication**

## 3. Replication Strategies:

- Synchronous Replication: Data changes are replicated to other services immediately as they occur. This approach ensures strong consistency but may introduce latency and affect performance.

- Asynchronous Replication: Data changes are replicated to other services after a delay. This approach improves performance and reduces latency but may lead to eventual consistency where the data might be stale for a short period.

## 4. Data Sources:

- The source of data replication is typically a service that owns the data, which shares or publishes data changes to other services.

## 5. Data Synchronization:

- Mechanisms need to be in place to handle synchronization issues, such as conflicts and data convergence, especially in distributed systems.

## Advantages of Data Replication Pattern

## 1. Improved Performance:

- By replicating data closer to where it is needed, read operations can be performed more quickly and efficiently, reducing the load on the central data store.

2. Increased Availability:
- Replicating data across multiple services ensures that data is available even if one service or data store fails, improving the overall resilience of the system.

3. Scalability:
- Data replication allows services to scale independently. Each service can handle its own data, improving the system's ability to handle increased load.

4. Reduced Latency:
- Local copies of data reduce the need for cross-service communication, leading to lower latency for data retrieval and processing.

**Challenges of Data Replication Pattern**

1. Data Consistency:
- Maintaining consistency across replicated data can be challenging. Different consistency models (eventual, strong) may need to be applied based on the specific requirements of the application.

2. Data Synchronization:
- Ensuring that all replicas are updated correctly and handling conflicts or inconsistencies can be complex. Mechanisms such as conflict resolution strategies are needed.

3. Increased Complexity:
- The system's complexity increases with data replication, as it requires additional logic for data synchronization, conflict resolution, and consistency management.

4. Storage Overhead:
- Replicating data increases storage requirements, as multiple copies of the data need to be maintained.

# Example Implementation of Data Replication in

# Microservices

## Scenario: E-commerce Application

Consider an e-commerce application with the following microservices:

1. Product Service: Manages product information.
2. Order Service: Handles order processing.
3. Inventory Service: Manages product inventory.

Data Replication Workflow

1. Data Ownership:
   - The Product Service owns the product data and provides a source of truth for product details.

2. Replication to Other Services:
   - The Inventory Service and Order Service need product information for their operations. They replicate data from the Product Service.

   Steps:
   - Product Updates: When the product details are updated in the Product Service, these changes are propagated to the Inventory Service and Order Service.
   - Data Replication: The product data is replicated either synchronously or asynchronously to the other services.

3. Synchronization Mechanism:
   - Event-Based Replication: The Product Service publishes events (e.g., `ProductUpdated`, `ProductDeleted`) to a message broker. The Inventory Service and Order Service subscribe to these events to update their local copies of product data.
   - Periodic Synchronization: The Inventory Service and Order Service periodically pull the latest product data from the Product Service to ensure their local copies are up-to-date.

4. Handling Inconsistencies:

- Conflict Resolution: If discrepancies occur (e.g., a product update conflicts with existing data), the system needs conflict resolution mechanisms to handle such cases.

- Consistency Checks: Regular consistency checks and reconciliation processes ensure that data across services remains accurate and synchronized.

5. Example Implementation:

- When a product's price is updated in the Product Service, it triggers an event `ProductPriceUpdated`. Both the Inventory Service and Order Service receive this event and update their local replicas of the product data accordingly.

Example Event:

**Json**

```
{
  "eventType": "ProductPriceUpdated",
  "productId": "prod1",
  "newPrice": 30.00,
  "timestamp": "2024-09-16T14:00:00Z"
}
```

**Optimizations**

1. Caching:

- Use caching mechanisms to reduce the load on the data replication system and improve performance. Cache data in local services to minimize the frequency of replication.

2. Data Compression:

- Compress data during replication to reduce network bandwidth usage and improve replication efficiency.

3. Partitioning:

- Partition data to distribute replication load and manage large datasets more effectively. This approach can help in scaling the replication process.

4. Monitoring and Logging:
  - Implement monitoring and logging to track replication status, detect anomalies, and ensure data consistency.

The Data Replication pattern is essential in microservices architecture for improving performance, availability, and scalability by duplicating data across services. While it provides significant benefits, such as faster data access and increased resilience, it also introduces challenges related to data consistency, synchronization, and system complexity. By implementing effective replication strategies, conflict resolution mechanisms, and optimizations, organizations can leverage data replication to build robust and scalable microservices systems.

# 4. Transaction Management

## Pattern: Saga Pattern

The SAGA pattern is a design pattern for managing distributed transactions in microservices architecture. Unlike traditional monolithic systems where transactions are handled in a single, atomic operation, microservices often involve complex interactions between multiple services. The SAGA pattern helps ensure data consistency across these services by breaking down transactions into a sequence of smaller, manageable steps.

### Key Concepts of the SAGA Pattern

1. SAGA:
  - A SAGA is a sequence of local transactions where each transaction updates a service's state and publishes an event or sends a message to trigger the next transaction in the sequence.

2. Local Transactions:
- Each service involved in a SAGA performs a local transaction. These transactions are typically short-lived and managed within the boundaries of the service.

3. Compensating Transactions:
- If a transaction fails, compensating transactions are executed to revert the changes made by previous transactions in the SAGA. This ensures that the system remains in a consistent state despite failures.

4. Orchestration and Choreography:
- Orchestration: A central orchestrator controls the flow of the SAGA, coordinating the execution of transactions and handling compensations.
- Choreography: Each service involved in the SAGA knows about the next steps and performs its part autonomously, publishing events that trigger the next transaction.

5. Failure Handling:
- In case of a failure, compensating transactions are invoked to undo the changes made by previous transactions. This process ensures that the system's state remains consistent even if some transactions fail.

**Advantages of the SAGA Pattern**

1. Consistency:
- Ensures eventual consistency across distributed systems by managing transactions in a distributed manner.

2. Resilience:
- Provides a mechanism to handle failures gracefully through compensating transactions, reducing the impact of failures on the overall system.

3. Scalability:
- Breaks down transactions into smaller, manageable units,

allowing services to scale independently and handle large volumes of transactions more efficiently.

4. Flexibility:

- Supports both orchestration and choreography, allowing for different approaches based on system requirements and complexity.

## Challenges of the SAGA Pattern

1. Complexity:

- Implementing and managing SAGA patterns can introduce complexity in terms of designing compensating transactions, handling failures, and ensuring consistency.

2. Performance:

- The overhead of managing multiple transactions and compensations can impact performance, especially if there are frequent failures or long-running transactions.

3. Monitoring and Debugging:

- Tracking and debugging SAGA executions and compensations can be challenging, requiring robust monitoring and logging to diagnose issues and ensure correctness.

4. Coordination Overhead:

- In orchestration, the central orchestrator can become a bottleneck or a single point of failure. In choreography, ensuring that all services correctly handle events and transitions requires careful design.

# Example Implementation of the SAGA Pattern

### Scenario: E-commerce Order Processing

Consider an e-commerce system where placing an order involves multiple services:

1. Order Service: Handles order creation.

2. Inventory Service: Manages stock levels.

3. Payment Service: Processes payments.

4. Shipping Service: Manages shipping and delivery.

SAGA Workflow

1. Start Transaction:
   - The customer places an order. The Order Service initiates the SAGA by creating an order.

   Step 1: Order Service creates a new order and publishes an `OrderCreated` event.

2. Process Order:
   - The Inventory Service listens for the `OrderCreated` event, reserves stock, and updates inventory.

   Step 2: Inventory Service reserves stock and publishes an `InventoryReserved` event.

3. Process Payment:
   - The Payment Service listens for the `InventoryReserved` event, processes the payment, and updates payment status.

   Step 3: Payment Service processes the payment and publishes a `PaymentProcessed` event.

4. Ship Order:
   - The Shipping Service listens for the `PaymentProcessed` event, schedules and manages shipping.

   Step 4: Shipping Service ships the order and publishes an `OrderShipped` event.

5. Handle Failures:
   - If at any step (e.g., payment processing) fails, compensating transactions are triggered to undo the previous steps:
      - If payment fails, Inventory Service would need to undo the stock reservation.
      - If inventory reservation fails after payment, the Order

Service might need to cancel the order.

Example Compensating Transactions:

- Cancel Inventory Reservation: If payment processing fails, the Inventory Service executes a compensating transaction to release the reserved stock.

- Refund Payment: If shipping fails, the Payment Service may need to issue a refund.

## Orchestration vs. Choreography

1. Orchestration:

- A central SAGA Orchestrator manages the entire process. It coordinates the execution of each step and handles compensations.

Orchestrator Workflow:

- Initiates the order creation.

- Calls each service in sequence (Inventory, Payment, Shipping).

- Handles failures and triggers compensations as needed.

2. Choreography:

- Each service knows about the next step and publishes events. Services react to these events and perform their tasks autonomously.

Choreography Workflow:

- Order Service creates an order and publishes an event.

- Inventory Service processes the event and publishes the next event.

- Payment Service processes the payment and publishes the next event.

- Shipping Service completes the order and publishes the final event.

The SAGA pattern is a crucial approach for managing distributed transactions in microservices architecture. It allows for handling complex, multi-step processes across various services while maintaining consistency and resilience. By implementing SAGA patterns effectively, organizations can build robust and scalable systems that handle transactions and failures gracefully, ensuring data integrity and smooth operational flow.

## Pattern: Two-Phase Commit (2PC)

The Two-Phase Commit (2PC) pattern is a protocol used for coordinating distributed transactions across multiple microservices or databases. It ensures that all participants in a transaction either commit (apply changes) or rollback (undo changes) their operations, maintaining consistency across distributed systems.

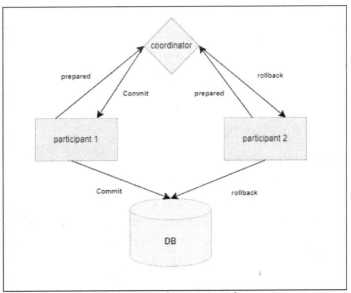

**8.5 Two-phase Commit**

### Key Concepts of Two-Phase Commit (2PC)

1. Distributed Transactions:

   - In a microservices architecture, transactions often span multiple services. Ensuring that all services either commit or rollback their changes is essential to maintain data consistency.

## 2. Coordinator:
- A central entity responsible for managing the transaction across multiple participants. The coordinator is typically a service or a component that oversees the 2PC process.

## 3. Participants:
- The services or databases involved in the transaction. Each participant performs local operations and communicates their status to the coordinator.

## 4. Two Phases:
- Prepare Phase: The coordinator sends a prepare request to all participants, asking them to prepare for committing the transaction. Participants perform the required operations and respond with their readiness.
- Commit/Rollback Phase: Based on the responses from all participants, the coordinator decides whether to commit or rollback the transaction. It sends the final commit or rollback request to each participant.

**Phases of Two-Phase Commit**

## 1. Prepare Phase:
- Coordinator: Sends a `Prepare` request to all participants.
- Participants: Each participant executes the transaction up to a point where it can commit, but does not finalize it yet. They then respond with a `Prepared` status if they are ready to commit or an `Abort` status if they encounter issues.

Example Prepare Request:

## Json

```
{
  "transactionId": "tx12345",
  "operation": "Prepare"
```

```
}
```

Example Prepared Response:

**Json**

```json
{
  "transactionId": "tx12345",
  "status": "Prepared"
}
```

2. Commit/Rollback Phase:

- Coordinator: Based on the responses from the prepare phase, the coordinator decides to either commit or rollback the transaction. It sends a `Commit` or `Rollback` request to all participants.

- Participants: Each participant performs the final commit or rollback operation based on the coordinator's decision and acknowledges the completion.

Example Commit Request:

**Json**

```json
{
  "transactionId": "tx12345",
  "operation": "Commit"
}
```

Example Rollback Request:

**Json**

```json
{
  "transactionId": "tx12345",
  "operation": "Rollback"
}
```

Example Commit Response:

## Json

```
{
  "transactionId": "tx12345",
  "status": "Committed"
}
```

Example Rollback Response:

## Json

```
{
  "transactionId": "tx12345",
  "status": "Rolled Back"
}
```

## Advantages of Two-Phase Commit

1. Consistency:
- Ensures that all participants either commit or rollback, maintaining data consistency across distributed systems.

2. Atomicity:
- Provides atomicity in distributed transactions, meaning all operations are completed successfully or none are applied.

3. Simplicity:
- Provides a clear and straightforward approach to managing distributed transactions with a well-defined protocol.

## Challenges of Two-Phase Commit

1. Single Point of Failure:
- The coordinator is a single point of failure. If the coordinator fails during the process, the outcome of the transaction may be uncertain, and recovery can be complex.

2. Blocking:
- Participants are blocked during the prepare phase, waiting for the coordinator's decision. This can lead to resource

contention and reduced system availability.

3. Performance:
   - The protocol can introduce latency and overhead due to the multiple rounds of communication and coordination between the coordinator and participants.

4. Complexity in Recovery:
   - Handling failures and recovering from partial failures can be complex, requiring sophisticated mechanisms for ensuring consistency and handling timeouts.

# Example Implementation of Two-Phase Commit in Microservices

### Scenario: E-commerce Order Processing

Consider an e-commerce application where placing an order involves multiple services:

1. Order Service: Creates an order.
2. Inventory Service: Updates stock levels.
3. Payment Service: Processes payment.

### 2PC Workflow

1. Start Transaction:
   - The Order Service initiates a distributed transaction and acts as the coordinator.

2. Prepare Phase:
   - The Order Service sends a `Prepare` request to the Inventory Service and Payment Service.

   Prepare Request:

### Json

```
{
  "transactionId": "tx12345",
  "operation": "Prepare"
```

}

- Inventory Service reserves stock and responds with `Prepared` if successful or `Abort` if it encounters issues.
- Payment Service performs a payment authorization and responds similarly.

3. Commit/Rollback Phase:
- If both services respond with `Prepared`, the Order Service decides to commit the transaction and sends a `Commit` request to the Inventory Service and Payment Service.

Commit Request:

**Json**

```json
{
  "transactionId": "tx12345",
  "operation": "Commit"
}
```

- Inventory Service updates stock and Payment Service completes payment processing. Both services acknowledge the commit.

- If any service responds with `Abort`, the Order Service sends a `Rollback` request to undo any changes.

Rollback Request:

**Json**

```json
{
  "transactionId": "tx12345",
  "operation": "Rollback"
}
```

- Services perform compensating actions to revert changes,

ensuring the system remains consistent.

**Handling Failures**

- Coordinator Failure: If the coordinator fails, participants may need to use timeouts and retry mechanisms to handle incomplete transactions.
- Participant Failure: If a participant fails, the coordinator should handle the failure and initiate compensating transactions as needed.

The Two-Phase Commit (2PC) pattern is a robust approach for ensuring data consistency and atomicity in distributed transactions across microservices. While it provides a clear protocol for managing transactions, it introduces challenges related to coordinator failure, blocking, and performance. Implementing 2PC requires careful consideration of these challenges and may be complemented with additional mechanisms for fault tolerance and recovery.

# 5. Data Security

Data security in microservices architecture involves implementing strategies and practices to protect data from unauthorized access, breaches, and other security threats. Given the distributed nature of microservices, ensuring data security requires addressing various aspects, including data encryption, access control, secure communication, and compliance with security standards.

**Key Concepts of Data Security in Microservices**

1. Data Encryption:
   - At Rest: Encrypting data stored in databases or file systems to protect it from unauthorized access. This ensures that even

if an attacker gains access to the storage medium, the data remains unreadable.

- In Transit: Encrypting data transmitted between services to prevent eavesdropping and tampering during communication. This is typically achieved using protocols like HTTPS or TLS.

2. Access Control:

- Authentication: Verifying the identity of users or services requesting access. Common methods include username/ password, OAuth tokens, API keys, and multi-factor authentication (MFA).

- Authorization: Determining whether a user or service has permission to access or modify specific resources. Role-based access control (RBAC) and attribute-based access control (ABAC) are common approaches.

3. Secure Communication:

- API Security: Implementing security measures for APIs, such as rate limiting, IP whitelisting, and input validation, to protect against abuse and attacks.

- Service-to-Service Communication: Securing communication between microservices using mutual TLS (mTLS) or other encryption methods to ensure that only authorized services can interact with each other.

4. Data Masking and Anonymization:

- Data Masking: Obscuring sensitive data within a database or application so that unauthorized users cannot view or access it.

- Data Anonymization: Transforming data to remove personally identifiable information (PII) or sensitive details while retaining its utility for analysis.

5. Audit Logging and Monitoring:

- Audit Logs: Recording security-related events and transactions to provide a trail for forensic analysis and compliance purposes.

- Monitoring: Implementing tools and practices to detect and respond to security incidents, anomalies, or breaches in real-time.

6. Compliance:

- Regulations and Standards: Adhering to industry standards and regulations such as GDPR, HIPAA, and PCI-DSS to ensure data security and privacy compliance.

## Implementing Data Security Patterns in Microservices

1. Data Encryption

- At Rest:
- Database Encryption: Enable encryption features in databases (e.g., AWS RDS, Azure SQL) to encrypt data at rest.
- File System Encryption: Use filesystem-level encryption for sensitive files (e.g., using tools like LUKS on Linux or BitLocker on Windows).

- In Transit:
- HTTPS/TLS: Secure communication between services by enforcing HTTPS/TLS for all API requests.
- mTLS: Implement mutual TLS for service-to-service communication to ensure both client and server authenticate each other.

Example:
- An e-commerce system encrypts customer payment information at rest in its database using AES-256 and secures API communication with TLS.

2. Access Control

- Authentication:
- OAuth 2.0: Use OAuth 2.0 for user authentication and authorization in web applications and APIs.
- JWT Tokens: Use JSON Web Tokens (JWT) to securely

transmit user claims and session information.

- Authorization:
  - RBAC: Define roles and permissions to control access to resources. For example, a user may have access to view but not modify product details.
  - ABAC: Use attributes and policies to define access rules based on user characteristics or resource attributes.

Example:
  - A microservice manages access to customer data based on roles, allowing only users with an "admin" role to modify records while other users can only view them.

3. Secure Communication

- API Security:
  - Rate Limiting: Implement rate limiting to prevent abuse and DDoS attacks.
  - Input Validation: Validate and sanitize all input data to prevent injection attacks.

- Service-to-Service Communication:
  - mTLS: Use mutual TLS for secure service-to-service communication, ensuring that only trusted services can communicate with each other.

Example:
  - A payment service and an order service use mutual TLS to encrypt and authenticate requests between them.

4. Data Masking and Anonymization

- Data Masking:
  - Masking Sensitive Data: Mask sensitive information (e.g., credit card numbers) in logs and non-production environments to prevent exposure.

- Data Anonymization:
  - Anonymize PII: Remove or obfuscate PII from datasets used

for analytics or testing.

Example:
- An analytics service receives anonymized user data to perform analysis without exposing personally identifiable information.

5. Audit Logging and Monitoring

- Audit Logs:
  - Logging: Implement comprehensive logging to capture security-related events, including access attempts, changes to sensitive data, and administrative actions.

- Monitoring:
  - Security Information and Event Management (SIEM): Use SIEM tools to aggregate, analyze, and respond to security events in real-time.

Example:
- A logging service records all authentication attempts and sensitive data access, with logs analyzed by a SIEM system for suspicious activity.

6. Compliance

- Regulations and Standards:
  - GDPR: Implement data protection measures to comply with GDPR requirements for handling personal data.
  - PCI-DSS: Follow PCI-DSS guidelines to secure payment card information and ensure compliance with industry standards.

Example:
- A healthcare application follows HIPAA regulations by implementing encryption for patient records and access controls to ensure data privacy and security.

The Data Security pattern in microservices architecture involves a comprehensive approach to protecting data across various dimensions. By implementing encryption, access control, secure communication, data masking, audit logging, and ensuring compliance, organizations can safeguard their data against threats and ensure the integrity and confidentiality of information in a distributed microservices environment.

In a microservices architecture, data management is multifaceted and requires careful consideration of various patterns. Key patterns include Data Ownership for decentralized management, Event Sourcing and CQRS for handling state and queries, API Composition and Data Replication for integration, and Saga Pattern and Two-Phase Commit for transaction management. Security and privacy concerns are managed through patterns like Data Encryption. Each pattern has its own benefits and challenges, and selecting the appropriate patterns depends on the specific requirements and constraints of the microservices architecture.

# Data pattern in Google cloud platform (GCP)

In Google Cloud Platform (GCP), implementing data patterns with microservices involves leveraging various GCP services to ensure efficient, scalable, and secure data management. Here's a detailed look at common data patterns and their implementations using GCP services:

1. Data Ownership Pattern

Description:
The Data Ownership pattern involves each microservice owning and managing its own data. This ensures that each service has control over its own database, reducing tight coupling between services and enhancing scalability.

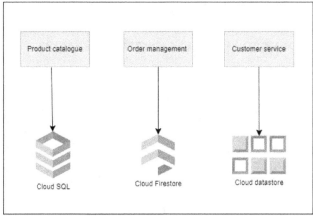

**8.6 Data ownership in GCP**

Example in GCP:

Consider an e-commerce application with microservices for Product Catalog, Order Management, and Customer Service.

- Product Catalog Service: Owns product data, stored in Cloud SQL (a managed relational database service).
- Order Management Service: Manages order data, stored in Cloud Firestore (a NoSQL document database).
- Customer Service: Maintains customer profiles, stored in Cloud Datastore (a NoSQL document database).

Implementation:

- Product Catalog: Stores product information in Cloud SQL and exposes RESTful APIs to interact with this data.
- Order Management: Uses Cloud Firestore to store orders, enabling real-time updates and offline support.
- Customer Service: Leverages Cloud Datastore for managing customer data with flexible data models.

Data Flow:

- Product Catalog Service provides product information to other services via APIs.
- Order Management Service creates orders and references product data from the Product Catalog.
- Customer Service handles customer profiles and provides

customer information to the Order Management Service.

## 2. CQRS (Command Query Responsibility Segregation) Pattern

Description:
CQRS separates read and write operations into different models, allowing optimized handling of queries and commands. This pattern improves scalability and performance by using different data storage and query mechanisms for reading and writing data.

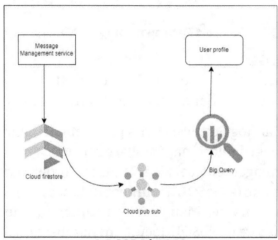

**8.7 CQRS in GCP**

Example in GCP:
Consider a real-time chat application with microservices for Message Management and User Profile.

- Message Management Service: Handles the writing of messages and reading of chat history.
- User Profile Service: Manages user profiles and preferences.

Implementation:
- Command Side (Writes): Message Management Service writes chat messages to Cloud Pub/Sub for real-time messaging and Cloud Firestore for storing chat history.
- Query Side (Reads): For optimized query performance, use BigQuery to aggregate and analyze chat messages and user

data.

Data Flow:
- Message Management Service writes messages to Cloud Firestore and publishes events to Cloud Pub/Sub.
- User Profile Service updates user preferences and integrates with BigQuery to provide analytics and reporting features.

3. Event Sourcing Pattern

Description:
Event Sourcing involves storing all changes to the application state as a sequence of events. Instead of storing the current state, the system stores a history of events that can be replayed to reconstruct the state.

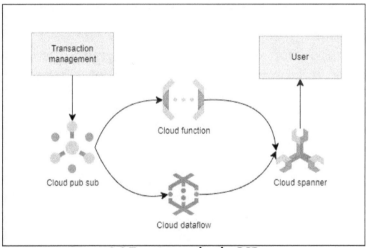

**8.8 Event sourcing in GCP**

Example in GCP:
Consider a financial application with microservices for Transaction Management and Account Balance.

- Transaction Management Service: Handles and stores financial transactions as events.
- Account Balance Service: Calculates and retrieves account balances based on transaction events.

Implementation:
- Event Store: Use Cloud Pub/Sub to capture and store transaction events as they occur.
- Event Processor: Cloud Functions or Dataflow processes events from Cloud Pub/Sub to update account balances in Cloud Spanner (a horizontally scalable relational database service).

Data Flow:
- Transaction Management Service publishes transaction events to Cloud Pub/Sub.
- Event Processor listens to Cloud Pub/Sub, processes events, and updates account balances in Cloud Spanner.

4. API Composition Pattern

Description:
API Composition involves creating a composite API from multiple microservices to aggregate data from different sources into a single response.

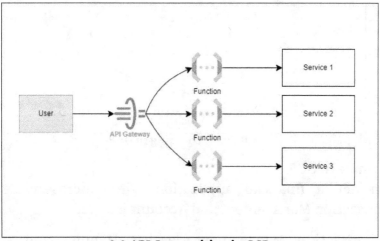

**8.9 API Composition in GCP**

Example in GCP:
Consider a travel booking application with microservices for Flights, Hotels, and Car Rentals.

- Flights Service: Provides flight availability information.
- Hotels Service: Provides hotel availability and booking details.
- Car Rentals Service: Provides car rental options.

Implementation:
- API Gateway: Use API Gateway to manage and route API requests.
- Composition Service: Implement a Cloud Function or Cloud Run service that aggregates data from Flights, Hotels, and Car Rentals services.

Data Flow:
- API Gateway routes requests to the Composition Service.
- Composition Service makes parallel API calls to Flights, Hotels, and Car Rentals services.
- Composition Service aggregates the responses and returns a combined result to the client.

5. Data Replication Pattern

Description:
Data Replication involves copying data across different microservices or databases to improve availability and performance. This pattern helps in scaling read operations and ensuring data consistency.

Example in GCP:
Consider an e-commerce platform with Product Catalog Service and Search Service.

- Product Catalog Service: Manages product data and updates.
- Search Service: Provides search functionality over product data.

Implementation:
- Replication: Use Cloud Pub/Sub to publish product updates from the Product Catalog Service.

- Search Service: Subscribes to Cloud Pub/Sub and updates its local index in Elasticsearch (a search and analytics engine).

Data Flow:
- Product Catalog Service publishes updates to Cloud Pub/Sub.
- Search Service processes these updates and maintains a search index in Elasticsearch.

6. Data Security Pattern

Description:
Data Security involves implementing measures to protect data from unauthorized access, breaches, and other security threats. This includes encryption, access control, and secure communication.

Example in GCP:
Consider a healthcare application with microservices for Patient Records, Appointment Scheduling, and Billing.

- Patient Records Service: Manages sensitive patient data.
-   Appointment   Scheduling   Service:   Manages   patient appointments.
- Billing Service: Handles payment information.

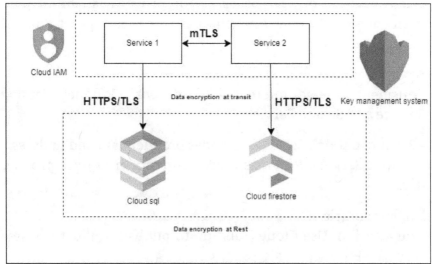

**8.10 Data security in GCP**

Implementation:

- Encryption: Use Cloud KMS (Key Management Service) for managing encryption keys. Encrypt data at rest in Cloud SQL and Cloud Storage, and use TLS for data in transit.
- Access Control: Implement IAM (Identity and Access Management) roles and policies to control access to services and data.
- Secure Communication: Enforce HTTPS for all API interactions and use mTLS for service-to-service communication.

Data Flow:

- Patient Records Service encrypts data before storing it in Cloud SQL.
- Appointment Scheduling Service and Billing Service communicate securely with each other using mutual TLS.

Implementing data patterns with microservices in Google Cloud Platform involves leveraging a range of GCP services to handle data ownership, consistency, security, and performance effectively. By using services such as Cloud SQL, Cloud Firestore, Cloud Pub/Sub, BigQuery, and Cloud Functions, organizations can build scalable, secure, and efficient microservices architectures that meet their specific data management needs.

# Data pattern in Azure

In Azure, implementing data patterns with microservices involves using Azure's extensive suite of services to manage, secure, and process data across distributed systems. Here's a detailed look at common data patterns and their implementations using Azure services:

1. Data Ownership Pattern

Description:

Each microservice owns and manages its own data store, which minimizes dependencies between services and enhances scalability and maintainability.

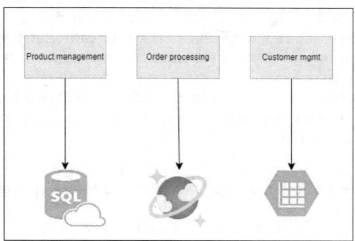

**8.11 Cloud ownership in Azure**

Example in Azure:
Consider an online retail application with microservices for Product Management, Order Processing, and Customer Management.

- Product Management Service: Owns product catalog data.
- Order Processing Service: Manages order data.
- Customer Management Service: Handles customer profiles.

Implementation:
- Product Management Service: Uses Azure SQL Database to store product information.
- Order Processing Service: Utilizes Azure Cosmos DB (NoSQL database) for order data to handle high throughput and global distribution.
- Customer Management Service: Stores customer profiles in Azure Table Storage (NoSQL storage for structured data).

Data Flow:
- Product Management Service exposes APIs for retrieving

product details.
- Order Processing Service uses product data via APIs from the Product Management Service and stores order data in Azure Cosmos DB.
- Customer Management Service provides customer data to other services as needed.

## 2. CQRS (Command Query Responsibility Segregation) Pattern

Description:
CQRS separates read and write operations, optimizing each for performance and scalability. Commands handle updates, while queries handle data retrieval.

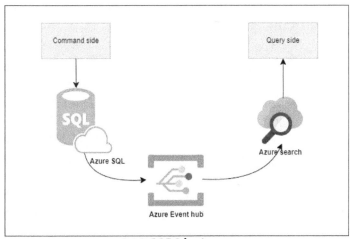

**8.12 CQRS in Azure**

Example in Azure:
Consider a real-time analytics application with microservices for User Activity Tracking and User Profile Management.

- User Activity Tracking Service: Handles write operations (e.g., logging user activities).
- User Profile Management Service: Manages read operations (e.g., fetching user profiles and activity reports).

Implementation:
- Command Side (Writes): Use Azure Event Hubs to collect and

store user activities. Data is processed and persisted in Azure SQL Database.
- Query Side (Reads): Use Azure Search to index user profiles and activity data for fast querying and searching.

Data Flow:
- User Activity Tracking Service writes activity data to Azure Event Hubs.
- Event Processing with Azure Stream Analytics or Azure Functions processes data from Event Hubs and updates Azure SQL Database.
- User Profile Management Service uses Azure Search to provide fast query capabilities for user profiles and activities.

3. Event Sourcing Pattern

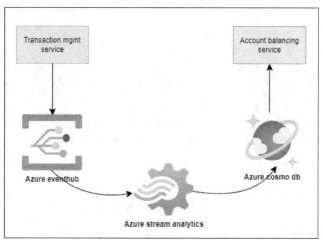

**8.13 Event sourcing in Azure**

Description:
Event Sourcing involves storing all changes to application state as a sequence of events. This allows for state reconstruction by replaying events.

Example in Azure:
Consider a financial transactions system with microservices for Transaction Management and Account Balance Calculation.

- Transaction Management Service: Records transactions as events.
- Account Balance Calculation Service: Computes account balances based on transaction events.

Implementation:
- Event Store: Use Azure Event Hubs to capture and store transaction events.
- Event Processor: Implement Azure Functions or Azure Stream Analytics to process events and update account balances in Azure SQL Database or Azure Cosmos DB.

Data Flow:
- Transaction Management Service sends transaction events to Azure Event Hubs.
- Event Processor processes events from Event Hubs, updating account balances accordingly.
- Account Balance Calculation Service queries the updated balances from the database.

4. API Composition Pattern

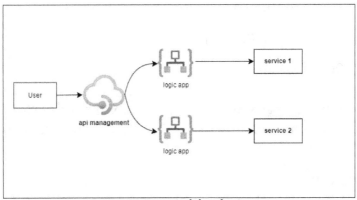

**8.14 API Composition in Azure**

Description:
API Composition involves aggregating data from multiple microservices into a single response. It simplifies data access by consolidating information from various sources.

Example in Azure:
Consider a travel booking application with microservices for Flight Search, Hotel Booking, and Car Rental.

- Flight Search Service: Provides flight data.
- Hotel Booking Service: Manages hotel reservations.
- Car Rental Service: Handles car rental options.

Implementation:
- API Gateway: Use Azure API Management to expose and manage APIs.
- Composition Service: Implement Azure Functions or Azure Logic Apps to aggregate data from the three services and return a combined result.

Data Flow:
- API Management routes requests to the Composition Service.
- Composition Service queries Flight Search, Hotel Booking, and Car Rental services.
- Composition Service aggregates the responses and provides a unified view to the client.

5. Data Replication Pattern

Description:
Data Replication involves copying data across different services or databases to enhance availability and performance. It is useful for scaling read operations and ensuring data redundancy.

Example in Azure:
Consider a content management system with microservices for Content Publishing and Content Search.

- Content Publishing Service: Manages and stores content data.
- Content Search Service: Provides search functionality over the content data.

Implementation:
- Replication: Use Azure Event Grid to publish content updates.
- Content Search Service subscribes to Event Grid and updates its index in Azure Cognitive Search.

Data Flow:
- Content Publishing Service publishes updates to Azure Event Grid.
- Content Search Service processes updates from Event Grid and maintains an up-to-date index in Azure Cognitive Search.

6. Data Security Pattern

Description:
Data Security involves implementing measures to protect data from unauthorized access, breaches, and other security threats. This includes encryption, access control, and secure communication.

Example in Azure:
Consider a healthcare application with microservices for Patient Records, Appointment Scheduling, and Billing.

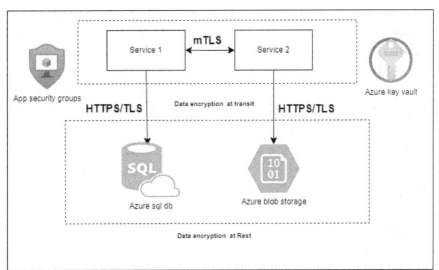

**8.15 Data security in Azure**

- Patient Records Service: Manages sensitive patient data.
- Appointment Scheduling Service: Manages appointment information.
- Billing Service: Handles payment and billing information.

Implementation:
- Encryption: Use Azure Key Vault to manage encryption keys. Encrypt data at rest in Azure SQL Database and Azure Blob Storage. Use TLS for encrypting data in transit.
- Access Control: Implement Azure Role-Based Access Control (RBAC) to manage access to Azure resources and data.
- Secure Communication: Enforce HTTPS for all API interactions and use Azure AD for authentication and authorization.

Data Flow:
- Patient Records Service encrypts data using keys from Azure Key Vault before storing it in Azure SQL Database.
- Appointment Scheduling Service and Billing Service communicate securely using HTTPS and authenticate via Azure AD.

Implementing data patterns with microservices in Azure involves leveraging a combination of Azure services to manage data efficiently and securely. By using services like Azure SQL Database, Azure Cosmos DB, Azure Event Hubs, Azure API Management, and Azure Key Vault, organizations can build scalable, secure, and efficient microservices architectures tailored to their specific data management needs.

# Data pattern in AWS

In AWS, implementing data patterns with microservices involves using a range of AWS services to manage, secure, and process data across distributed systems. Here's a detailed look at common data patterns and their implementations using

AWS services:

1. Data Ownership Pattern

Description:
In the Data Ownership pattern, each microservice is responsible for its own data store, reducing dependencies between services and enabling independent scaling and maintenance.

Example in AWS:
Consider an e-commerce application with microservices for Product Catalog, Order Management, and Customer Service.

- Product Catalog Service: Manages product information.
- Order Management Service: Handles order data.
- Customer Service: Manages customer profiles.

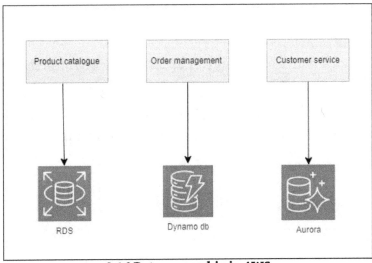

**8.16 Data ownership in AWS**

Implementation:
- Product Catalog Service: Uses Amazon RDS (Relational Database Service) to store product details.
- Order Management Service: Utilizes Amazon DynamoDB (NoSQL database) for storing orders to handle high throughput and low latency.

- Customer Service: Stores customer profiles in Amazon Aurora (a MySQL-compatible database) for high availability and performance.

Data Flow:
- Product Catalog Service exposes APIs to retrieve product data.
- Order Management Service interacts with the Product Catalog Service to fetch product information and stores order data in DynamoDB.
- Customer Service provides customer information and integrates with other services as needed.

2. CQRS (Command Query Responsibility Segregation) Pattern

Description:
CQRS separates read and write operations into different models, optimizing performance and scalability by using different data stores for reads and writes.

Example in AWS:
Consider a real-time analytics application with microservices for User Activity Tracking and User Analytics.

- User Activity Tracking Service: Handles write operations.
- User Analytics Service: Manages read operations.

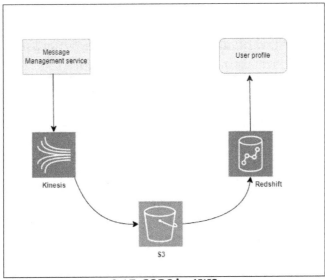

**8.17 CQRS in AWS**

Implementation:
- Command Side (Writes): Use Amazon Kinesis (for real-time data streaming) to collect and process user activity data, and store it in Amazon S3 for durable storage.
- Query Side (Reads): Use Amazon Redshift (data warehouse) to query and analyze user data efficiently.

Data Flow:
- User Activity Tracking Service streams activity data to Amazon Kinesis.
- Data is processed by AWS Lambda or Amazon Kinesis Data Firehose and stored in Amazon S3.
- User Analytics Service queries data from Amazon Redshift for reporting and analysis.

3. Event Sourcing Pattern

Description:
Event Sourcing involves capturing all changes to the application state as a sequence of events, allowing state reconstruction by replaying these events.

Example in AWS:
Consider a financial application with microservices for Transaction Processing and Account Balance Calculation.

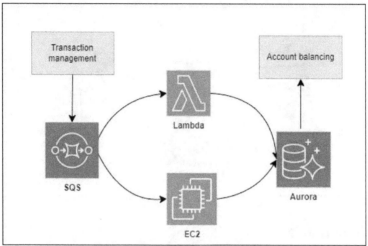

**8.18 Event sourcing in AWS**

- Transaction Processing Service: Manages and stores transactions as events.
- Account Balance Calculation Service: Computes account balances based on events.

Implementation:
- Event Store: Use Amazon Kinesis Data Streams or Amazon SQS (Simple Queue Service) to capture and store transaction events.
- Event Processor: Use AWS Lambda or Amazon EC2 to process events and update account balances in Amazon Aurora.

Data Flow:
- Transaction Processing Service publishes events to Amazon Kinesis Data Streams.
- Event Processor reads events from the stream, processes them, and updates account balances in Amazon Aurora.

4. API Composition Pattern

Description:
API Composition involves aggregating data from multiple microservices into a single response. This pattern simplifies data access by consolidating information from various sources.

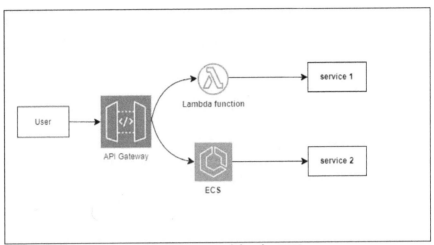

**8.19 API composition in AWS**

Example in AWS:
Consider a travel booking application with microservices for Flight Search, Hotel Booking, and Car Rental.

- Flight Search Service: Provides flight information.
- Hotel Booking Service: Manages hotel reservations.
- Car Rental Service: Handles car rental options.

Implementation:
- API Gateway: Use Amazon API Gateway to manage and route API requests.
- Composition Service: Implement an AWS Lambda function or Amazon ECS (Elastic Container Service) task that aggregates data from the three services and returns a unified response.

Data Flow:
- API Gateway routes requests to the Composition Service.
- Composition Service calls Flight Search, Hotel Booking, and

Car Rental services.
- Composition Service aggregates responses and provides a unified result to the client.

5. Data Replication Pattern

Description:
Data Replication involves copying data across different services or databases to enhance availability, performance, and redundancy.

Example in AWS:
Consider a content management system with microservices for Content Management and Content Search.

- Content Management Service: Manages and stores content data.
- Content Search Service: Provides search functionality over the content data.

Implementation:
- Replication: Use Amazon SNS (Simple Notification Service) to publish content updates.
- Content Search Service subscribes to SNS and updates its index in Amazon Elasticsearch Service.

Data Flow:
- Content Management Service publishes updates to Amazon SNS.
- Content Search Service processes updates from SNS and maintains a search index in Amazon Elasticsearch Service.

6. Data Security Pattern

Description:
Data Security involves implementing measures to protect data from unauthorized access, breaches, and other security threats. This includes encryption, access control, and secure communication.

Example in AWS:

Consider a healthcare application with microservices for Patient Records, Appointment Scheduling, and Billing.

- Patient Records Service: Manages sensitive patient data.
- Appointment Scheduling Service: Manages appointment information.
- Billing Service: Handles payment and billing information.

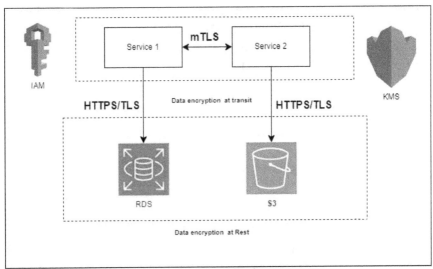

**8.20 Data security in AWS**

Implementation:

- Encryption: Use AWS Key Management Service (KMS) to manage encryption keys. Encrypt data at rest in Amazon RDS and Amazon S3, and use TLS for data in transit.
- Access Control: Implement IAM (Identity and Access Management) roles and policies to control access to AWS resources and data.
- Secure Communication: Enforce HTTPS for all API interactions and use AWS IAM for authentication and authorization.

Data Flow:

- Patient Records Service encrypts data using AWS KMS before storing it in Amazon RDS.

- Appointment Scheduling Service and Billing Service communicate securely using HTTPS and authenticate via AWS IAM.

Implementing data patterns with microservices in AWS involves using various AWS services to manage data effectively and securely. By leveraging services like Amazon RDS, Amazon DynamoDB, Amazon Kinesis, Amazon S3, Amazon Redshift, AWS Lambda, and AWS KMS, organizations can build scalable, secure, and efficient microservices architectures that address their specific data management needs.

# CHAPTER 9. CIRCUIT BREAKER PATTERN

The Circuit Breaker pattern is a design pattern used in microservices architecture to handle faults and prevent cascading failures. It is inspired by the electrical circuit breaker, which protects electrical circuits from overloads and short circuits. In the context of microservices, the Circuit Breaker pattern helps manage failures gracefully and improve system resilience.

## Overview of the Circuit Breaker Pattern

Purpose
The Circuit Breaker pattern aims to detect and handle failures in a distributed system by:
- Preventing the system from making repeated requests to a failing service.
- Allowing the system to recover and retry operations once the failing service is deemed to be back online.
- Providing fallback mechanisms to ensure that the system remains functional even when certain services are down.

## Components of the Circuit Breaker Pattern

### 1. Closed State:

- In this state, requests are allowed to pass through to the service. The circuit breaker monitors for failures and tracks the health of the service.
- If the failure rate exceeds a predefined threshold, the circuit

breaker transitions to the Open State.

### 2. Open State:

- In the Open State, requests are immediately failed and not sent to the failing service. This prevents the service from being overwhelmed with requests while it is recovering.

- The circuit breaker periodically transitions to the Half-Open State to check if the service is back to normal.

### 3. Half-Open State:

- In this state, the circuit breaker allows a limited number of requests to pass through to the service to test if it has recovered.

- If these requests succeed, the circuit breaker transitions back to the Closed State. If failures occur, it returns to the Open State.

### 4. Fallback Mechanism:

- Provides an alternative response or behavior when the service is in the Open State. This could involve returning cached data, default values, or a predefined error message.

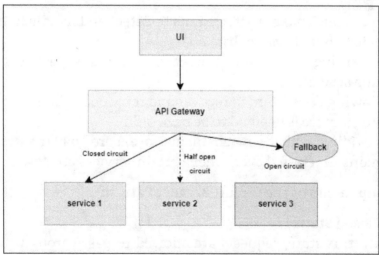

**9.1 Circuit breaker**

## Implementation of the Circuit Breaker Pattern

## 1. Design Considerations

- Thresholds: Define thresholds for failure rates and response times that trigger state transitions.
- Timeouts: Set timeouts for how long the circuit breaker stays in each state.
- Recovery Mechanism: Implement logic for transitioning between states, including periodic checks during the Half-Open State.

## 2. Libraries and Tools

Several libraries and tools can be used to implement the Circuit Breaker pattern, including:
- Hystrix: A popular library from Netflix that provides circuit breaker functionality.
- Resilience4j: A lightweight library designed for Java applications that offers circuit breaker functionality.
- Spring Cloud Circuit Breaker: An abstraction over several circuit breaker implementations, integrated with the Spring ecosystem.

Example Scenario

Scenario Description
Consider an e-commerce application with microservices for Order Management, Inventory Management, and Payment Processing. If the Payment Processing service becomes overloaded or fails, we want to prevent cascading failures and provide a fallback mechanism.

### Implementation Steps:

1. Define Circuit Breaker Configuration:
    - Failure Threshold: If more than 50% of requests to the Payment Processing service fail, trigger the Open State.
    - Timeout: Set a timeout of 30 seconds before transitioning to the Half-Open State.

2. Implement Circuit Breaker Logic:

- Closed State: Requests from the Order Management service to the Payment Processing service pass through. The circuit breaker tracks failures and response times.

- Open State: If the failure rate exceeds the threshold, the circuit breaker transitions to the Open State. All requests to the Payment Processing service are immediately failed.

- Half-Open State: After a predefined time, the circuit breaker allows a limited number of requests to the Payment Processing service to test if it has recovered. If these requests succeed, it transitions back to the Closed State. If they fail, it returns to the Open State.

3. Configure Fallback Mechanism:

- Fallback Response: If the Payment Processing service is in the Open State, the Order Management service returns a fallback response, such as an error message indicating that the payment service is currently unavailable.

### Example Code (Using Resilience4j in Java)

__Java__

```
import io.github.resilience4j.circuitbreaker.CircuitBreaker;
import io.github.resilience4j.circuitbreaker.CircuitBreakerConfig;
import io.github.resilience4j.circuitbreaker.CircuitBreakerRegistry;
import io.github.resilience4j.circuitbreaker.callables.CheckedRunnable;
import io.github.resilience4j.circuitbreaker.callables.CheckedCallable;

import java.time.Duration;

public class PaymentServiceClient {
```

```java
    private final CircuitBreaker circuitBreaker;

    public PaymentServiceClient() {
        CircuitBreakerConfig          config          =
CircuitBreakerConfig.custom()
            .failureRateThreshold(50) // 50% failure rate to
open the circuit
            .waitDurationInOpenState(Duration.ofSeconds(30
)) // Time to wait before transitioning to Half-Open State
            .slidingWindowSize(100) // Number of requests to
evaluate for failure rate
            .build();

        CircuitBreakerRegistry          registry          =
CircuitBreakerRegistry.of(config);
        this.circuitBreaker                              =
registry.circuitBreaker("paymentServiceCircuitBreaker");
    }

    public void processPayment() {
        CheckedRunnable runnable = CheckedRunnable.of(() -> {
            // Code to call Payment Processing service
        });

        try {
            CircuitBreaker.decorateCheckedRunnable(circuitBrea
ker, runnable).run();
        } catch (Exception e) {
            // Fallback logic here
            System.out.println("Payment  service  is  currently
unavailable. Please try again later.");
        }
    }
}
```

The Circuit Breaker pattern is crucial for building resilient microservices architectures. By preventing cascading failures and managing service interactions intelligently, the Circuit Breaker pattern helps maintain system stability and reliability. Implementing this pattern involves careful configuration of thresholds, timeouts, and fallback mechanisms to effectively handle service failures and recovery.

# Circuit breaker pattern in Google cloud platform

In Google Cloud Platform (GCP), implementing the Circuit Breaker pattern involves using various GCP services and tools to manage failures and ensure system resilience. Here's a detailed description of how to implement the Circuit Breaker pattern with microservices in GCP, along with an example scenario.

### Overview of the Circuit Breaker Pattern

The Circuit Breaker pattern helps prevent cascading failures by managing the interaction between services and handling failures gracefully. It consists of three states:
- Closed: Requests are allowed and monitored.
- Open: Requests are failed immediately, and the system does not attempt to contact the failing service.
- Half-Open: A limited number of requests are allowed to test if the service has recovered.

### Implementing the Circuit Breaker Pattern in GCP

1. Design Considerations

- Failure Thresholds: Define how many failures or timeouts are acceptable before switching to the Open State.
- Timeouts: Determine how long the Circuit Breaker should stay open before transitioning to Half-Open.
- Recovery Strategy: Implement logic for transitioning between states and defining fallback mechanisms.

## 2. GCP Services and Tools

- Google Cloud Functions: Use for implementing lightweight, serverless components that handle requests and apply Circuit Breaker logic.
- Google Cloud Run: Deploy microservices with built-in scaling and manage circuit breaker logic in your service code.
- Google Cloud Pub/Sub: Use for asynchronous messaging, which can help in implementing fallback strategies and retry mechanisms.
- Google Cloud Monitoring and Logging: Monitor service health and performance metrics to make informed decisions about state transitions.

## Example Scenario

### Scenario Description
Consider an e-commerce application with microservices for Order Processing, Inventory Management, and Payment Processing. We want to prevent the Order Processing service from overwhelming the Payment Processing service if it fails or is slow to respond.

## Implementation Steps

1. Define Circuit Breaker Configuration:
   - Failure Threshold: More than 50% of requests to Payment Processing service fail within a 5-minute window.
   - Timeout: Keep the circuit open for 30 seconds before checking if the Payment Processing service has recovered.

2. Implement Circuit Breaker Logic in Google Cloud Functions

Implementation with Cloud Functions:

- Create a Google Cloud Function for the Order Processing service that incorporates Circuit Breaker logic.

### **Python**

```
from google.cloud import pubsub_v1
from google.cloud import logging
import time
import requests

# Set up Pub/Sub and Logging
publisher = pubsub_v1.PublisherClient()
project_id = 'your-project-id'
topic_id = 'payment-service-failure'

logging_client = logging.Client()
logger = logging_client.logger('order-processing-logs')

def process_order(request):
    payment_service_url = 'https://payment-service-url.com/process'

    # Define Circuit Breaker state
    state = 'CLOSED'
    failure_count = 0
    success_count = 0
    failure_threshold = 5
    timeout = 30

    try:
        # Circuit Breaker logic
        if state == 'OPEN':
            logger.log_text('Circuit is OPEN. Returning fallback response.')
            return 'Payment Service is currently unavailable. Please try again later.'

        # Send request to Payment Processing service
        response = requests.post(payment_service_url, json=request.json)

        if response.status_code == 200:
            success_count += 1
```

```
    if success_count > failure_threshold:
        state = 'CLOSED'
    return 'Order processed successfully!'
else:
    failure_count += 1
    if failure_count > failure_threshold:
        state = 'OPEN'
        # Publish failure event to Pub/Sub for monitoring
and fallback
        publisher.publish(topic_id,    b'Payment    Service
Failure Detected')
        time.sleep(timeout)
    return 'Failed to process payment.'

except Exception as e:
    logger.log_text(f'Error occurred: {str(e)}')
    return 'An error occurred while processing your order.'
```

## 3. Configure Google Cloud Pub/Sub for Fallback and Monitoring

- Set Up Pub/Sub Topic: Create a Pub/Sub topic to publish failure events.

- Create a Subscriber: Implement a Google Cloud Function or a service that subscribes to the failure topic to handle fallback actions or alerts.

## 4. Monitor Service Health with Google Cloud Monitoring

- Use Google Cloud Monitoring to set up dashboards and alerts based on the performance metrics of your services.
- Create alerts to notify you when the failure rate exceeds thresholds or when the Circuit Breaker transitions.

Implementing the Circuit Breaker pattern in GCP involves using Cloud Functions, Cloud Run, Pub/Sub, and Monitoring to handle service failures and ensure resilience. By defining thresholds, implementing state transitions, and integrating with GCP's monitoring and logging tools, you can effectively manage failures and maintain system stability.

This example demonstrates how to incorporate Circuit Breaker logic into a Cloud Function, but similar principles can be applied using other GCP services based on your architecture and requirements.

# Circuit Breaker pattern in Azure

Implementing the Circuit Breaker pattern in Azure involves using various Azure services and tools to manage failures and enhance system resilience. Here's a detailed description of how to implement the Circuit Breaker pattern with microservices in Azure, along with an example scenario.

### Overview of the Circuit Breaker Pattern

The Circuit Breaker pattern helps to handle failures gracefully and prevent cascading failures in distributed systems. It consists of three main states:
- Closed State: Requests are allowed, and failures are monitored.
- Open State: Requests are not allowed, and the service is bypassed until it recovers.
- Half-Open State: Limited requests are allowed to check if the service has recovered.

### Implementing the Circuit Breaker Pattern in Azure

1. Design Considerations

- Failure Thresholds: Define how many failures or timeouts are acceptable before the circuit breaker opens.
- Timeouts: Determine the duration for how long the circuit breaker remains open before checking for recovery.
- Fallback Mechanisms: Implement fallback responses or

alternate actions if the circuit breaker is open.

2. Azure Services and Tools

- Azure Functions: Implement serverless functions that can apply Circuit Breaker logic.
- Azure API Management: Use to handle and route API requests, and can integrate with custom policies for Circuit Breaker logic.
- Azure Application Insights: Monitor service health and performance metrics to determine circuit breaker states.
- Azure Service Bus: Use for messaging and implementing fallback strategies.

**Example Scenario**

**Scenario Description**

Consider an e-commerce application with microservices for Order Processing, Inventory Management, and Payment Processing. We need to ensure that if the Payment Processing service fails or is slow, the Order Processing service does not get overwhelmed.

**Implementation Steps**

1. Define Circuit Breaker Configuration:
   - Failure Threshold: More than 50% of requests to the Payment Processing service fail within a 5-minute window.
   - Timeout: Keep the circuit open for 30 seconds before transitioning to the Half-Open State.

2. Implement Circuit Breaker Logic in Azure Functions

**Implementation with Azure Functions:**

- Create an Azure Function for the Order Processing service with integrated Circuit Breaker logic.

**Python**

```python
import logging
import requests
import azure.functions as func
from datetime import datetime, timedelta

# Global variables for Circuit Breaker state
circuit_state = 'CLOSED'
failure_count = 0
success_count = 0
failure_threshold = 5
timeout_duration = timedelta(seconds=30)
last_failure_time = datetime.now()

def main(req: func.HttpRequest) -> func.HttpResponse:
    global circuit_state, failure_count, success_count, last_failure_time

    payment_service_url = 'https://payment-service-url.com/process'

    # Circuit Breaker logic
    if circuit_state == 'OPEN':
        logging.info('Circuit is OPEN. Returning fallback response.')
        return func.HttpResponse('Payment Service is currently unavailable. Please try again later.', status_code=503)

    try:
        # Send request to Payment Processing service
        response = requests.post(payment_service_url, json=req.get_json())

        if response.status_code == 200:
            success_count += 1
            if success_count > failure_threshold:
                circuit_state = 'CLOSED'
            return func.HttpResponse('Order processed successfully!')
```

```
    else:
        failure_count += 1
        if failure_count > failure_threshold:
            circuit_state = 'OPEN'
            last_failure_time = datetime.now()
            # Trigger fallback or alert
            logging.error('Payment Service Failure Detected')
            return  func.HttpResponse('Failed  to  process
payment.', status_code=502)

    except Exception as e:
        logging.error(f'Error occurred: {str(e)}')
        return  func.HttpResponse('An  error  occurred  while
processing your order.', status_code=500)

    # Periodically check and transition to Half-Open State
    if  circuit_state  ==  'OPEN'  and  datetime.now()  -
last_failure_time > timeout_duration:
        circuit_state = 'HALF-OPEN'
        # Implement logic to test service recovery
        try:
            test_response = requests.get(payment_service_url)
            if test_response.status_code == 200:
                circuit_state = 'CLOSED'
            else:
                circuit_state = 'OPEN'
        except:
            circuit_state = 'OPEN'

    return func.HttpResponse('Order processing completed.')
```

3. Configure Azure Application Insights for Monitoring

- Use Azure Application Insights to monitor the performance and health of the microservices. Set up alerts based on failure rates, response times, and circuit breaker state transitions.

Configuration:
- Create Application Insights resources.
- Integrate Application Insights SDK into your Azure Functions.
- Configure custom metrics and alerts for failure rates and circuit breaker status.

4. Fallback and Recovery Mechanisms

- Fallback Responses: Implement fallback responses or alternative actions when the circuit breaker is open.
- Service Bus: Use Azure Service Bus for queuing messages or implementing retry logic for failed requests.

Example:
- If the Payment Processing service is down, use Azure Service Bus to queue payment requests and process them when the service is back online.

Implementing the Circuit Breaker pattern in Azure involves leveraging Azure Functions, API Management, Application Insights, and Service Bus to handle service failures and maintain resilience. By defining thresholds, implementing Circuit Breaker logic in Azure Functions, and integrating with monitoring tools, you can effectively manage failures and ensure that your microservices architecture remains stable and responsive.

This example illustrates how to incorporate Circuit Breaker logic into an Azure Function, but similar principles can be applied across different Azure services based on your architecture and requirements.

# Circuit Breaker pattern in AWS

Implementing the Circuit Breaker pattern in AWS involves using AWS services and tools to manage failures and ensure the resilience of your microservices architecture. Here's a detailed description of how to implement the Circuit Breaker pattern with microservices in AWS, along with an example scenario.

## Overview of the Circuit Breaker Pattern

The Circuit Breaker pattern helps prevent cascading failures and maintain system stability by managing service interactions and handling failures gracefully. It consists of three main states:
- Closed State: Requests are allowed to pass through and are monitored.
- Open State: Requests are blocked, and the system does not interact with the failing service.
- Half-Open State: Limited requests are allowed to test if the service has recovered.

## Implementing the Circuit Breaker Pattern in AWS

1. Design Considerations

- Failure Thresholds: Define how many failures or timeouts are acceptable before opening the circuit.
- Timeouts: Set the duration for how long the circuit remains open before checking for recovery.
- Fallback Mechanisms: Implement fallback strategies to ensure system functionality even when the service is down.

2. AWS Services and Tools

- AWS Lambda: Implement serverless functions that can incorporate Circuit Breaker logic.
- Amazon API Gateway: Manage and route API requests, and apply custom logic for Circuit Breaker functionality.
- Amazon CloudWatch: Monitor metrics and set up alarms to

track service health and Circuit Breaker state transitions.
- Amazon SQS (Simple Queue Service): Use for queuing requests and implementing retry logic.
- Amazon SNS (Simple Notification Service): Publish failure alerts and notifications.

**Example Scenario**

**Scenario Description**

Consider an e-commerce application with microservices for Order Processing, Inventory Management, and Payment Processing. We want to ensure that the Order Processing service does not overwhelm the Payment Processing service if it fails or experiences high latency.

**Implementation Steps**

1. Define Circuit Breaker Configuration

- Failure Threshold: More than 50% of requests to the Payment Processing service fail within a 5-minute window.
- Timeout: Keep the circuit open for 30 seconds before checking if the Payment Processing service has recovered.

2. Implement Circuit Breaker Logic in AWS Lambda

Implementation with AWS Lambda:

- Create an AWS Lambda function for the Order Processing service that includes Circuit Breaker logic.

## Python

```
import json
import requests
import boto3
from datetime import datetime, timedelta

# Set up SNS and CloudWatch
```

```python
sns_client = boto3.client('sns')
cloudwatch_client = boto3.client('cloudwatch')
topic_arn       =       'arn:aws:sns:your-region:your-account-
id:payment-service-failure'

# Global variables for Circuit Breaker state
circuit_state = 'CLOSED'
failure_count = 0
success_count = 0
failure_threshold = 5
timeout_duration = timedelta(seconds=30)
last_failure_time = datetime.now()

def lambda_handler(event, context):
    global    circuit_state,    failure_count,    success_count,
last_failure_time

    payment_service_url = 'https://payment-service-url.com/
process'

    if circuit_state == 'OPEN':
        return {
          'statusCode': 503,
          'body': json.dumps('Payment Service is currently
unavailable. Please try again later.')
        }

    try:
        response    =    requests.post(payment_service_url,
json=event)

        if response.status_code == 200:
            success_count += 1
            if success_count > failure_threshold:
                circuit_state = 'CLOSED'
            return {
              'statusCode': 200,
              'body': json.dumps('Order processed successfully!')
```

```
            }
        else:
            failure_count += 1
            if failure_count > failure_threshold:
                circuit_state = 'OPEN'
                last_failure_time = datetime.now()
                sns_client.publish(
                    TopicArn=topic_arn,
                    Message='Payment Service Failure Detected',
                    Subject='Payment Service Failure'
                )
                return {
                    'statusCode': 502,
                    'body': json.dumps('Failed to process payment.')
                }

    except Exception as e:
        return {
            'statusCode': 500,
            'body': json.dumps(f'An error occurred: {str(e)}')
        }

    # Check for recovery in Half-Open State
    if circuit_state == 'OPEN' and datetime.now() -
last_failure_time > timeout_duration:
        circuit_state = 'HALF-OPEN'
        try:
            test_response = requests.get(payment_service_url)
            if test_response.status_code == 200:
                circuit_state = 'CLOSED'
            else:
                circuit_state = 'OPEN'
        except:
            circuit_state = 'OPEN'

    return {
        'statusCode': 200,
```

'body': json.dumps('Order processing completed.')
}

## 3. Configure CloudWatch for Monitoring

- CloudWatch Alarms: Set up alarms to monitor the failure rate and performance metrics of the Payment Processing service and the Lambda function.
- Custom Metrics: Publish custom metrics related to Circuit Breaker state transitions and failure rates.

Configuration:
- Create CloudWatch metrics and alarms to alert when the failure rate exceeds the threshold or when the circuit breaker transitions states.

## 4. Implement Fallback Mechanisms

- SQS for Retry Logic: Use Amazon SQS to queue payment requests and process them later when the service recovers.
- SNS for Notifications: Use Amazon SNS to send notifications about service failures and recovery status.

Example:
- If the Payment Processing service is down, queue payment requests in an SQS queue and process them once the service is available again.

Implementing the Circuit Breaker pattern in AWS involves leveraging services such as AWS Lambda, API Gateway, CloudWatch, SQS, and SNS to handle failures and ensure system resilience. By defining thresholds, incorporating Circuit Breaker logic in Lambda functions, and integrating with monitoring tools, you can effectively manage service failures and maintain a stable and responsive microservices architecture.

This example illustrates how to incorporate Circuit Breaker

logic into an AWS Lambda function, but similar principles can be applied using other AWS services based on your specific architecture and requirements.

# CHAPTER 10.
# SECURITY PATTERNS

In microservices architecture, securing services is crucial due to the distributed nature of the system and the potential for increased attack surfaces. Various security patterns help ensure that microservices are protected against threats while maintaining data integrity and confidentiality. Here are key security patterns commonly used in microservices architecture:

## API Gateway Security Pattern

The API Gateway Security Pattern is a fundamental approach in microservices architecture to manage and enforce security across multiple services. The API Gateway acts as a single entry point for all client requests, and it plays a critical role in implementing various security measures to protect backend microservices.

### Key Components and Functions of the API Gateway Security Pattern

1. Centralized Access Control
   - Authentication: Verifies the identity of the client making the request. Common methods include OAuth 2.0, JWT (JSON Web Tokens), API keys, or integration with Identity Providers (IdPs).
   - Authorization: Determines whether an authenticated client has permission to access specific resources or perform

certain actions. Role-Based Access Control (RBAC) and Attribute-Based Access Control (ABAC) are often used.

## 2. Traffic Management and Rate Limiting

- Rate Limiting: Controls the number of requests a client can make within a specified time period to prevent abuse and ensure fair usage. Rate limits can be set based on IP address, API key, or user identity.

- Throttling: Limits the request rate to prevent overloading services. This helps maintain system performance and availability.

## 3. Input Validation and Request Filtering

- Input Validation: Ensures that incoming requests conform to expected formats and constraints, preventing injection attacks and malformed requests.

- Request Filtering: Blocks or sanitizes potentially harmful requests based on patterns or content types to protect backend services from malicious data.

## 4. TLS Termination

- TLS/SSL Termination: Encrypts communication between clients and the API Gateway to ensure data confidentiality and integrity. The API Gateway can handle the TLS handshake and decryption, forwarding requests to backend services in plaintext or re-encrypted.

## 5. Threat Protection

- Web Application Firewall (WAF): Filters and monitors HTTP traffic to detect and block malicious requests. WAF rules can protect against common web vulnerabilities such as SQL injection, cross-site scripting (XSS), and cross-site request forgery (CSRF).

- DDoS Protection: Mitigates Distributed Denial of Service (DDoS) attacks by absorbing or filtering out malicious traffic before it reaches backend services.

## 6. Logging and Monitoring

- Request Logging: Records details about incoming requests, including source IP, request paths, and response status codes. This helps with auditing and troubleshooting.

- Monitoring and Alerts: Tracks API usage patterns, performance metrics, and security events. Alerts can be set up for anomalies or suspicious activities.

7. Authentication and Authorization Delegation

- Token Management: Handles token issuance, validation, and revocation. The API Gateway can delegate token validation to an external service or IdP.

- Claims-Based Authorization: Uses claims from tokens (e.g., user roles or permissions) to enforce authorization policies.

**Example Implementations**

1. AWS API Gateway

Features:
- AWS Cognito Integration: Manages user authentication and access control directly through AWS Cognito, providing user pools, identity pools, and federated identities.
- AWS WAF: Protects APIs by applying rules to filter out malicious traffic.
- API Keys and Usage Plans: Controls access and rate limits by requiring API keys for different usage plans.

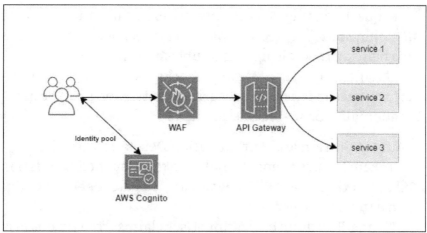

**10.1 API Gateway security in AWS**

Example Configuration:
- Configure AWS API Gateway to use AWS Cognito for user authentication. Set up AWS WAF to apply rules for common web vulnerabilities.
- Define usage plans with API Keys to manage access and rate limiting.

## 2. Azure API Management

Features:
- OAuth 2.0 and OpenID Connect: Supports authentication and authorization through OAuth 2.0 and OpenID Connect providers.
- Policy-Based Security: Allows the implementation of custom policies for rate limiting, IP filtering, and request validation.
- Azure Application Gateway WAF: Provides a Web Application Firewall to protect APIs from common threats.

Example Configuration:
- Configure Azure API Management to use OAuth 2.0 for authentication and apply custom policies for input validation and rate limiting.
- Integrate with Azure Application Gateway to use WAF rules for additional protection.

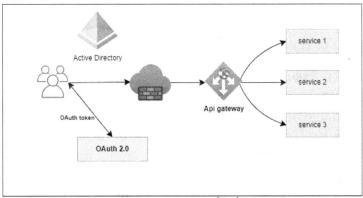

**10.2 API Gateway security in Azure**

3. Google Cloud API Gateway

Features:
- Google Identity Platform: Integrates with Identity Platform for authentication and authorization.
- Cloud Armor: Provides DDoS protection and WAF capabilities to protect APIs from attacks.
- Quota Management: Manages usage quotas and rate limits to control API consumption.

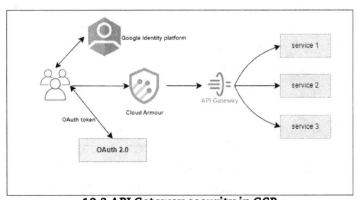

**10.3 API Gateway security in GCP**

Example Configuration:
- Set up Google Cloud API Gateway with Google Identity Platform for authentication and use Cloud Armor to apply security policies.
- Configure quotas and rate limits to manage API access and

prevent abuse.

### Benefits of the API Gateway Security Pattern

- Centralized Security Management: Simplifies the management of security policies and controls by consolidating them at a single entry point.
- Enhanced Protection: Provides comprehensive protection against various threats, including malicious traffic, DDoS attacks, and unauthorized access.
- Scalability: Improves scalability by offloading security functions from backend services, allowing them to focus on their core logic.
- Simplified Client Integration: Clients interact with a single API Gateway rather than multiple microservices, simplifying authentication and authorization.

### Challenges

- Single Point of Failure: The API Gateway becomes a critical component; its failure can affect the entire system. Implement redundancy and failover strategies to mitigate this risk.
- Performance Overhead: Adding security checks and processing at the API Gateway may introduce latency. Optimize performance through caching and efficient processing.

The API Gateway Security Pattern is a powerful approach for managing and enforcing security across microservices. By centralizing authentication, authorization, traffic management, and threat protection, the API Gateway helps maintain a secure and resilient microservices architecture. Implementing this pattern using services like AWS API Gateway, Azure API Management, or Google Cloud API Gateway can provide robust security features tailored to the needs of your system.

# Service-to-Service Authentication Pattern

The Service-to-Service Authentication Pattern is a key approach in microservices architecture for ensuring secure communication between services. This pattern is crucial in a distributed system where multiple microservices need to interact with each other while maintaining strict security and privacy.

**Key Concepts**

1. Authentication: Verifying the identity of a service or component before allowing it to interact with other services.
2. Authorization: Ensuring that the authenticated service has the appropriate permissions to perform the requested actions.

**Components of Service-to-Service Authentication**

1. Authentication Tokens: Tokens or credentials used by services to prove their identity.
2. Certificate-Based Authentication: Uses certificates to validate the identity of services.
3. OAuth 2.0 / JWT: Commonly used standards for token-based authentication and authorization.
4. Mutual TLS (mTLS): A method of using TLS certificates to authenticate both the client and the server.

**Patterns for Service-to-Service Authentication**

1. Token-Based Authentication

Description:
In this approach, services use tokens to authenticate requests to other services. Tokens are often issued by an identity provider and are included in request headers or as query parameters.

Key Aspects:
- JWT (JSON Web Tokens): A popular format for tokens that encodes claims and metadata, which services can use to verify the token's validity and extract information.

- OAuth 2.0: Provides a framework for issuing and validating tokens, and managing permissions.

Example Workflow:
1. Service A requests a token from an OAuth 2.0 authorization server.
2. Service A includes the token in the Authorization header of requests to Service B.
3. Service B validates the token using a public key or through the OAuth 2.0 server to ensure the request is from an authenticated and authorized service.

Example in AWS:
- AWS Lambda functions can use Amazon Cognito for token-based authentication. Service A gets a token from Cognito and includes it in requests to other AWS services.

2. Certificate-Based Authentication

Description:
Certificate-Based Authentication involves using X.509 certificates to authenticate services. Each service has a certificate issued by a trusted certificate authority (CA), and services use these certificates to prove their identity.

Key Aspects:
- Public Key Infrastructure (PKI): A framework for managing certificates and keys.
- X.509 Certificates: Standard format for certificates used in many secure communication protocols.

Example Workflow:
1. Service A presents its certificate to Service B when making a request.
2. Service B verifies Service A's certificate against a trusted CA.
3. If the certificate is valid, Service B allows the request to proceed.

Example in Google Cloud Platform:

- Google Kubernetes Engine (GKE) can use Istio service mesh to handle certificate-based authentication using mTLS for secure service-to-service communication.

3. Mutual TLS (mTLS)

Description:
Mutual TLS (mTLS) extends TLS by requiring both the client and the server to authenticate each other using certificates. This provides a strong form of authentication and ensures that both parties are trusted.

Key Aspects:
- Client and Server Certificates: Both client and server have certificates that are validated during the TLS handshake.
- Automatic Key Management: Service meshes often handle certificate issuance and rotation.

Example Workflow:
1. During the TLS handshake, Service A presents its certificate to Service B.
2. Service B validates the certificate and presents its own certificate.
3. Both services establish a secure connection and can verify each other's identity.

Example in Azure:
- Azure Kubernetes Service (AKS) can use Istio or Linkerd service meshes to implement mTLS for secure communication between microservices.

4. API Keys

Description:
API Keys are simple tokens used to identify and authenticate services. Although less secure than token-based or certificate-based methods, API keys are sometimes used for service authentication.

Key Aspects:
- Simple Implementation: API keys are straightforward to implement but may lack the robustness of other methods.
- Secret Management: API keys should be securely managed and rotated regularly.

Example Workflow:
1. Service A includes its API key in the request header or as a query parameter when calling Service B.
2. Service B validates the API key against a list of known keys.
3. If the key is valid, Service B processes the request.

Example in AWS:
- Amazon API Gateway can be configured to require API keys for accessing certain API methods, though this is typically more for client API management rather than inter-service communication.

**Best Practices for Service-to-Service Authentication**

1. Use Strong Authentication Methods: Prefer token-based authentication or certificate-based methods over simple API keys for higher security.
2. Implement Role-Based Access Control (RBAC): Ensure services have the minimum necessary permissions to reduce the impact of a compromised service.
3. Regularly Rotate Credentials: Periodically update and rotate authentication tokens or certificates to minimize security risks.
4. Secure Key and Certificate Storage: Use secure storage solutions, such as AWS Secrets Manager, Azure Key Vault, or Google Cloud Secret Manager, to manage sensitive credentials.
5. Monitor and Audit: Track authentication events and access patterns to detect anomalies or potential security issues.

The Service-to-Service Authentication Pattern is essential for maintaining security in a microservices architecture. By using methods like token-based authentication, certificate-based authentication, mutual TLS, and API keys, you can ensure that microservices communicate securely and that only authorized services can interact with each other. Implementing these practices helps protect your system from unauthorized access and reduces the risk of security breaches.

# Data Encryption Pattern

The Data Encryption Pattern in microservices architecture focuses on ensuring that sensitive data is protected both in transit and at rest. This pattern is crucial for maintaining data confidentiality and integrity, particularly in distributed systems where data traverses multiple services and storage systems.

### Key Concepts of Data Encryption

1. Encryption in Transit: Protects data as it moves between services or between clients and services, preventing unauthorized interception or tampering.
2. Encryption at Rest: Secures data stored in databases, file systems, or other storage solutions, safeguarding it from unauthorized access even if physical storage is compromised.

### Components of the Data Encryption Pattern

1. Encryption Algorithms: Defines the methods used to encode data. Common algorithms include AES (Advanced Encryption Standard), RSA (Rivest-Shamir-Adleman), and ECC (Elliptic Curve Cryptography).
2. Key Management: Involves the generation, storage, rotation, and distribution of encryption keys. Key management services (KMS) provide secure handling of cryptographic keys.
3. Certificates: Used in encryption protocols like TLS to verify the identity of communicating parties and establish secure connections.

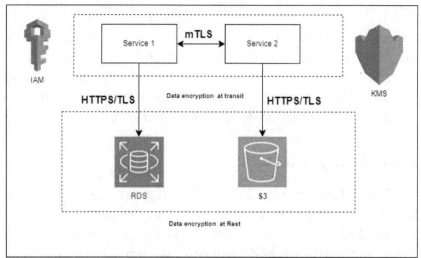

**10.4 Data security in AWS**

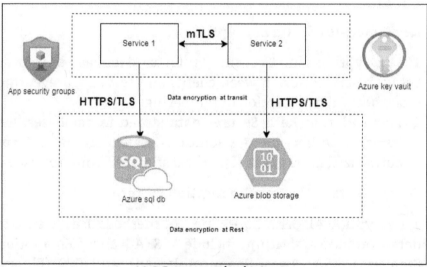

**10.5 Data security in Azure**

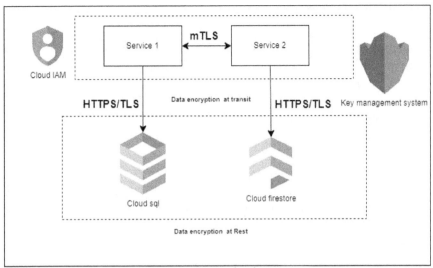

**10.6 Data security in GCP**

## Patterns for Data Encryption

### 1. Encryption in Transit

Description:
Encryption in transit involves securing data as it travels between microservices, clients, and other external systems. This prevents data from being intercepted or tampered with during transmission.

Key Aspects:
- TLS/SSL: Use Transport Layer Security (TLS) or Secure Sockets Layer (SSL) to encrypt data sent over the network.
- HTTPS: Ensures that HTTP traffic is encrypted using TLS, protecting data between clients and services.

Example Workflow:
1. A client makes an HTTPS request to a microservice.
2. The TLS protocol encrypts the data before it is sent over the network.
3. The microservice decrypts the data upon receipt and processes the request.

Example in AWS:
- Amazon API Gateway and AWS Elastic Load Balancing can be configured to use HTTPS to encrypt data in transit between clients and services.

## 2. Encryption at Rest

Description:
Encryption at rest protects data stored in databases, file systems, or other persistent storage solutions. It ensures that data remains secure even if the storage system is accessed without authorization.

Key Aspects:
- Database Encryption: Encrypts data stored in databases, including both structured and unstructured data.
- File System Encryption: Protects data stored in file systems using encryption at the file or disk level.

Example Workflow:
1. Data is written to a database or file system.
2. The encryption service encrypts the data before it is saved.
3. When the data is read, it is decrypted by the encryption service before being returned to the requesting service.

Example in Azure:
- Azure SQL Database provides built-in encryption for data at rest using Transparent Data Encryption (TDE).
- Azure Blob Storage supports server-side encryption with options for AES-256 encryption.

## 3. Key Management

Description:
Key Management involves securely handling encryption keys used for encrypting and decrypting data. Proper key management ensures that keys are protected, rotated, and retired according to best practices.

Key Aspects:
- Key Rotation: Periodically updates encryption keys to enhance security.
- Key Storage: Uses secure systems for storing encryption keys, such as hardware security modules (HSMs) or cloud-based key management services.
- Key Access Control: Restricts access to encryption keys to authorized entities only.

Example Workflow:
1. Encryption keys are generated and stored securely in a Key Management Service (KMS).
2. Microservices request encryption keys from the KMS as needed.
3. The KMS handles key rotation and access control, ensuring that keys are used securely.

Example in Google Cloud Platform (GCP):
- Google Cloud Key Management Service (KMS) provides centralized management for cryptographic keys used in GCP services, including encryption key rotation and access control.

## 4. Data Masking and Tokenization

Description:
Data Masking and Tokenization involve replacing sensitive data with non-sensitive representations to protect it from unauthorized access.

Key Aspects:
- Data Masking: Alters data to hide sensitive information, such as replacing actual values with dummy values.
- Tokenization: Replaces sensitive data with tokens that can be mapped back to the original data only by authorized systems.

Example Workflow:
1. Sensitive data is replaced with tokens or masked values before storage or processing.

2. Only authorized systems can access the tokenization service to retrieve the original data.

Example in AWS:
- AWS Glue DataBrew supports data masking for sensitive data during data preparation and transformation tasks.

Best Practices for Data Encryption

1. Use Strong Encryption Algorithms: Employ industry-standard algorithms such as AES-256 for encryption to ensure robust protection.
2. Manage Encryption Keys Securely: Use key management services or hardware security modules to handle encryption keys, ensuring they are rotated and protected.
3. Encrypt Sensitive Data: Apply encryption to all sensitive data, including personal information, financial data, and confidential business information.
4. Secure Communication Channels: Use TLS/SSL for encrypting data in transit to protect it from interception and tampering.
5. Regularly Review and Update Encryption Practices: Stay updated with security best practices and emerging threats, and adjust encryption practices accordingly.

The Data Encryption Pattern is a critical aspect of securing a microservices architecture. By implementing encryption both in transit and at rest, managing keys effectively, and applying techniques like data masking and tokenization, organizations can ensure that sensitive data remains protected throughout its lifecycle. Properly implementing these encryption practices helps safeguard data against unauthorized access and maintains its confidentiality and integrity.

# Identity and Access Management (IAM) Pattern

The Identity and Access Management (IAM) Pattern is crucial in microservices architecture for managing and securing access to resources. It involves controlling who can access which resources and what actions they can perform, ensuring that each service and user has appropriate permissions.

**Key Concepts of IAM in Microservices Architecture**

1. Identity: Refers to the unique identification of users, services, or applications within the system. Each identity must be authenticated to verify its legitimacy.
2. Access Control: Determines what authenticated identities are allowed to do. This involves defining permissions and policies that specify access rights.
3. Authorization: Ensures that an authenticated identity has the necessary permissions to perform specific actions on resources.

**Components of IAM**

1. Authentication: Verifying the identity of users or services.
2. Authorization: Defining and enforcing what authenticated users or services can access and perform.
3. Roles and Permissions: Structuring permissions into roles that can be assigned to users or services.
4. Policy Management: Creating and managing policies that define access rules and permissions.
5. Identity Providers: Services that manage and authenticate identities, such as OAuth 2.0 providers or identity services.

**Patterns for IAM**

**1. Centralized Identity Management**

Description:
Centralized Identity Management involves using a single system or service to handle authentication and authorization for all microservices. This approach simplifies identity

management and provides a consistent security model across the system.

Key Aspects:
- Single Sign-On (SSO): Allows users to authenticate once and gain access to multiple services without re-authenticating.
- Unified Identity Store: Central repository for managing user identities and their attributes.

Example Workflow:
1. A user logs in through a centralized identity provider (e.g., an SSO service).
2. The identity provider issues an authentication token (e.g., JWT) to the user.
3. The user includes the token in requests to various microservices.
4. Each microservice validates the token and enforces access control based on the user's roles and permissions.

Example in AWS:
- Amazon Cognito can be used to manage user authentication and integrate with other AWS services to provide centralized identity management and SSO capabilities.

## 2. Role-Based Access Control (RBAC)

Description:
RBAC assigns permissions based on roles rather than individual users or services. Roles represent a set of permissions, and users or services are assigned roles according to their needs.

Key Aspects:
- Role Definition: Define roles with specific permissions.
- Role Assignment: Assign roles to users or services based on their responsibilities.

Example Workflow:
1. Define roles such as "Admin," "Developer," and "Viewer" with

specific permissions.

2. Assign these roles to users or services based on their functions.

3. Services or users access resources according to the permissions granted by their roles.

Example in Azure:

- Azure Role-Based Access Control (RBAC) allows you to define roles and permissions and assign them to users, groups, or applications to control access to Azure resources.

### 3. Attribute-Based Access Control (ABAC)

Description:

ABAC uses attributes (such as user attributes, resource attributes, and environmental conditions) to define access policies. This approach allows for more fine-grained access control based on various factors.

Key Aspects:

- Policy Definitions: Create policies based on attributes like user department, resource type, or access time.
- Dynamic Access Control: Adjust access rights dynamically based on the context of the request.

Example Workflow:

1. Define policies that allow access based on attributes, such as "Allow access to financial records if the user's department is Finance."

2. When a request is made, the system evaluates the attributes of the user and resource to enforce the policy.

Example in Google Cloud Platform:

- Google Cloud IAM supports ABAC by allowing the creation of policies that grant permissions based on attributes such as resource labels and user groups.

### 4. Policy-Based Access Control

Description:
Policy-Based Access Control involves creating policies that define access rules and conditions for resources. These policies are evaluated when a user or service attempts to access a resource.

Key Aspects:
- Policy Creation: Define policies that specify who can access which resources and under what conditions.
- Policy Evaluation: Evaluate policies in real-time to make access decisions.

Example Workflow:
1. Create policies that define access rules, such as "Only users with the 'Admin' role can modify resource configurations."
2. When a user requests access, the system evaluates the policies to determine if the user is authorized.

Example in AWS:
- AWS IAM Policies define permissions for AWS resources. You create policies with specific actions and resources and attach them to IAM roles or users.

## 5. Federated Identity Management

Description:
Federated Identity Management allows users to authenticate using credentials from an external identity provider. This approach supports SSO across different systems and services.

Key Aspects:
- Federation Protocols: Use protocols like SAML (Security Assertion Markup Language) or OpenID Connect for federated authentication.
- Trust Relationships: Establish trust between the identity provider and the services that rely on it.

Example Workflow:

1. A user authenticates with an external identity provider (e.g., Google or Facebook).
2. The identity provider issues a federated token.
3. The user presents the token to microservices that accept federated identities.
4. The microservices validate the token and grant access based on the user's identity.

Example in Azure:
- Azure Active Directory (AAD) supports federated authentication with external identity providers and can be used to provide SSO for applications and services.

**Best Practices for IAM**

1. Implement Least Privilege: Ensure that users and services have only the permissions they need to perform their functions.
2. Use Strong Authentication Methods: Implement multi-factor authentication (MFA) to enhance security.
3. Regularly Review and Update Roles and Permissions: Periodically review and adjust roles and permissions to reflect changes in responsibilities.
4. Securely Manage Credentials: Use secure storage solutions for managing and rotating credentials and keys.
5. Monitor and Audit Access: Continuously monitor and audit access patterns to detect and respond to unauthorized access or anomalies.


The IAM Pattern in microservices architecture is essential for managing and securing access to resources. By implementing centralized identity management, RBAC, ABAC, policy-based access control, and federated identity management, organizations can effectively control who has access to their services and resources. Adhering to best practices for IAM helps ensure a secure and well-governed microservices environment, protecting sensitive data and maintaining system integrity.

# Secure API Design Pattern

The Secure API Design Pattern is essential for ensuring that APIs within a microservices architecture are designed with robust security practices. Secure APIs are critical for protecting data and services from unauthorized access, ensuring data integrity, and maintaining the overall security of the system.

### Key Concepts of Secure API Design

1. Authentication: Verifying the identity of clients or services making requests to the API.
2. Authorization: Determining whether an authenticated entity has the appropriate permissions to perform specific actions.
3. Data Protection: Ensuring that data transmitted through APIs is protected from unauthorized access and tampering.
4. Input Validation: Validating input data to prevent attacks such as injection or data corruption.
5. Logging and Monitoring: Tracking API usage and security events to detect and respond to potential threats.

### Components of Secure API Design

1. Authentication Mechanisms: Methods for verifying the identity of clients, such as API keys, tokens, or certificates.
2. Authorization Controls: Rules and policies that define what authenticated clients are allowed to do.
3. Encryption: Protecting data in transit and at rest to ensure confidentiality and integrity.
4. Rate Limiting and Throttling: Controlling the rate of requests to prevent abuse and ensure fair usage.
5. Input Validation and Sanitization: Ensuring that input data meets expected formats and constraints to prevent malicious activities.

6. Error Handling: Managing error responses securely to avoid exposing sensitive information.

**Patterns for Secure API Design**

**1. Authentication and Authorization**

Description:
Authentication verifies the identity of clients or services, while authorization determines their permissions. Effective API security requires both to ensure that only authorized entities can access and perform actions on the API.

Key Aspects:
- Token-Based Authentication: Use tokens such as JWT (JSON Web Tokens) for stateless authentication. Tokens are included in request headers and verified by the API.
- OAuth 2.0: A widely used framework for authentication and authorization, supporting various grant types and scopes.
- API Keys: Simple tokens used for identifying and authenticating clients, though they are less secure than tokens or certificates.

Example Workflow:
1. A client requests an authentication token from an authorization server.
2. The client includes the token in the Authorization header of API requests.
3. The API validates the token and checks the associated permissions before processing the request.

Example in AWS:
- Amazon API Gateway integrates with AWS Cognito to handle authentication using JWT tokens and OAuth 2.0.

**2. Data Encryption**

Description:
Data encryption ensures that sensitive data is protected

during transmission and while stored. Encryption helps maintain data confidentiality and integrity.

Key Aspects:
- Encryption in Transit: Use TLS (Transport Layer Security) or HTTPS to encrypt data transmitted between clients and the API.
- Encryption at Rest: Encrypt data stored in databases or file systems to protect it from unauthorized access.

Example Workflow:
1. A client connects to the API over HTTPS.
2. Data transmitted between the client and the API is encrypted using TLS.
3. Sensitive data stored in the database is encrypted at rest using AES (Advanced Encryption Standard).

Example in Azure:
- Azure API Management supports HTTPS for encrypting data in transit and integrates with Azure Key Vault for managing encryption keys.

### 3. Input Validation and Sanitization

Description:
Input validation and sanitization ensure that data received by the API adheres to expected formats and constraints, reducing the risk of security vulnerabilities such as injection attacks.

Key Aspects:
- Validation: Check that input data meets specific criteria, such as type, format, length, and range.
- Sanitization: Clean or modify input data to remove potentially harmful content before processing.

Example Workflow:
1. The API validates input data against defined schemas or constraints.
2. Malformed or malicious input is rejected or sanitized before

further processing.

Example in Google Cloud Platform:
- Google Cloud Endpoints supports input validation using OpenAPI specifications to define expected data formats and constraints.

## 4. Rate Limiting and Throttling

Description:
Rate limiting and throttling control the rate of API requests to prevent abuse and ensure fair usage. These mechanisms protect APIs from being overwhelmed by excessive or malicious requests.

Key Aspects:
- Rate Limiting: Restrict the number of requests a client can make within a specified time period.
- Throttling: Temporarily limit or block requests when a client exceeds defined usage thresholds.

Example Workflow:
1. The API Gateway applies rate limits based on IP address or API key.
2. Clients exceeding the rate limit receive a 429 Too Many Requests response.

Example in AWS:
- Amazon API Gateway allows you to set rate limits and quotas to manage API request rates and prevent abuse.

## 5. Error Handling

Description:
Error handling ensures that error responses do not expose sensitive information and provide useful feedback to clients. Secure error handling helps prevent information leakage and improves the user experience.

Key Aspects:

- Generic Error Messages: Provide generic error messages that do not disclose internal details or stack traces.
- Error Logging: Log detailed error information internally for troubleshooting and monitoring.

Example Workflow:
1. The API returns a standard error message with a general description of the issue.
2. Detailed error information is logged securely for internal review.

Example in Azure:
- Azure Application Insights can be used to log and monitor errors while providing generic error messages to users.

Best Practices for Secure API Design

1. Use Strong Authentication and Authorization: Implement robust authentication mechanisms like OAuth 2.0 and secure token management.
2. Encrypt Sensitive Data: Apply encryption for data in transit and at rest to protect data confidentiality and integrity.
3. Validate and Sanitize Inputs: Ensure all input data is validated and sanitized to prevent injection attacks and data corruption.
4. Implement Rate Limiting and Throttling: Protect APIs from abuse and ensure fair usage by controlling the rate of requests.
5. Handle Errors Securely: Provide generic error messages to users and log detailed information internally for security monitoring.

The Secure API Design Pattern is essential for safeguarding microservices and their interactions. By implementing strong authentication and authorization, encrypting data, validating inputs, controlling request rates, and handling errors securely, you can protect your APIs from various threats and vulnerabilities. Adhering to these practices helps ensure that your microservices architecture remains secure, resilient, and reliable.

# Service Mesh Security Pattern

The Service Mesh Security Pattern is a comprehensive approach to securing communication and interactions between microservices in a distributed system. A service mesh provides a dedicated infrastructure layer for managing and securing service-to-service communications, offering advanced security features beyond what traditional approaches can achieve.

### Key Concepts of Service Mesh Security

1. Service-to-Service Communication: Secure interactions between microservices, including mutual authentication and encryption.
2. Traffic Management: Control and monitor the flow of traffic between services, including routing, load balancing, and policy enforcement.
3. Security Policies: Define and enforce security rules and policies for accessing and interacting with services.
4. Observability: Monitor and log service interactions to detect and respond to security incidents.

### Components of Service Mesh Security

1. Sidecar Proxies: Lightweight proxies deployed alongside each microservice instance to handle communication and security features.
2. Control Plane: Manages the configuration and policies for the service mesh, including security rules and traffic management.
3. Data Plane: Handles the actual data transfer between microservices, including encryption and traffic routing.

## Patterns for Service Mesh Security

### 1. Mutual TLS (mTLS)

Description:
Mutual TLS (mTLS) is a method of securing service-to-service communication by requiring both parties to authenticate each other using certificates. This ensures that only trusted services can communicate and that data is encrypted in transit.

Key Aspects:
- Certificate-Based Authentication: Services present certificates to authenticate themselves to each other.
- Encryption: Data transmitted between services is encrypted using TLS.

Example Workflow:
1. Service A and Service B exchange certificates during the TLS handshake.
2. Both services verify each other's certificates and establish a secure connection.
3. Data transmitted between the services is encrypted, ensuring confidentiality and integrity.

Example in Google Cloud Platform:
- Istio on Google Kubernetes Engine (GKE) uses mTLS to secure communication between microservices.

### 2. Traffic Encryption

Description:
Traffic Encryption involves encrypting data as it moves between services within the mesh. This protects data from being intercepted or tampered with during transmission.

Key Aspects:
- Automatic Encryption: Encryption is handled automatically by the service mesh, without requiring changes to application code.

- End-to-End Encryption: Ensures that data remains encrypted from the source service to the destination service.

Example Workflow:
1. Service A sends a request to Service B.
2. The service mesh automatically encrypts the request data.
3. Service B decrypts the data upon receipt and processes the request.

Example in AWS:
- AWS App Mesh supports TLS encryption for securing traffic between services in the mesh.

### 3. Fine-Grained Access Control

Description:
Fine-Grained Access Control involves defining and enforcing detailed policies that specify which services can access which resources and perform specific actions. This is managed by the service mesh control plane.

Key Aspects:
- Policy Definition: Create policies based on service identities, roles, or attributes.
- Policy Enforcement: The service mesh enforces policies at runtime, ensuring that only authorized services can access protected resources.

Example Workflow:
1. Define access policies that specify which services can access certain endpoints or resources.
2. The service mesh enforces these policies when services make requests to each other.

Example in Azure:
- Azure Service Fabric integrates with Azure Active Directory (AAD) to provide fine-grained access control based on service identities.

## 4. Secure Service Discovery

Description:
Secure Service Discovery involves ensuring that service-to-service communication is only established with trusted and verified services. The service mesh handles service discovery securely, often using encrypted communication channels.

Key Aspects:
- Service Registry: Maintains a list of available services and their endpoints.
- Secure Communication: Ensures that services are discovered and communicated securely.

Example Workflow:
1. Services register themselves with the service registry in the service mesh.
2. The service mesh uses encrypted channels to discover and communicate with services.

Example in Google Cloud Platform:
- Istio provides secure service discovery and communication within Google Kubernetes Engine (GKE) clusters.

## 5. Observability and Logging

Description:
Observability and Logging involve monitoring and recording service interactions to detect security incidents and understand system behavior. The service mesh provides tools for comprehensive visibility into service communications and security events.

Key Aspects:
- Distributed Tracing: Track requests as they flow through the service mesh to diagnose performance issues and security incidents.
- Centralized Logging: Collect and analyze logs from all

services and proxies to detect anomalies and respond to incidents.

Example Workflow:
1. Service mesh proxies log details of service interactions and security events.
2. Logs are collected and analyzed to detect unusual patterns or potential threats.

Example in AWS:
- AWS App Mesh integrates with Amazon CloudWatch for monitoring and logging service interactions.

Best Practices for Service Mesh Security

1. Implement mTLS for Service Communication: Use mutual TLS to secure and authenticate service-to-service communication.
2. Encrypt Traffic End-to-End: Ensure that data is encrypted from the source to the destination service.
3. Define and Enforce Security Policies: Use fine-grained access control policies to manage service interactions and resource access.
4. Secure Service Discovery: Use secure methods for service discovery to ensure trusted communication between services.
5. Monitor and Log Interactions: Implement comprehensive observability and logging to detect and respond to security incidents.

The Service Mesh Security Pattern is a powerful approach to securing communication and interactions in a microservices architecture. By leveraging mutual TLS, traffic encryption, fine-grained access control, secure service discovery, and observability, organizations can enhance the security of their microservices environment. Implementing these practices helps protect against unauthorized access, data breaches, and other security threats, ensuring a robust and secure microservices infrastructure.

# Security Logging and Monitoring Pattern

The Security Logging and Monitoring Pattern in microservices architecture is crucial for detecting, analyzing, and responding to security incidents. It involves systematically capturing, storing, and analyzing logs and metrics to maintain visibility into the system's security posture, detect potential threats, and ensure compliance with security policies.

## Key Concepts of Security Logging and Monitoring

1. Logging: The process of recording events, transactions, and changes within the system. Logs provide a historical record of system activities, including security-related events.
2. Monitoring: Continuously observing system activities to identify anomalies, potential threats, or performance issues. Monitoring involves analyzing logs and metrics to ensure the system operates securely and efficiently.
3. Alerting: Notifying administrators or security teams when suspicious or anomalous activity is detected. Alerts help in timely response to potential security incidents.
4. Compliance: Ensuring that logging and monitoring practices meet regulatory and organizational standards for data protection and privacy.

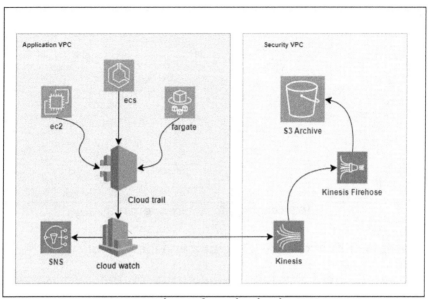

**10.7 Logging and monitoring in AWS**

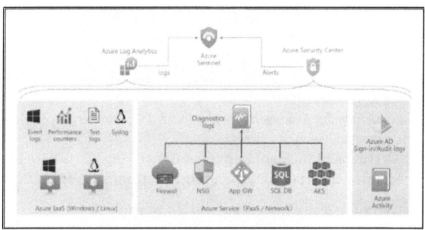

**10.8 Logging and monitoring in Azure**

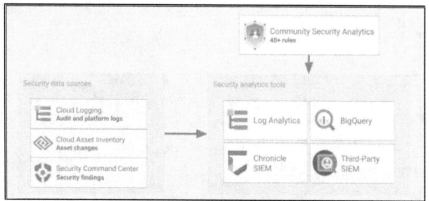

**10.9 Logging and monitoring in GCP**

## Components of Security Logging and Monitoring

1. Log Sources: Various components of the microservices architecture that generate logs, including application code, infrastructure, and network devices.
2. Log Aggregation: Collecting logs from different sources and consolidating them into a centralized location for analysis.
3. Log Storage: Storing logs securely and ensuring they are retained for the required duration to meet compliance and investigative needs.
4. Log Analysis: Analyzing logs to identify patterns, anomalies, and potential security threats.
5. Alerting and Incident Response: Generating alerts based on predefined criteria and responding to detected incidents.

Patterns for Security Logging and Monitoring

1. Centralized Logging

Description:
Centralized Logging involves aggregating logs from all microservices and infrastructure components into a single, centralized repository. This simplifies log management and analysis.

Key Aspects:

- Log Collection Agents: Deploy agents or use built-in features to collect logs from various sources.
- Central Log Repository: Use a centralized logging system or service to store and manage logs.

Example Workflow:
1. Each microservice and infrastructure component sends logs to a central logging service.
2. Logs are collected and stored in a centralized repository.
3. Security analysts access and analyze logs from the central repository.

Example in AWS:
- Amazon CloudWatch Logs collects and aggregates logs from various AWS services and applications into a central location.

2. Log Aggregation and Normalization

Description:
Log Aggregation and Normalization involve collecting logs from multiple sources, transforming them into a consistent format, and storing them in a central repository for easier analysis.

Key Aspects:
- Aggregation: Collect logs from different microservices, databases, and infrastructure components.
- Normalization: Convert logs into a consistent format to facilitate analysis.

Example Workflow:
1. Logs from different microservices are collected by aggregation agents.
2. Logs are normalized to a common format (e.g., JSON) for consistency.
3. Normalized logs are stored in a central log management system.

Example in Google Cloud Platform:

- Google Cloud Logging aggregates and normalizes logs from Google Cloud services and custom applications.

## 3. Security Monitoring and Anomaly Detection

Description:
Security Monitoring and Anomaly Detection involve continuously observing logs and metrics to identify unusual patterns or behaviors that may indicate security threats.

Key Aspects:
- Real-Time Monitoring: Continuously monitor logs and metrics for suspicious activities.
- Anomaly Detection: Use algorithms or rules to identify deviations from normal behavior.

Example Workflow:
1. Logs and metrics are continuously monitored by a security information and event management (SIEM) system.
2. Anomalies or deviations from expected patterns trigger alerts.
3. Security teams investigate and respond to identified anomalies.

Example in Azure:
- Azure Monitor provides real-time monitoring and anomaly detection for Azure resources and applications.

## 4. Alerting and Incident Response

Description:
Alerting and Incident Response involve notifying security teams of detected anomalies or threats and providing mechanisms to respond to incidents.

Key Aspects:
- Alert Configuration: Define thresholds and conditions for generating alerts.
- Incident Response: Implement procedures for investigating

and responding to security incidents.

Example Workflow:
1. Anomalies detected by monitoring systems trigger alerts based on predefined rules.
2. Alerts are sent to security teams through channels like email or SMS.
3. Security teams investigate the incident and take appropriate actions.

Example in AWS:
- Amazon CloudWatch Alarms can be configured to trigger notifications or automated responses based on specific conditions.

5. Compliance and Auditing

Description:
Compliance and Auditing involve ensuring that logging and monitoring practices meet regulatory requirements and organizational policies. This includes maintaining log integrity and retention.

Key Aspects:
- Log Retention: Store logs for a specified period to meet compliance requirements.
- Audit Trails: Maintain records of log access and changes to ensure accountability.

Example Workflow:
1. Logs are retained in compliance with regulatory requirements and internal policies.
2. Auditing tools track access to logs and changes to ensure integrity.

Example in Google Cloud Platform:
- Google Cloud Audit Logs provide detailed logs of administrative activities and access to Google Cloud resources, helping meet compliance requirements.

Best Practices for Security Logging and Monitoring

1. Implement Centralized Logging: Aggregate logs from all components into a central repository to simplify management and analysis.
2. Normalize Logs: Ensure logs are in a consistent format to facilitate effective analysis and correlation.
3. Monitor in Real-Time: Continuously monitor logs and metrics to detect and respond to threats promptly.
4. Define Alerting Rules: Set up alerts based on security events and anomalies to ensure timely responses.
5. Ensure Compliance: Maintain logs in accordance with regulatory requirements and organizational policies.
6. Review and Update: Regularly review and update logging and monitoring practices to adapt to evolving security threats.

The Security Logging and Monitoring Pattern is essential for maintaining a secure microservices architecture. By implementing centralized logging, log aggregation and normalization, security monitoring, alerting, and compliance practices, organizations can effectively detect, analyze, and respond to security incidents. This pattern enhances visibility into system activities, supports proactive security measures, and ensures compliance with regulatory requirements.

# Data Privacy Pattern

The Data Privacy Pattern in microservices architecture focuses on ensuring that personal and sensitive data is handled in a way that protects privacy and complies with relevant regulations. This pattern addresses the challenges of managing and safeguarding data across distributed services while maintaining compliance with privacy laws and regulations.

### Key Concepts of Data Privacy

1. Data Minimization: Only collect and retain the minimum amount of personal data necessary for a specific purpose.
2. Data Encryption: Protect data through encryption to ensure it is secure both in transit and at rest.
3. Access Control: Implement strict access controls to ensure that only authorized individuals or services can access sensitive data.
4. Data Masking: Hide or obfuscate sensitive data to protect it from unauthorized access or exposure.
5. Auditing and Monitoring: Continuously monitor and audit data access and usage to detect and respond to privacy breaches.

**Components of Data Privacy Pattern**

1. Data Classification: Categorize data based on its sensitivity and privacy requirements.
2. Data Encryption: Encrypt data to protect it from unauthorized access.
3. Access Control: Implement policies and mechanisms to control who can access and modify data.
4. Data Masking and Anonymization: Use techniques to obscure or anonymize data to protect privacy.
5. Compliance and Auditing: Ensure that data handling practices meet regulatory requirements and are subject to regular audits.

**Patterns for Data Privacy**

1. Data Classification

Description:
Data Classification involves categorizing data based on its sensitivity and privacy requirements. This helps determine appropriate handling, security measures, and compliance requirements for different types of data.

Key Aspects:

- Classification Levels: Define classification levels (e.g., Public, Internal, Confidential, Restricted) based on data sensitivity.
- Tagging: Tag data with its classification level to enforce appropriate handling and security measures.

Example Workflow:
1. Identify and categorize data types based on sensitivity and privacy requirements.
2. Apply classification tags to data to guide its handling and protection.

Example in Azure:
- Azure Information Protection allows you to classify and label data based on its sensitivity.

2. Data Encryption

Description:
Data Encryption involves protecting data from unauthorized access by converting it into a secure format that can only be decrypted by authorized entities.

Key Aspects:
- Encryption in Transit: Use TLS or HTTPS to encrypt data as it travels between services.
- Encryption at Rest: Encrypt data stored in databases, files, or other storage systems.

Example Workflow:
1. Data is encrypted using encryption algorithms (e.g., AES) before storage or transmission.
2. Authorized entities decrypt the data using secure keys when needed.

Example in AWS:
- AWS Key Management Service (KMS) provides encryption keys for securing data in transit and at rest.

3. Access Control

Description:
Access Control involves defining and enforcing policies to control who can access and modify sensitive data. This ensures that only authorized users or services can interact with the data.

Key Aspects:
- Role-Based Access Control (RBAC): Assign roles to users and services, and define permissions based on these roles.
- Attribute-Based Access Control (ABAC): Use attributes (e.g., user role, data classification) to determine access permissions.

Example Workflow:
1. Define roles and permissions for accessing sensitive data.
2. Enforce access control policies using authentication and authorization mechanisms.

Example in Google Cloud Platform:
- Google Cloud Identity and Access Management (IAM) allows you to define and enforce access control policies for Google Cloud resources.

4. Data Masking and Anonymization

Description:
Data Masking and Anonymization involve obscuring or transforming data to protect privacy while maintaining its usability for development, testing, or analysis.

Key Aspects:
- Data Masking: Replace sensitive data with masked values that retain the data's structure but hide its original content.
- Data Anonymization: Remove or obfuscate personal identifiers to prevent the identification of individuals.

Example Workflow:
1. Apply masking or anonymization techniques to sensitive data before sharing or using it in non-production

environments.
2. Ensure that masked or anonymized data cannot be traced back to individuals.

Example in AWS:
- AWS Glue DataBrew provides data transformation capabilities, including masking and anonymizing data.

5. Compliance and Auditing

Description:
Compliance and Auditing involve ensuring that data privacy practices adhere to regulatory requirements and internal policies. Regular audits and monitoring help detect and address any non-compliance issues.

Key Aspects:
- Compliance: Ensure data handling practices meet regulations such as GDPR, CCPA, or HIPAA.
- Auditing: Regularly review data access and handling practices to identify and address any issues.

Example Workflow:
1. Implement compliance checks to ensure adherence to privacy regulations.
2. Conduct regular audits to review data access logs and handling practices.

Example in Azure:
- Azure Security Center provides security management and compliance monitoring for Azure resources.

Best Practices for Data Privacy

1. Classify Data: Identify and classify data based on sensitivity and privacy requirements to guide handling and protection measures.
2. Encrypt Data: Use encryption to secure data both in transit and at rest.

3. Implement Access Controls: Define and enforce access control policies to restrict data access to authorized entities.

4. Mask and Anonymize Data: Use masking and anonymization techniques to protect privacy while retaining data usability.

5. Ensure Compliance: Adhere to relevant privacy regulations and regularly audit data handling practices.

The Data Privacy Pattern is essential for safeguarding personal and sensitive data in a microservices architecture. By implementing data classification, encryption, access control, masking, and compliance practices, organizations can effectively protect privacy and meet regulatory requirements. Adhering to these practices helps ensure that data is handled securely and responsibly across the microservices ecosystem.

# Distributed Denial of Service (DDoS) Protection Pattern

The Distributed Denial of Service (DDoS) Protection Pattern in a microservices architecture focuses on defending against DDoS attacks, where an attacker attempts to overwhelm a service or system with an excessive amount of traffic, rendering it unavailable to legitimate users. In a microservices environment, protecting against DDoS attacks requires a comprehensive approach to ensure the availability and reliability of the services.

### Key Concepts of DDoS Protection

1. Traffic Filtering: Identifying and filtering malicious traffic to prevent it from reaching your microservices.

2. Rate Limiting: Controlling the rate at which requests are accepted from clients to mitigate the impact of large-scale attacks.

3. Load Balancing: Distributing traffic across multiple

instances or servers to handle high volumes of requests and reduce the impact of attacks.

4. Scaling: Automatically adjusting resources to accommodate increased traffic and maintain service availability.

5. Monitoring and Alerting: Continuously monitoring traffic patterns and setting up alerts to detect and respond to potential DDoS attacks.

## Components of DDoS Protection Pattern

1. Traffic Management: Techniques to manage and filter incoming traffic to prevent malicious requests from overwhelming the system.

2. Scaling Mechanisms: Methods to scale infrastructure dynamically in response to traffic spikes.

3. Load Balancing: Distributing traffic across multiple servers or instances to ensure high availability and reliability.

4. Monitoring and Response: Tools and processes to monitor traffic patterns, detect anomalies, and respond to potential DDoS attacks.

## Patterns for DDoS Protection

1. Traffic Filtering

Description:
Traffic Filtering involves inspecting incoming traffic to identify and block malicious requests before they reach the microservices. This helps prevent DDoS attacks from overwhelming the system.

Key Aspects:
- IP Blacklisting: Block requests from known malicious IP addresses.
- Rate-Based Filtering: Use rate limiting to filter out excessive requests from individual IP addresses.

Example Workflow:
1. Incoming traffic is inspected by a traffic filtering

mechanism.

2. Malicious requests are identified and blocked based on predefined rules or patterns.

3. Legitimate traffic is allowed to pass through to the microservices.

Example in AWS:

- AWS WAF (Web Application Firewall) provides traffic filtering capabilities to protect against common web exploits and DDoS attacks.

## 2. Rate Limiting

Description:
Rate Limiting involves controlling the number of requests a client can make to the microservices within a given timeframe. This helps mitigate the impact of high-volume attacks and ensures fair usage.

Key Aspects:
- IP-Based Rate Limiting: Limit the number of requests from individual IP addresses.
- Service-Level Rate Limiting: Apply rate limits based on service endpoints or resource types.

Example Workflow:
1. Configure rate limits for different services or endpoints.
2. Monitor incoming requests and enforce rate limits based on the defined thresholds.
3. Block or throttle requests that exceed the allowed rate.

Example in Google Cloud Platform:
- Google Cloud Armor provides rate limiting and DDoS protection for applications running on Google Cloud.

## 3. Load Balancing

Description:
Load Balancing distributes incoming traffic across multiple

instances or servers to prevent any single instance from being overwhelmed. This helps maintain high availability and reliability during DDoS attacks.

Key Aspects:
- Horizontal Scaling: Add more instances or servers to handle increased traffic.
- Load Distribution: Distribute traffic evenly across available instances.

Example Workflow:
1. Incoming traffic is directed to a load balancer.
2. The load balancer distributes traffic across multiple instances based on predefined algorithms.
3. The instances process the requests, reducing the load on any single instance.

Example in Azure:
- Azure Load Balancer distributes traffic across multiple virtual machines to handle high volumes of requests.

4. Auto-Scaling

Description:
Auto-Scaling automatically adjusts the number of instances or resources based on traffic patterns and load. This helps ensure that the system can handle sudden spikes in traffic without manual intervention.

Key Aspects:
- Dynamic Scaling: Increase or decrease the number of instances based on real-time traffic and load metrics.
- Scaling Policies: Define policies for when and how to scale resources.

Example Workflow:
1. Monitor traffic and resource utilization metrics.
2. Automatically add or remove instances based on predefined scaling policies.

3. Ensure that sufficient resources are available to handle traffic spikes.

Example in AWS:
- Amazon EC2 Auto Scaling automatically adjusts the number of EC2 instances based on traffic and load conditions.

5. Monitoring and Alerting

Description:
Monitoring and Alerting involve continuously tracking traffic patterns, system performance, and security events to detect and respond to potential DDoS attacks. Timely alerts help in taking appropriate actions to mitigate the impact of attacks.

Key Aspects:
- Traffic Monitoring: Track incoming traffic volumes and patterns to identify anomalies.
- Alerts: Set up alerts based on traffic thresholds or detected anomalies.

Example Workflow:
1. Monitor traffic and system performance using monitoring tools.
2. Configure alerts to notify administrators of potential DDoS attacks or anomalies.
3. Respond to alerts by implementing mitigation measures or adjusting configurations.

Example in Azure:
- Azure Monitor provides comprehensive monitoring and alerting capabilities for Azure resources and applications.

**Best Practices for DDoS Protection**

1. Implement Traffic Filtering: Use traffic filtering mechanisms to block malicious requests and protect microservices.
2. Apply Rate Limiting: Control the rate of incoming requests

to prevent abuse and ensure fair usage.

3. Use Load Balancing: Distribute traffic across multiple instances to maintain availability and reliability.

4. Enable Auto-Scaling: Automatically adjust resources to handle traffic spikes and ensure sufficient capacity.

5. Monitor and Alert: Continuously monitor traffic patterns and set up alerts to detect and respond to potential DDoS attacks.

The Distributed Denial of Service (DDoS) Protection Pattern is essential for maintaining the availability and reliability of microservices in the face of large-scale attacks. By implementing traffic filtering, rate limiting, load balancing, auto-scaling, and monitoring, organizations can effectively mitigate the impact of DDoS attacks and ensure that their microservices remain accessible and performant. Adhering to these best practices helps protect against disruptions and maintain a resilient microservices architecture.

# Zero Trust Architecture Pattern

The Zero Trust Architecture (ZTA) Pattern is a security model designed to protect systems by assuming that threats may exist both outside and inside the network. In a microservices architecture, Zero Trust ensures that every request, regardless of its origin, is verified and validated before granting access to resources. This approach enhances security by minimizing trust assumptions and enforcing rigorous access controls.

### Key Principles of Zero Trust Architecture

1. Never Trust, Always Verify: Assume that threats can be present anywhere and require continuous verification of users, devices, and requests.

2. Least Privilege Access: Grant the minimum level of access necessary for users and services to perform their tasks.

3. Micro-Segmentation: Divide the network into smaller segments to limit lateral movement of threats within the environment.

4. Assume Breach: Design systems with the assumption that a breach may occur, and implement controls to limit its impact.

## Components of Zero Trust Architecture

1. Identity and Access Management (IAM): Systems that authenticate and authorize users and services based on their identity and roles.

2. Network Segmentation: Dividing the network into segments to control and monitor traffic flows.

3. Application and Data Security: Protecting applications and data through encryption, access controls, and secure coding practices.

4. Continuous Monitoring: Continuously observing and analyzing traffic, access patterns, and system behavior to detect anomalies and threats.

5. Security Policies and Enforcement: Implementing and enforcing security policies based on the Zero Trust model.

## Patterns for Implementing Zero Trust Architecture

1. Identity and Access Management (IAM)

Description:
IAM systems manage authentication and authorization to ensure that only verified users and services can access resources. Zero Trust requires robust IAM practices to continuously validate identities and their permissions.

Key Aspects:
- Multi-Factor Authentication (MFA): Use multiple methods of authentication (e.g., passwords, tokens, biometrics) to verify identity.
- Role-Based Access Control (RBAC): Define and enforce access policies based on roles and responsibilities.

- Attribute-Based Access Control (ABAC): Use attributes (e.g., department, location) to determine access permissions.

Example Workflow:
1. A user or service requests access to a resource.
2. The IAM system verifies the identity using MFA.
3. The access request is evaluated against RBAC or ABAC policies.
4. Access is granted or denied based on the policies.

Example in AWS:
- AWS Identity and Access Management (IAM) provides fine-grained access control and supports MFA for enhanced security.

2. Micro-Segmentation

Description:
Micro-Segmentation involves dividing the network into smaller, isolated segments to control and monitor traffic between them. This limits the potential impact of a breach by preventing unauthorized lateral movement.

Key Aspects:
- Network Segmentation: Create network segments based on function, sensitivity, or other criteria.
- Security Policies: Define policies for traffic flow between segments and enforce them using firewalls or other security controls.

Example Workflow:
1. Define network segments based on application, environment, or sensitivity.
2. Implement firewalls or security controls to enforce traffic policies between segments.
3. Monitor and log traffic between segments to detect and respond to anomalies.

Example in Google Cloud Platform:

- Google Cloud VPC Service Controls provide network segmentation and access control to protect data and applications.

3. Application and Data Security

Description:
Protecting applications and data involves implementing security measures to ensure that data is encrypted, applications are secure, and access is controlled based on Zero Trust principles.

Key Aspects:
- Encryption: Encrypt data both in transit and at rest to protect it from unauthorized access.
- Secure Coding Practices: Follow secure coding guidelines to prevent vulnerabilities in applications.
- Data Classification: Classify data based on sensitivity and apply appropriate security controls.

Example Workflow:
1. Encrypt sensitive data using strong encryption algorithms.
2. Apply secure coding practices during application development.
3. Classify data and apply access controls based on its classification.

Example in Azure:
- Azure Key Vault provides encryption key management and secrets management for protecting sensitive data.

4. Continuous Monitoring

Description:
Continuous Monitoring involves observing and analyzing network traffic, access patterns, and system behavior to detect and respond to anomalies and potential threats in real-time.

Key Aspects:

- Traffic Analysis: Monitor network traffic for unusual patterns or behaviors.
- Behavioral Analysis: Analyze user and service behavior to detect deviations from normal patterns.
- Alerting: Set up alerts for suspicious activities or policy violations.

Example Workflow:
1. Collect and analyze logs and metrics from various sources.
2. Use monitoring tools to detect anomalies or deviations from normal behavior.
3. Generate alerts and take action based on detected threats.

Example in AWS:
- Amazon GuardDuty provides continuous threat detection and monitoring for AWS resources.

5. Security Policies and Enforcement

Description:
Security Policies and Enforcement involve defining and implementing policies that align with Zero Trust principles. This includes access control policies, data protection policies, and network security policies.

Key Aspects:
- Policy Definition: Create detailed policies for access control, data protection, and network security.
- Policy Enforcement: Implement controls to enforce policies and ensure compliance.

Example Workflow:
1. Define security policies based on Zero Trust principles.
2. Implement policies using access control systems, firewalls, and other security controls.
3. Regularly review and update policies to adapt to evolving threats.

Example in Google Cloud Platform:

- Google Cloud Identity-Aware Proxy (IAP) enforces access policies for applications and services based on user identity and context.

Best Practices for Zero Trust Architecture

1. Adopt Multi-Factor Authentication (MFA): Implement MFA for all users and services to enhance identity verification.
2. Implement Micro-Segmentation: Divide the network into isolated segments to limit lateral movement and reduce attack surfaces.
3. Encrypt Data: Ensure that data is encrypted both in transit and at rest to protect against unauthorized access.
4. Continuously Monitor and Analyze: Use monitoring tools to detect and respond to anomalies and potential threats in real-time.
5. Define and Enforce Security Policies: Create and implement detailed security policies to govern access, data protection, and network security.

The Zero Trust Architecture Pattern is a proactive approach to security that ensures every request and interaction within a microservices architecture is verified and validated. By implementing IAM, micro-segmentation, application and data security, continuous monitoring, and robust security policies, organizations can significantly enhance their security posture and mitigate the risks associated with modern cyber threats. Adopting Zero Trust principles helps maintain a secure and resilient microservices environment.

Securing a microservices architecture involves multiple patterns and practices to protect against various threats and vulnerabilities. By implementing patterns like API Gateway Security, Service-to-Service Authentication, Data Encryption, IAM, Secure API Design, Service Mesh Security, Security Logging and Monitoring, Data Privacy, DDoS Protection, and Zero Trust Architecture, you can build a robust security framework for your microservices.

These patterns and practices help ensure that your microservices are resilient to attacks, compliant with regulations, and capable of maintaining data integrity and confidentiality.

# CHAPTER 11. USER INTERFACE PATTERN

The User Interface (UI) Pattern in a microservices architecture focuses on how the front-end or client-facing interfaces interact with the underlying microservices. This pattern addresses how to effectively design and manage user interfaces that integrate with microservices to deliver a cohesive and responsive user experience.

## Key Concepts of UI Pattern in Microservices

**1. Decoupling Front-End and Back-End:** Separating the user interface from the back-end services to allow for independent development and deployment.

**2. API Gateway:** Using an API gateway to provide a unified entry point for the front-end to interact with various microservices.

**3. Service Composition:** Aggregating data from multiple microservices to present a unified view to the user.

**4. Client-Side Aggregation:** Fetching data from multiple microservices directly in the client application and aggregating it on the front-end.

**5. Backend for Frontend (BFF):** Creating specialized back-end services tailored to the needs of specific front-end applications or user experiences.

### Components of UI Pattern

**1. API Gateway:** Acts as a single entry point for the front-end, routing requests to appropriate microservices and aggregating responses.

**2. Service Composition:** Aggregates and composes data from multiple microservices to provide a unified response to the front-end.

**3. Client-Side Aggregation:** The front-end application makes multiple requests to different microservices and combines the data on the client side.

**4. Backend for Frontend (BFF):** Provides tailored back-end services that are specific to the needs of different front-end applications, improving performance and user experience.

# Patterns for Implementing UI in Microservices

## 1. API Gateway

Description:
An API Gateway provides a single entry point for the front-end application to interact with various microservices. It simplifies the interaction between the client and the microservices by routing requests, handling authentication, and aggregating responses.

Key Aspects:
- Request Routing: Directs requests from the front-end to the appropriate microservice.
- Response Aggregation: Combines responses from multiple microservices into a single response for the front-end.
- Cross-Cutting Concerns: Handles tasks such as authentication, logging, and rate limiting.

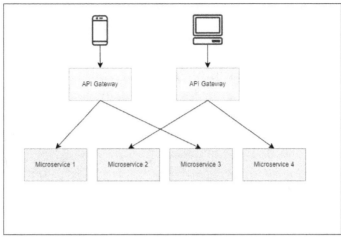

**11.1 API Gateway**

Example Workflow:
1. The front-end application sends a request to the API Gateway.
2. The API Gateway routes the request to the appropriate microservices.
3. The microservices process the request and return responses to the API Gateway.
4. The API Gateway aggregates the responses and sends a unified response to the front-end application.

Example in AWS:
- Amazon API Gateway provides a managed service for creating and deploying APIs, including request routing and response aggregation.

## 2. Service Composition

Description:
Service Composition involves aggregating data from multiple microservices to provide a cohesive response to the front-end application. This can be achieved either on the server-side (using an API Gateway or BFF) or on the client-side.

Key Aspects:

- Backend Aggregation: The API Gateway or BFF combines data from multiple microservices before sending it to the front-end.
- Client-Side Aggregation: The front-end application makes separate requests to different microservices and combines the data.

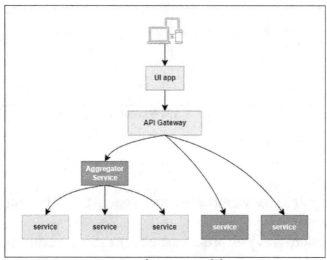

**11.2 Service composition**

Example Workflow:
1. The API Gateway or BFF makes calls to multiple microservices to gather the required data.
2. The responses from the microservices are combined into a single response.
3. The unified response is sent to the front-end application.

Example in Google Cloud Platform:
- Google Cloud Endpoints can be used to manage APIs, including composing data from multiple microservices.

## 3. Client-Side Aggregation

Description:
Client-Side Aggregation involves fetching data from multiple microservices directly in the client application and combining

it to present a unified view to the user.

Key Aspects:
- Multiple Requests: The front-end application makes separate requests to different microservices.
- Data Combination: The front-end application combines the responses to present a cohesive user experience.

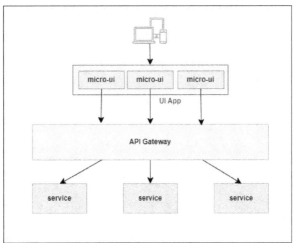

**11.3 Client side aggregation**

Example Workflow:
1. The front-end application sends multiple requests to different microservices.
2. Each microservice returns its data to the front-end application.
3. The front-end application aggregates the data and presents it to the user.

Example in Azure:
- Azure API Management can be used to expose multiple APIs and manage client-side aggregation.

# 4. Backend for Frontend (BFF)

Description:
The BFF pattern involves creating specialized back-end

services that cater to the specific needs of different front-end applications. This helps optimize performance and user experience by tailoring the back-end responses to the front-end requirements.

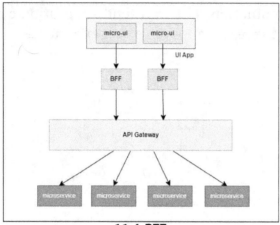

**11.4 BFF**

Key Aspects:
- Tailored Back-End Services: Create back-end services that are optimized for specific front-end applications (e.g., web, mobile).
- Performance Optimization: Improve performance by reducing the amount of data sent to the front-end and optimizing responses.

Example Workflow:
1. The front-end application requests data from the BFF.
2. The BFF communicates with various microservices to gather and aggregate the data.
3. The BFF sends a tailored response to the front-end application based on its needs.

Example in AWS:
- AWS Lambda can be used to implement BFF services, handling requests and aggregating data from microservices.

## Best Practices for UI in Microservices

1. Use API Gateway: Implement an API Gateway to provide a unified entry point, manage cross-cutting concerns, and aggregate responses.
2. Consider BFF for Complex UIs: Use the BFF pattern for applications with complex front-end requirements to optimize performance and user experience.
3. Implement Client-Side Aggregation When Appropriate: Use client-side aggregation for simpler use cases where combining data in the front-end is feasible.
4. Design for Scalability: Ensure that the UI pattern can scale with the number of microservices and the volume of traffic.
5. Ensure Consistent User Experience: Maintain a consistent user experience by integrating and presenting data in a cohesive manner.

The User Interface Pattern in microservices architecture is crucial for delivering a cohesive and responsive user experience. By leveraging patterns such as API Gateway, Service Composition, Client-Side Aggregation, and Backend for Frontend (BFF), organizations can effectively manage interactions between the front-end and the underlying microservices. Adopting these patterns helps ensure that the UI is scalable, performant, and capable of handling complex interactions with distributed services.

# User Interface Pattern in Google cloud platform

Implementing the User Interface (UI) Pattern in Google Cloud Platform (GCP) involves using various GCP services and tools to manage interactions between the front-end application and microservices. Below, I'll describe how to implement this pattern on GCP using key components and services.

## Key Components and Services

1. Google Cloud Endpoints: Provides API management, including request routing and response aggregation.
2. Google Cloud Functions: Implements Backend for Frontend (BFF) services to tailor responses to specific front-end needs.
3. Google Cloud Storage and CDN: Hosts static assets and improves performance by caching content.
4. Google App Engine or Google Kubernetes Engine: Hosts microservices and handles scaling and load balancing.
5. Google Cloud Monitoring and Logging: Provides visibility into application performance and user interactions.

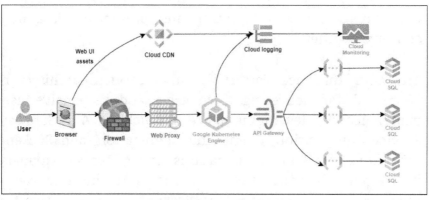

**11.5 UI Pattern in GCP**

## Patterns and Examples

## 1. API Gateway with Google Cloud Endpoints

Description:
Google Cloud Endpoints provides API management capabilities, including request routing, response aggregation, and API security. It serves as a unified entry point for the front-end to interact with multiple microservices.

Key Aspects:

- Request Routing: Directs incoming requests to the appropriate microservices.
- Response Aggregation: Combines responses from multiple microservices into a single response.
- API Management: Provides monitoring, logging, and security features for APIs.

Example Workflow:
1. Setup API Gateway:
   - Define API specifications using OpenAPI or gRPC.
   - Deploy the API using Google Cloud Endpoints.

2. Frontend Integration:
   - Configure the front-end application to send API requests to the Google Cloud Endpoints API gateway.
   - The gateway routes these requests to the appropriate microservices.

3. Response Handling:
   - The microservices return responses to the API gateway.
   - The gateway aggregates these responses if needed and sends them back to the front-end.

Example Implementation:
- Use Google Cloud Endpoints to manage APIs for a shopping application. The API gateway routes requests for product details, user information, and order processing to different microservices and combines the results into a single response for the front-end application.

## 2. Backend for Frontend (BFF) with Google Cloud Functions

Description:
The BFF pattern involves creating specialized back-end services tailored to the needs of specific front-end applications. Google Cloud Functions can be used to implement these services, optimizing performance and user experience.

Key Aspects:
- Tailored Services: Develop serverless functions that provide data aggregation or transformation specific to the front-end needs.
- Performance Optimization: Reduce data processing on the client side and deliver optimized responses.

Example Workflow:
1. Create Cloud Functions:
   - Write Cloud Functions that aggregate data from various microservices.
   - Deploy these functions on Google Cloud.

2. Frontend Integration:
   - Configure the front-end application to call the Cloud Functions for specific tasks.

3. Data Aggregation:
   - Cloud Functions gather and process data from different microservices.
   - Return the aggregated data to the front-end.

Example Implementation:
- For a travel booking application, use Google Cloud Functions to create a BFF that fetches and aggregates data from microservices handling flights, hotels, and car rentals, providing a unified response to the front-end application.

### 3. Client-Side Aggregation

Description:
Client-Side Aggregation involves making multiple requests from the front-end application to different microservices and combining the data on the client side.

Key Aspects:
- Multiple Requests: The front-end application communicates with various microservices.

- Data Combination: The front-end application processes and combines responses.

Example Workflow:
1. Front-End Application:
   - Make concurrent API requests to different microservices.

2. Data Processing:
   - Combine the responses from microservices in the front-end code.

3. Display Data:
   - Render the combined data in the user interface.

Example Implementation:
- In a news aggregator app, the front-end makes requests to microservices for articles, images, and user comments. It then combines and displays this data to provide a cohesive view of the news content.

## 4. Hosting Static Assets with Google Cloud Storage and CDN

Description:
Google Cloud Storage can be used to host static assets such as HTML, CSS, and JavaScript files. Google Cloud CDN improves performance by caching these assets closer to the users.

Key Aspects:
- Static Asset Hosting: Store and serve static files from Google Cloud Storage.
- Content Delivery: Use Google Cloud CDN to cache and deliver content globally, reducing latency.

Example Workflow:

1. Upload Assets:
   - Upload static files to a Google Cloud Storage bucket.

2. Configure CDN:
   - Set up Google Cloud CDN to cache and serve the static files.

## 3. Frontend Access:

- The front-end application retrieves static assets from the CDN.

Example Implementation:
- For a corporate website, host the website's static assets (e.g., HTML, CSS, images) in Google Cloud Storage and use Google Cloud CDN to ensure fast and reliable delivery of these assets to users around the world.

## 5. Monitoring and Logging with Google Cloud Monitoring and Logging

Description:
Google Cloud Monitoring and Logging provide visibility into application performance, user interactions, and system health. This helps in tracking UI performance and identifying issues.

Key Aspects:
- Performance Metrics: Monitor metrics such as request latency and error rates.
- Logging: Collect and analyze logs to troubleshoot issues and understand user behavior.

Example Workflow:
1. Set Up Monitoring:
   - Configure Google Cloud Monitoring to track metrics for your microservices and front-end application.

2. Configure Logging:
   - Use Google Cloud Logging to collect logs from various services.

3. Analyze Data:
   - Review metrics and logs to identify performance bottlenecks or errors.

Example Implementation:

- In an e-commerce platform, use Google Cloud Monitoring to track the performance of the product search feature and Google Cloud Logging to analyze errors and user interactions, helping improve the overall user experience.

Best Practices for UI in GCP

1. Use API Gateway: Implement Google Cloud Endpoints to manage API interactions and provide a unified entry point.
2. Implement BFF for Optimization: Utilize Google Cloud Functions to create tailored back-end services for specific front-end needs.
3. Leverage Client-Side Aggregation: Make efficient use of client-side aggregation when appropriate, while considering the impact on performance.
4. Host and Cache Static Assets: Use Google Cloud Storage and CDN to efficiently manage and deliver static assets.
5. Monitor and Log: Utilize Google Cloud Monitoring and Logging to gain insights into application performance and user interactions.

The User Interface Pattern in Google Cloud Platform involves leveraging various GCP services to effectively manage and optimize the interaction between the front-end and microservices. By using API Gateways, Backend for Frontend (BFF), client-side aggregation, static asset hosting, and monitoring, organizations can build scalable, performant, and secure user interfaces for their microservices architectures.

# User Interface pattern in Azure

Implementing the User Interface (UI) Pattern in Azure involves using Azure services to efficiently manage interactions between the front-end application and microservices. Azure provides a range of tools to support API management, data aggregation, and scalable front-end deployment.

## Key Components and Services

1. Azure API Management: Acts as an API gateway, managing API requests and responses.
2. Azure Functions: Implements Backend for Frontend (BFF) services, providing tailored responses.
3. Azure Blob Storage and Azure CDN: Hosts static assets and improves performance with content caching.
4. Azure App Service or Azure Kubernetes Service (AKS): Hosts microservices and handles scaling.
5. Azure Monitor and Azure Log Analytics: Provides monitoring and logging for application performance and user interactions.

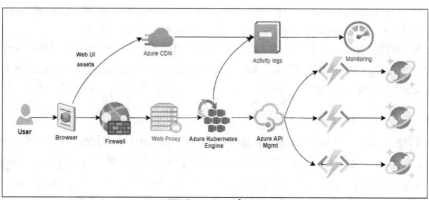

**11.6 UI Patterns in Azure**

## Patterns and Examples

### 1. API Gateway with Azure API Management

Description:
Azure API Management provides a unified entry point for the front-end to interact with various microservices. It handles request routing, response aggregation, security, and monitoring.

Key Aspects:
- Request Routing: Routes incoming requests to the

appropriate microservices.

- Response Aggregation: Combines responses from multiple microservices into a single response.
- API Management: Includes features like API versioning, caching, and monitoring.

Example Workflow:
1. Setup API Gateway:
   - Define APIs using Azure API Management.
   - Configure routes, policies, and security settings.

2. Frontend Integration:
   - Configure the front-end application to send API requests to Azure API Management.

3. Response Handling:
   - Azure API Management routes requests to microservices.
   - Aggregates responses and returns a unified response to the front-end application.

Example Implementation:
- For an e-commerce platform, Azure API Management can be used to route requests for product details, user profiles, and order processing to different microservices and aggregate responses into a single view for the front-end application.

## 2. Backend for Frontend (BFF) with Azure Functions

Description:
Azure Functions can be used to implement the Backend for Frontend (BFF) pattern, creating specialized back-end services that cater to the specific needs of different front-end applications.

Key Aspects:
- Tailored Services: Develop serverless functions to handle data aggregation and transformation based on front-end requirements.
- Performance Optimization: Reduce client-side processing

and deliver optimized responses.

Example Workflow:
1. Create Azure Functions:
   - Develop Azure Functions that aggregate data from various microservices.
   - Deploy these functions in Azure.

2. Frontend Integration:
   - Configure the front-end application to call the Azure Functions for specific data needs.

3. Data Aggregation:
   - Azure Functions retrieve and process data from different microservices.
   - Return the aggregated data to the front-end.

Example Implementation:
- In a travel booking application, use Azure Functions to aggregate data from microservices handling flights, hotels, and car rentals. This function will provide a unified response to the front-end application.

### 3. Client-Side Aggregation

Description:
Client-Side Aggregation involves making multiple requests from the front-end application to various microservices and combining the data on the client side.

Key Aspects:
- Multiple Requests: The front-end application communicates with different microservices.
- Data Combination: The front-end application processes and combines responses.

Example Workflow:
1. Front-End Application:
   - Send concurrent API requests to different microservices.

2. Data Processing:
 - Combine the responses in the front-end application logic.

3. Display Data:
 - Render the combined data to the user interface.

Example Implementation:
- For a content management system, the front-end makes requests to microservices for articles, images, and user comments. It then combines and displays this information in a cohesive manner.

## 4. Hosting Static Assets with Azure Blob Storage and Azure CDN

Description:
Azure Blob Storage can be used to host static assets such as HTML, CSS, and JavaScript files. Azure CDN (Content Delivery Network) improves performance by caching and delivering these assets globally.

Key Aspects:
- Static Asset Hosting: Store and serve static files from Azure Blob Storage.
- Content Delivery: Use Azure CDN to cache and deliver static assets with low latency.

Example Workflow:
1. Upload Assets:
 - Store static files (e.g., HTML, CSS, JavaScript) in an Azure Blob Storage container.

2. Configure CDN:
 - Set up Azure CDN to cache and deliver content from the Blob Storage.

3. Frontend Access:
 - The front-end application accesses static assets through the Azure CDN endpoint.

Example Implementation:
- Host a company's static website assets in Azure Blob Storage and use Azure CDN to ensure fast and efficient delivery to users globally.

## 5. Monitoring and Logging with Azure Monitor and Azure Log Analytics

Description:
Azure Monitor and Azure Log Analytics provide tools to track application performance, user interactions, and system health. This helps in diagnosing issues and improving the UI.

Key Aspects:
- Performance Metrics: Monitor application performance and user interactions.
- Logging: Collect and analyze logs for troubleshooting and insights.

Example Workflow:
1. Set Up Monitoring:
    - Configure Azure Monitor to track metrics for your microservices and front-end application.

2. Configure Logging:
    - Use Azure Log Analytics to collect logs from various services.

3. Analyze Data:
    - Review performance metrics and logs to identify issues and optimize the user experience.

Example Implementation:
- For an online banking application, use Azure Monitor to track user login times and transaction processing performance, and Azure Log Analytics to analyze logs for potential issues and improve service reliability.

**Best Practices for UI in Azure**

1. Use API Management: Implement Azure API Management to manage API interactions and provide a unified entry point.

2. Implement BFF for Optimization: Utilize Azure Functions for tailored back-end services that cater to specific front-end needs.

3. Leverage Client-Side Aggregation: When appropriate, use client-side aggregation to handle data from multiple services, while being mindful of performance implications.

4. Host and Cache Static Assets: Use Azure Blob Storage and Azure CDN to efficiently manage and deliver static assets.

5. Monitor and Log: Utilize Azure Monitor and Azure Log Analytics for visibility into application performance and user behavior.

The User Interface Pattern in Azure involves leveraging Azure services to manage and optimize the interactions between the front-end application and microservices. By using Azure API Management, Azure Functions, client-side aggregation, Azure Blob Storage, Azure CDN, and Azure Monitor, organizations can build scalable, efficient, and secure user interfaces for their microservices architectures. This approach ensures that applications are responsive, performant, and capable of providing a seamless user experience.

## User Interface Pattern in AWS

Implementing the User Interface (UI) Pattern in AWS involves leveraging various AWS services to effectively manage interactions between the front-end application and microservices. AWS provides a range of tools for API management, data aggregation, static asset hosting, and monitoring.

### Key Components and Services

1. Amazon API Gateway: Manages API requests and responses, acts as an API gateway.
2. AWS Lambda: Implements Backend for Frontend (BFF) services, providing tailored responses.
3. Amazon S3 and Amazon CloudFront: Hosts static assets and improves performance with content caching.
4. Amazon ECS, Amazon EKS, or AWS Fargate: Hosts microservices and handles scaling.
5. Amazon CloudWatch: Provides monitoring and logging for application performance and user interactions.

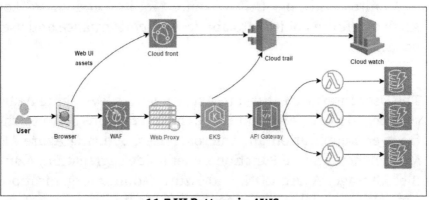

**11.7 UI Pattern in AWS**

## Patterns and Examples

### 1. API Gateway with Amazon API Gateway

Description:
Amazon API Gateway provides a unified entry point for the front-end application to interact with multiple microservices. It handles request routing, response aggregation, security, and monitoring.

Key Aspects:
- Request Routing: Routes incoming API requests to appropriate microservices.
- Response Aggregation: Combines responses from multiple microservices into a single response.

- API Management: Includes features like request throttling, caching, and API key management.

Example Workflow:

1. Setup API Gateway:

   - Define RESTful or WebSocket APIs using Amazon API Gateway.

   - Configure routes, methods, and security settings (e.g., authorization, throttling).

2. Frontend Integration:

   - Configure the front-end application to send API requests to the Amazon API Gateway.

3. Response Handling:

   - Amazon API Gateway routes requests to microservices.

   - Aggregates and processes responses, then sends a unified response back to the front-end.

Example Implementation:

- For a ride-sharing app, Amazon API Gateway can route requests for user profiles, ride requests, and payment processing to various microservices and aggregate these responses for the front-end application.

## 2. Backend for Frontend (BFF) with AWS Lambda

Description:

AWS Lambda can be used to implement the Backend for Frontend (BFF) pattern, creating specialized back-end services that provide data aggregation or transformation specific to the needs of different front-end applications.

Key Aspects:

- Tailored Services: Develop serverless functions to handle specific data needs for different front-end applications.
- Performance Optimization: Optimize the response for front-end applications by handling data aggregation on the server side.

Example Workflow:
1. Create AWS Lambda Functions:
   - Develop Lambda functions that aggregate data from multiple microservices.
   - Deploy these functions on AWS Lambda.

2. Frontend Integration:
   - Configure the front-end application to call the AWS Lambda functions for specific data requirements.

3. Data Aggregation:
   - Lambda functions gather and process data from different microservices.
   - Return the aggregated data to the front-end.

Example Implementation:
- For a media streaming application, use AWS Lambda to create a BFF function that collects and processes data from microservices handling videos, user recommendations, and playback history. The Lambda function provides a tailored response to the front-end application.

### 3. Client-Side Aggregation

Description:
Client-Side Aggregation involves making multiple requests from the front-end application to various microservices and combining the data on the client side.

Key Aspects:
- Multiple Requests: The front-end application communicates directly with different microservices.
- Data Combination: The front-end application processes and combines responses.

Example Workflow:
1. Front-End Application:
   - Make concurrent API requests to different microservices.

2. Data Processing:
 - Combine responses from various microservices on the client side.

3. Display Data:
 - Render the aggregated data in the user interface.

Example Implementation:
- In a financial dashboard application, the front-end makes requests to microservices for account balances, transaction history, and market data. It combines this data on the client side to provide a unified financial overview.

## 4. Hosting Static Assets with Amazon S3 and Amazon CloudFront

Description:
Amazon S3 is used to host static assets such as HTML, CSS, and JavaScript files. Amazon CloudFront is a Content Delivery Network (CDN) that caches and delivers these assets globally, improving performance.

Key Aspects:
- Static Asset Hosting: Store and serve static files from Amazon S3.
- Content Delivery: Use Amazon CloudFront to cache and deliver assets with low latency.

Example Workflow:
1. Upload Assets:
 - Store static files (e.g., HTML, CSS, JavaScript) in an Amazon S3 bucket.

2. Configure CDN:
 - Set up Amazon CloudFront to distribute and cache content from the S3 bucket.

3. Frontend Access:
 - The front-end application retrieves static assets from the

CloudFront endpoint.

Example Implementation:
- For a marketing website, host static assets in Amazon S3 and use Amazon CloudFront to ensure fast and efficient delivery of content to users worldwide.

## 5. Monitoring and Logging with Amazon CloudWatch

Description:
Amazon CloudWatch provides monitoring and logging services to track application performance, user interactions, and system health.

Key Aspects:
- Performance Metrics: Monitor application performance and health metrics.
- Logging: Collect and analyze logs from various services to troubleshoot issues and gain insights.

Example Workflow:
1. Set Up Monitoring:
   - Configure Amazon CloudWatch to track metrics for microservices and the front-end application.

2. Configure Logging:
   - Use CloudWatch Logs to collect logs from AWS Lambda, API Gateway, and other services.

3. Analyze Data:
   - Review CloudWatch metrics and logs to identify performance issues and optimize the user experience.

Example Implementation:
- For an online retail platform, use Amazon CloudWatch to monitor the performance of product search functionality and CloudWatch Logs to analyze error logs from various microservices, improving overall application reliability.

## Best Practices for UI in AWS

1. Use API Gateway: Implement Amazon API Gateway to manage API interactions and provide a unified entry point.

2. Implement BFF for Optimization: Utilize AWS Lambda for tailored back-end services that cater to specific front-end needs.

3. Leverage Client-Side Aggregation: When applicable, use client-side aggregation to combine data from multiple services, while considering performance impacts.

4. Host and Cache Static Assets: Use Amazon S3 and Amazon CloudFront to efficiently manage and deliver static assets.

5. Monitor and Log: Utilize Amazon CloudWatch for visibility into application performance and user behavior.

The User Interface Pattern in AWS involves leveraging AWS services to manage and optimize interactions between the front-end application and microservices. By using Amazon API Gateway, AWS Lambda, Amazon S3, Amazon CloudFront, and Amazon CloudWatch, organizations can build scalable, performant, and secure user interfaces. This approach ensures that applications are responsive, reliable, and capable of delivering a seamless user experience.

# CHAPTER 12.
# OBSERVABILITY
# PATTERNS

The Observability Pattern in microservices architecture refers to the practice of monitoring and understanding the internal state of a system based on the external outputs it produces. This involves collecting and analyzing metrics, logs, and traces to ensure that the system is functioning correctly and to diagnose issues when they arise.

## Key Components of Observability

**1. Metrics:** Quantitative data that represents the performance and health of services (e.g., latency, error rates, throughput).
**2. Logs:** Textual records generated by services, capturing events and state changes (e.g., errors, transactions).
**3. Traces:** Records of the flow of requests through various microservices, helping to visualize how data moves through the system.

## Observability Pattern in Microservices

### 1. Metrics Collection

**Description:**
Metrics provide quantitative insight into the performance and health of microservices. Common metrics include request latency, error rates, and resource utilization.

**Implementation Steps:**
1. Instrument Code: Integrate monitoring libraries into your microservices code to collect relevant metrics (e.g., Prometheus client libraries for various languages).
2. Export Metrics: Expose these metrics via endpoints or push them to a monitoring system.
3. Monitor Metrics: Use a monitoring platform to visualize and analyze these metrics.

**Example Implementation:**

- **Prometheus and Grafana:** Use Prometheus to collect metrics from microservices and Grafana to visualize them. For example, you can track metrics like request duration and error rates for an e-commerce service, which helps in identifying performance bottlenecks and issues.

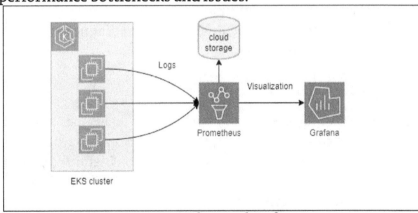

**12.1 Prometheus and Grafana**

## 2. Log Aggregation

**Description:**
Logs are crucial for understanding events that occur within microservices. They provide detailed information about the behavior of applications and can help in diagnosing issues.

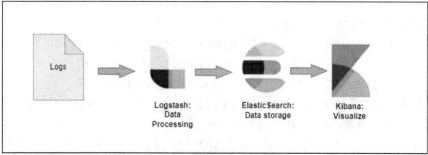

**12.2 EKS Stack**

## Implementation Steps:

1. Log Collection: Implement logging libraries in your microservices to generate logs (e.g., using libraries like Log4j, Winston).
2. Centralize Logs: Use a centralized logging service to aggregate logs from all microservices (e.g., ELK Stack - Elasticsearch, Logstash, Kibana).
3. Analyze Logs: Search and analyze logs to diagnose issues or understand system behavior.

## Example Implementation:

- ELK Stack: Collect logs from various microservices and send them to Elasticsearch. Use Logstash to process and filter logs, and Kibana to visualize and query logs. For instance, you can track user login attempts and errors across different services to identify failed login issues.

### 3. Distributed Tracing

### Description:
Distributed tracing helps track the flow of requests across multiple microservices, allowing you to understand how requests are processed through the system and identify bottlenecks.

### Implementation Steps:
1. Instrument Code: Use tracing libraries to instrument your

code (e.g., OpenTelemetry, Jaeger).

2. Collect Traces: Collect and propagate trace information across service boundaries.

3. Visualize Traces: Use a tracing system to visualize and analyze traces.

**Example Implementation:**

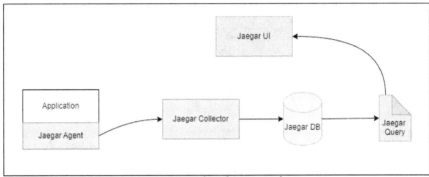

**12.3 Jaegar implementation**

**Jaeger:** Instrument microservices with Jaeger client libraries to create and propagate trace data. Visualize traces using the Jaeger UI to track a user's journey from the web front-end to the backend services and identify where delays or errors occur.

# Example Implementation in AWS

## 1. Metrics Collection with Amazon CloudWatch

**Description:**
Amazon CloudWatch provides metrics collection and monitoring capabilities, allowing you to track the performance and health of your microservices.

**Implementation Steps:**
1. Instrument Code: Use AWS SDKs to send custom metrics from your microservices to CloudWatch.
2. Create Alarms: Set up CloudWatch Alarms to notify you of critical issues based on metric thresholds (e.g., high error rates).
3. Visualize Metrics: Use CloudWatch Dashboards to visualize

metrics.

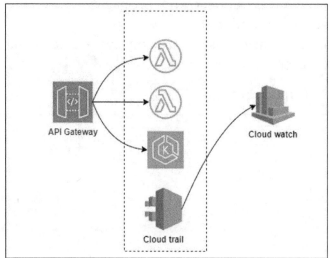

**12.4 Monitoring using cloud watch in AWS**

### Example Implementation:
- Monitor Lambda functions' performance, including invocation count, duration, and errors, using CloudWatch Metrics. Create dashboards to visualize these metrics and set up alarms for high error rates.

### 2. Log Aggregation with Amazon CloudWatch Logs

### Description:
CloudWatch Logs aggregates and manages log data from various AWS services and applications.

### Implementation Steps:
1. Send Logs: Configure your microservices to send logs to CloudWatch Logs.
2. Create Log Groups: Organize logs into log groups and streams.
3. Analyze Logs: Use CloudWatch Logs Insights to query and analyze logs.

**Example Implementation:**
- Configure an EC2 instance to send application logs to CloudWatch Logs. Use CloudWatch Logs Insights to query logs for specific error patterns or performance issues.

### 3. Distributed Tracing with AWS X-Ray

**Description:**
AWS X-Ray provides distributed tracing capabilities, helping you visualize and analyze request flows across microservices.

**Implementation Steps:**
1. Instrument Code: Integrate AWS X-Ray SDK into your microservices.
2. Collect Traces: X-Ray collects trace data and visualizes request flows.
3. Analyze Traces: Use the X-Ray console to view and analyze traces.

**Example Implementation:**
- Instrument a microservices application to use AWS X-Ray. Visualize the flow of a request as it passes through different services, identifying latency issues or errors in the request path.

## Best Practices for Observability in Microservices

1. Consistency: Ensure consistent instrumentation across all microservices for metrics, logs, and traces.
2. Centralization: Use centralized tools and platforms for aggregating and analyzing metrics, logs, and traces.
3. Automated Alerts: Set up automated alerts for critical issues based on predefined thresholds.
4. Visualization: Use dashboards and visualizations to monitor and understand system behavior.
5. Continuous Improvement: Regularly review and update your observability practices based on operational experience and evolving needs.

The Observability Pattern in microservices architecture involves leveraging metrics, logs, and distributed tracing to monitor, understand, and troubleshoot the system. By using tools such as Prometheus, ELK Stack, and Jaeger or AWS services like CloudWatch and AWS X-Ray, organizations can gain deep insights into their microservices, ensuring they operate reliably and efficiently while enabling rapid issue detection and resolution.

# Observability pattern in Google cloud platform

The Observability Pattern in Google Cloud Platform (GCP) involves leveraging GCP's tools and services to monitor, analyze, and troubleshoot microservices applications. Observability in GCP includes metrics collection, log aggregation, and distributed tracing, each of which plays a crucial role in understanding and managing the performance and health of your applications.

## Key Components and Services in GCP

1. Google Cloud Monitoring: For collecting and visualizing metrics.
2. Google Cloud Logging: For aggregating and analyzing logs.
3. Google Cloud Trace: For distributed tracing and visualizing request flows.
4. Google Cloud Error Reporting: For aggregating and alerting on application errors.
5. Google Cloud Profiler: For continuous profiling of your applications to understand performance characteristics.

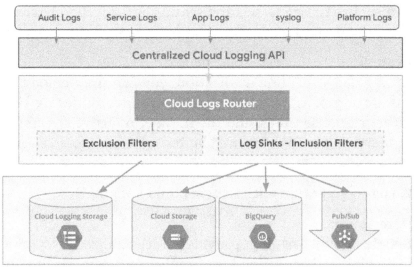

**12.4 Google cloud monitoring**

# Patterns and Examples

## 1. Metrics Collection with Google Cloud Monitoring

**Description:**
Google Cloud Monitoring allows you to collect, visualize, and analyze metrics from your microservices. It provides dashboards, charts, and alerts based on performance and health metrics.

**Implementation Steps:**
1. Instrument Code: Use Google Cloud Monitoring client libraries to instrument your microservices for metrics collection.
2. Export Metrics: Metrics can be exported directly to Google Cloud Monitoring or via OpenTelemetry.
3. Monitor and Alert: Set up dashboards and create alerts based on metric thresholds.

**Example Implementation:**
- Application Performance: Instrument a set of microservices to export metrics such as request latency, error rates, and throughput to Google Cloud Monitoring. Create a dashboard

to visualize these metrics and set up alerts for high latency or increased error rates.

**Example:**
For a video streaming application, you can use Google Cloud Monitoring to track metrics such as video buffering times, server response times, and the number of active streams. Set up alerts to notify the team if buffering times exceed a certain threshold.

## 2. Log Aggregation with Google Cloud Logging

**Description:**
Google Cloud Logging provides a centralized system for managing and analyzing logs from various services. It allows you to aggregate logs, set up alerts, and query log data.

**Implementation Steps:**
1. Configure Logging: Set up logging for your microservices using Google Cloud Logging libraries or agents.
2. Centralize Logs: Send logs to Google Cloud Logging for aggregation and storage.
3. Analyze and Alert: Use Log Explorer to search, filter, and analyze logs. Create alerts based on log patterns.

**Example Implementation:**
- Error Tracking: Configure Google Cloud Logging to collect logs from your microservices. Set up log-based alerts to notify the team of specific error patterns or anomalies. Use Log Explorer to investigate and troubleshoot issues based on log data.

**Example:**
For an e-commerce platform, collect logs related to transaction failures and user authentication issues. Use Google Cloud Logging to aggregate these logs, create alerts for high rates of transaction failures, and analyze the logs to identify the root cause.

### 3. Distributed Tracing with Google Cloud Trace

**Description:**
Google Cloud Trace provides distributed tracing capabilities, allowing you to trace and visualize the flow of requests through various microservices. It helps in understanding latency and pinpointing performance bottlenecks.

**Implementation Steps:**
1. Instrument Code: Integrate Google Cloud Trace SDKs into your microservices to capture trace data.
2. Collect and Propagate Traces: Ensure trace data is collected and propagated across service boundaries.
3. Visualize Traces: Use Google Cloud Trace to view and analyze traces, identifying latency and performance issues.

**Example Implementation:**
- Request Tracking: Instrument microservices with Google Cloud Trace to capture end-to-end traces of user requests. Visualize the trace data to understand the request flow and identify bottlenecks in the system.

**Example:**
For a travel booking application, use Google Cloud Trace to track a user's journey from searching for flights to booking and payment. Analyze the trace data to identify which services contribute to latency and optimize them.

### 4. Error Reporting with Google Cloud Error Reporting

**Description:**
Google Cloud Error Reporting aggregates and alerts on application errors, providing real-time insights into issues and trends.

**Implementation Steps:**
1. Integrate Error Reporting: Use the Google Cloud Error Reporting client library to report errors from your

microservices.

2. Aggregate Errors: Errors are automatically aggregated and categorized in Google Cloud Error Reporting.

3. Analyze and Alert: Set up alerts and analyze error reports to address recurring issues.

## Example Implementation:

- Real-Time Error Alerts: Integrate Google Cloud Error Reporting into your microservices to capture and aggregate errors. Set up notifications to alert the development team of new or increased error rates.

## Example:

For a financial application, use Google Cloud Error Reporting to capture and aggregate errors related to transaction processing. Set up alerts to notify the team if error rates exceed a certain threshold and use the aggregated data to diagnose and fix issues.

## 5. Continuous Profiling with Google Cloud Profiler

## Description:

Google Cloud Profiler continuously profiles your applications to understand performance characteristics, including CPU and memory usage.

## Implementation Steps:

1. Enable Profiling: Integrate Google Cloud Profiler into your applications.

2. Collect Profiles: Collect profiling data over time to understand application performance.

3. Analyze Profiles: Use the Google Cloud Profiler interface to analyze performance data and identify optimization opportunities.

## Example Implementation:

- Performance Optimization: Use Google Cloud Profiler to profile a microservice and identify performance bottlenecks such as high CPU or memory usage. Optimize code based on the profiling data to improve overall application performance.

**Example:**
For a high-traffic web application, use Google Cloud Profiler to continuously monitor CPU and memory usage across different microservices. Analyze the profiling data to identify and address performance bottlenecks.

**Best Practices for Observability in GCP**

1. Consistent Instrumentation: Ensure all microservices are consistently instrumented for metrics, logs, and traces.
2. Centralized Management: Use Google Cloud services to centralize metrics, logs, and traces for easier management and analysis.
3. Automated Alerts: Set up automated alerts to proactively respond to performance issues or errors.
4. Comprehensive Dashboards: Create comprehensive dashboards in Google Cloud Monitoring to visualize and monitor key metrics and performance indicators.
5. Regular Reviews: Regularly review observability data to improve system performance and address emerging issues.

The Observability Pattern in GCP involves using tools like Google Cloud Monitoring, Google Cloud Logging, Google Cloud Trace, Google Cloud Error Reporting, and Google Cloud Profiler to monitor and analyze the performance and health of microservices. By effectively utilizing these services, organizations can gain deep insights into their applications, ensuring they operate reliably and efficiently while enabling rapid issue detection and resolution.

# Observability pattern in Azure

The Observability Pattern in Microsoft Azure involves

leveraging Azure's suite of monitoring and diagnostic tools to ensure that microservices applications are performant, reliable, and well-understood. Observability encompasses collecting and analyzing metrics, logs, and traces to monitor the health and performance of applications.

### Key Components and Services in Azure

1. Azure Monitor: For collecting and analyzing metrics and logs.
2. Azure Application Insights: For application performance monitoring and distributed tracing.
3. Azure Log Analytics: For querying and analyzing log data.
4. Azure Security Center: For security-related monitoring and threat detection.
5. Azure Advisor: For recommendations based on best practices.

## Patterns and Examples

### 1. Metrics Collection with Azure Monitor

**Description:**
Azure Monitor provides a comprehensive solution for collecting, analyzing, and acting on telemetry data from your applications and infrastructure.

**Implementation Steps:**
1. Instrument Code: Use Azure Monitor SDKs or agents to collect metrics from your microservices.
2. Export Metrics: Metrics are exported to Azure Monitor for visualization and analysis.
3. Create Dashboards and Alerts: Use Azure Monitor to create dashboards and set up alerts based on metric thresholds.

**Example Implementation:**
- Performance Metrics: Instrument your microservices with Azure Monitor to collect metrics such as CPU usage, memory usage, and request latency. Set up dashboards to visualize

these metrics and configure alerts for high CPU usage or latency spikes.

**Example:**
For a web application, use Azure Monitor to track metrics like response times and server health. Create a dashboard to visualize these metrics and set up alerts to notify you if response times exceed a threshold or if server health drops below acceptable levels.

## 2. Log Aggregation with Azure Log Analytics

**Description:**
Azure Log Analytics is part of Azure Monitor and provides a centralized repository for aggregating and analyzing logs from various sources.

**Implementation Steps:**
1. Configure Logging: Set up logging for your microservices to send log data to Azure Log Analytics.
2. Centralize Logs: Aggregate logs into Azure Log Analytics.
3. Query and Analyze: Use Kusto Query Language (KQL) in Log Analytics to search and analyze logs.

**Example Implementation:**
- Error Tracking: Configure your microservices to send logs to Azure Log Analytics. Use KQL queries to identify patterns in log data, such as error rates or specific error messages. Set up alerts based on these log patterns.

**Example:**
For a financial transaction system, send logs related to transaction processing and user interactions to Azure Log Analytics. Use KQL to query logs for specific error patterns or performance issues and set up alerts to address any critical issues.

## 3. Distributed Tracing with Azure Application Insights

**Description:**
Azure Application Insights provides distributed tracing capabilities, allowing you to track the flow of requests through various microservices and visualize performance bottlenecks.

**Implementation Steps:**
1. Instrument Code: Integrate Application Insights SDKs into your microservices to enable distributed tracing.
2. Collect and Propagate Traces: Ensure trace data is captured and propagated across service boundaries.
3. Visualize and Analyze: Use Application Insights to visualize traces and identify performance issues.

**Example Implementation:**
- Request Tracking: Instrument your microservices with Application Insights to track the flow of requests from the front-end to the back-end services. Visualize the end-to-end trace data to identify where delays or errors occur.

**Example:**
For a supply chain management system, use Application Insights to track a request's journey from order placement to fulfillment. Analyze the trace data to find out which microservices are causing delays and optimize those services.

**4. Error Reporting with Azure Monitor and Application Insights**

**Description:**
Azure Monitor and Application Insights provide error reporting and alerting capabilities, helping you detect and address application errors in real-time.

**Implementation Steps:**
1. Configure Error Reporting: Set up your microservices to report errors to Azure Application Insights.
2. Aggregate and Analyze: Errors are aggregated in Application Insights, allowing you to view and analyze them.

3. Create Alerts: Set up alerts for specific error types or thresholds.

**Example Implementation:**
- Error Alerts: Configure your microservices to send error data to Application Insights. Set up alerts to notify you of increased error rates or specific error types.

**Example:**
For a customer support platform, configure Application Insights to report and aggregate errors related to ticket submissions and user interactions. Set up alerts to notify the support team if there is a spike in errors, allowing for timely investigation and resolution.

## 5. Continuous Profiling with Azure Application Insights Profiler

**Description:**
Azure Application Insights Profiler helps you understand application performance characteristics by profiling your code and identifying performance bottlenecks.

**Implementation Steps:**
1. Enable Profiling: Integrate the Application Insights Profiler with your application.
2. Collect Profiling Data: Gather profiling data to understand CPU and memory usage.
3. Analyze Performance: Use the profiling data to identify and address performance issues.

**Example Implementation:**
- Performance Optimization: Use Application Insights Profiler to profile a microservice and identify CPU and memory usage patterns. Optimize the code based on profiling data to improve application performance.

**Example:**
For a media streaming application, use Application Insights

Profiler to monitor and optimize performance bottlenecks such as high CPU usage during video encoding. Analyze the profiling data to improve efficiency and reduce processing time.

**Best Practices for Observability in Azure**

1. Consistent Instrumentation: Ensure all microservices are consistently instrumented for metrics, logs, and traces using Azure services.
2. Centralized Monitoring: Use Azure Monitor and Application Insights to centralize monitoring and observability.
3. Automated Alerts: Set up automated alerts based on predefined thresholds for metrics and log patterns.
4. Comprehensive Dashboards: Create detailed dashboards in Azure Monitor and Application Insights to visualize and monitor key performance indicators.
5. Regular Review and Improvement: Continuously review observability data and refine monitoring strategies based on operational needs and emerging issues.

The Observability Pattern in Azure involves utilizing tools such as Azure Monitor, Azure Log Analytics, Azure Application Insights, and Azure Application Insights Profiler to monitor and analyze the performance and health of microservices. By effectively implementing these tools, organizations can gain deep insights into their applications, enabling efficient troubleshooting, performance optimization, and proactive issue resolution.

# Observability pattern in AWS

The Observability Pattern in AWS involves leveraging AWS's suite of monitoring and diagnostic tools to ensure the health, performance, and reliability of microservices applications. Observability encompasses the collection and analysis of metrics, logs, and traces to provide a comprehensive view of system behavior and performance.

**Key Components and Services in AWS**

1. Amazon CloudWatch: For collecting and visualizing metrics and logs.
2. AWS X-Ray: For distributed tracing and visualizing request flows.
3. AWS CloudTrail: For tracking API activity and security-related events.
4. AWS CodeDeploy and CodePipeline: For deployment tracking and monitoring.
5. Amazon CloudWatch Logs Insights: For querying and analyzing log data.

# Patterns and Examples

### 1. Metrics Collection with Amazon CloudWatch

**Description:**
Amazon CloudWatch collects and tracks metrics from AWS services and custom applications, allowing you to monitor performance and set up alarms for critical thresholds.

**Implementation Steps:**
1. Instrument Code: Use the AWS SDKs or CloudWatch Agent to collect metrics from your microservices.
2. Export Metrics: Send metrics to CloudWatch, where they can be aggregated and visualized.
3. Create Dashboards and Alerts: Set up CloudWatch Dashboards to visualize metrics and create alarms to notify you of anomalies.

**Example Implementation:**
- Application Performance Metrics: Instrument your microservices to send metrics like CPU utilization, memory usage, and request latency to CloudWatch. Create a CloudWatch Dashboard to visualize these metrics and set up

alarms for high CPU usage or latency spikes.

**Example:**
For an e-commerce platform, use CloudWatch to track metrics such as page load times and order processing times. Create dashboards to monitor these metrics in real-time and set up alerts to notify you if processing times exceed acceptable limits.

## 2. Log Aggregation with Amazon CloudWatch Logs

**Description:**
Amazon CloudWatch Logs provides a centralized system for aggregating, storing, and analyzing log data from various sources.

**Implementation Steps:**
1. Configure Logging: Set up your microservices to send logs to CloudWatch Logs using the CloudWatch Logs agent or SDKs.
2. Centralize Logs: Aggregate logs into CloudWatch Logs for storage and analysis.
3. Analyze and Alert: Use CloudWatch Logs Insights to query and analyze log data. Create alerts based on log patterns.

**Example Implementation:**
- Error and Activity Logs: Configure CloudWatch Logs to collect logs from your microservices. Use CloudWatch Logs Insights to search for error messages or unusual activity patterns and set up alerts based on these log findings.

**Example:**
For a social media application, aggregate logs related to user interactions and error messages into CloudWatch Logs. Use Logs Insights to query for patterns such as failed login attempts and set up alerts for increased error rates.

## 3. Distributed Tracing with AWS X-Ray

**Description:**

AWS X-Ray provides distributed tracing capabilities to track the flow of requests across microservices, helping you understand performance bottlenecks and latency issues.

**Implementation Steps:**
1. Instrument Code: Integrate AWS X-Ray SDKs into your microservices to capture tracing data.
2. Collect and Propagate Traces: Ensure trace data is collected and propagated across service boundaries.
3. Visualize and Analyze: Use the X-Ray console to view and analyze traces, identifying areas for optimization.

**Example Implementation:**
- Request Flow Tracking: Instrument your microservices with AWS X-Ray to capture and trace requests from the front-end to the back-end services. Visualize the trace data to identify latency issues and optimize the performance of the slowest services.

**Example:**
For an online banking system, use AWS X-Ray to track a customer's journey from login to transaction completion. Analyze the traces to identify bottlenecks in the authentication or transaction processing services.

### 4. API Activity Tracking with AWS CloudTrail

**Description:**
AWS CloudTrail tracks API activity and user actions within your AWS environment, providing an audit trail for security and compliance purposes.

**Implementation Steps:**
1. Enable CloudTrail: Set up CloudTrail to record API activity and user actions.
2. Collect Logs: CloudTrail captures and stores logs of API calls and user activities.
3. Analyze and Audit: Use CloudTrail logs to perform security

audits and track changes to your AWS environment.

**Example Implementation:**
- Security Monitoring: Enable CloudTrail to monitor API calls related to resource management and access. Review CloudTrail logs to detect unauthorized access or changes to sensitive resources.

**Example:**
For a data warehouse environment, use CloudTrail to track API calls related to data access and modifications. Analyze the logs to ensure compliance with data access policies and detect any unauthorized changes.

## 5. Log Querying and Analysis with Amazon CloudWatch Logs Insights

**Description:**
Amazon CloudWatch Logs Insights provides a powerful query language to analyze log data, helping you gain insights and troubleshoot issues.

**Implementation Steps:**
1. Send Logs to CloudWatch Logs: Ensure your microservices are configured to send logs to CloudWatch Logs.
2. Use Logs Insights: Query and analyze log data using CloudWatch Logs Insights.
3. Create Dashboards and Alerts: Set up dashboards to visualize query results and create alerts based on log patterns.

**Example Implementation:**
- Log Analysis: Use CloudWatch Logs Insights to analyze logs for specific error messages or performance metrics. Create dashboards to visualize log data and set up alerts for anomalies.

**Example:**
For a web application, use CloudWatch Logs Insights to query logs for slow page loads or error messages. Set up a dashboard

to monitor these logs and create alerts for spikes in error rates or performance issues.

**Best Practices for Observability in AWS**

1. Consistent Instrumentation: Ensure all microservices are instrumented for metrics, logs, and traces using AWS services.
2. Centralized Monitoring: Use Amazon CloudWatch and AWS X-Ray to centralize monitoring and observability.
3. Automated Alerts: Set up automated alerts for critical thresholds and anomalies.
4. Comprehensive Dashboards: Create detailed dashboards in CloudWatch to visualize key performance indicators and system health.
5. Regular Reviews: Continuously review observability data and refine your monitoring strategy based on operational needs and emerging issues.

The Observability Pattern in AWS involves leveraging tools such as Amazon CloudWatch, AWS X-Ray, AWS CloudTrail, and Amazon CloudWatch Logs Insights to monitor and analyze the performance and health of microservices. By effectively implementing these services, organizations can gain deep insights into their applications, enabling efficient troubleshooting, performance optimization, and proactive issue resolution.

# CHAPTER 13.
# TESTING STRATEGY

Testing microservices architecture requires a multifaceted approach due to the complexity and distributed nature of microservices. Each microservice needs to be tested in isolation, as well as in conjunction with other services to ensure that they work together as expected. Here's a detailed look at various testing strategies for microservices architecture:

## 1. Unit Testing

**Description:**
Unit testing involves testing individual microservices or components in isolation to ensure that they work correctly based on their specifications. These tests are typically written by developers and are focused on testing the smallest units of code, such as functions or methods.

**Key Aspects:**
- Isolation: Each unit test should be isolated from external dependencies (e.g., databases, message queues).
- Mocking: Use mocks and stubs to simulate interactions with external dependencies.
- Frequency: Unit tests are run frequently during the development process to catch errors early.

**Example:**
For a user authentication microservice, write unit tests

to verify that authentication logic correctly validates user credentials and handles edge cases (e.g., incorrect password).

## 2. Integration Testing

### Description:
Integration testing focuses on verifying the interactions between different components or services. It ensures that individual microservices work together as expected and that data flows correctly between them.

### Key Aspects:
- Service Interactions: Test the interactions between microservices to verify that they correctly handle requests and responses.
- Data Consistency: Ensure that data is correctly passed and maintained across service boundaries.
- Test Environments: Use integration testing environments that closely resemble production.

### Example:
For an e-commerce platform, integration tests could verify that the order service correctly interacts with the inventory service and the payment service, ensuring that an order is processed correctly from placing to payment.

## 3. Contract Testing

### Description:
Contract testing ensures that the interactions between microservices adhere to predefined contracts or APIs. This type of testing verifies that services meet the expectations of their consumers and producers, reducing integration issues.

### Key Aspects:
- Consumer-Driven Contracts: Consumers define expectations, and providers ensure they meet those expectations.
- Automated Contracts: Automate contract tests to run as part of the CI/CD pipeline.

- Tools: Use tools like Pact for contract testing.

**Example:**
For a travel booking system, define a contract for the booking service API, and test that the service adheres to this contract when interacting with the search service and payment service.

## 4. End-to-End Testing

**Description:**
End-to-end (E2E) testing verifies the complete workflow of a microservices-based application, ensuring that the entire system functions as expected from the user's perspective.

**Key Aspects:**
- Workflow Testing: Test user journeys or workflows across multiple microservices.
- Realistic Data: Use realistic data and scenarios that mimic actual usage.
- Complexity: E2E tests can be complex and time-consuming, so they are typically run less frequently than unit or integration tests.

**Example:**
For an online shopping application, end-to-end tests could simulate a user journey from searching for products, adding items to the cart, checking out, and receiving an order confirmation.

## 5. Performance Testing

**Description:**
Performance testing assesses how well microservices perform under various conditions, including normal and peak loads. It helps identify bottlenecks and ensures that services meet performance requirements.

**Key Aspects:**
- Load Testing: Test how microservices handle increasing

loads.

- Stress Testing: Assess the system's behavior under extreme conditions.
- Benchmarking: Measure response times, throughput, and resource usage.

**Example:**

For a video streaming service, performance testing could simulate thousands of simultaneous users to ensure that the service can handle high traffic without degradation in quality or performance.

## 6. Security Testing

**Description:**

Security testing ensures that microservices are protected against vulnerabilities and threats. It involves testing for common security issues and verifying that services comply with security standards and best practices.

**Key Aspects:**

- Vulnerability Scanning: Scan for known vulnerabilities in code and dependencies.
- Penetration Testing: Simulate attacks to find weaknesses in the system.
- Compliance Testing: Ensure that services adhere to security regulations and standards.

**Example:**

For a financial services application, security testing might involve penetration testing to identify vulnerabilities and checking for compliance with regulations like PCI-DSS for handling payment information.

## 7. Chaos Testing

**Description:**

Chaos testing (or chaos engineering) involves intentionally introducing failures and disruptions to test the system's resilience and recovery capabilities. It helps ensure that microservices can handle unexpected issues gracefully.

**Key Aspects:**
- Failure Injection: Introduce faults such as service outages, network latency, or data corruption.
- Resilience Testing: Test the system's ability to recover from failures and continue functioning.
- Automated Chaos Experiments: Use tools to automate chaos testing and run experiments regularly.

**Example:**
For a cloud-based application, chaos testing might involve simulating the failure of a service instance to ensure that the system can continue operating with minimal impact.

## 8. Regression Testing

**Description:**
Regression testing ensures that new code changes do not introduce new bugs or break existing functionality. It involves running a suite of tests that cover existing features and functionality.

**Key Aspects:**
- Automated Regression Tests: Automate regression tests to run as part of the CI/CD pipeline.
- Test Coverage: Ensure that regression tests cover critical functionality and user workflows.
- Frequent Execution: Run regression tests frequently to catch issues early.

**Example:**
After adding a new feature to a microservice, run regression tests to verify that existing features, such as user authentication and data retrieval, continue to work correctly.

## Best Practices for Testing Microservices

1. Automate Testing: Automate unit, integration, and regression tests to ensure consistent and rapid feedback.
2. Use Test Containers: Use containerized environments for testing to replicate production-like conditions and avoid dependency issues.
3. Monitor Test Results: Continuously monitor test results and integrate them into the CI/CD pipeline for early detection of issues.
4. Test in Isolation: Ensure that each microservice is tested in isolation to identify issues specific to that service.
5. Integrate Testing into Development: Integrate testing practices into the development process to ensure that issues are identified and resolved early.

Testing strategies for microservices architecture involve a combination of unit testing, integration testing, contract testing, end-to-end testing, performance testing, security testing, chaos testing, and regression testing. By employing these strategies, organizations can ensure that their microservices-based applications are reliable, performant, secure, and resilient, leading to better overall system quality and user experience.

# CHAPTER 14.
# DEPLOYMENT
# PATTERNS

Deploying microservices effectively requires adopting specific patterns and practices tailored to the cloud platform in use. Here's a detailed look at deployment patterns for microservices in Google Cloud Platform (GCP), Microsoft Azure, and Amazon Web Services (AWS).

## 1. Google Cloud Platform (GCP)

### 1.1. Google Kubernetes Engine (GKE)

**Description:**
GKE is a managed Kubernetes service that automates the deployment, scaling, and management of containerized applications. It's ideal for microservices architectures due to Kubernetes' robust orchestration capabilities.

**Deployment Pattern:**

**1. Containerized Microservices**: Package each microservice into Docker containers.
**2. Create Kubernetes Deployments:** Define Kubernetes deployments for each microservice, specifying desired replicas, container images, and resource limits.
**3. Service Discovery:** Use Kubernetes Services to enable

communication between microservices.

**4. Scaling and Management:** Utilize Kubernetes' auto-scaling and rolling updates to manage and scale microservices.

**Example:**

Deploy a multi-tier e-commerce application where the user service, product service, and order service are each packaged into separate Docker containers. Deploy them on GKE with Kubernetes deployments and services to handle scaling and traffic management.

## 1.2. Google Cloud Run

**Description:**

Cloud Run is a fully managed compute platform that automatically scales your containerized applications. It abstracts away infrastructure management, making it easier to deploy and manage microservices.

**Deployment Pattern:**

1. Build Containers: Package each microservice into a Docker container.
2. Deploy to Cloud Run: Deploy each container to Cloud Run, which automatically handles scaling and load balancing.
3. Manage Traffic: Configure routing and manage traffic between different versions of services.

**Example:**

Deploy a set of microservices such as a user authentication service and a product catalog service on Cloud Run. Each service scales automatically based on demand and is accessible via HTTP endpoints.

## 1.3. Google App Engine

**Description:**

Google App Engine is a fully managed platform for building and deploying applications without managing the underlying infrastructure. It supports deploying microservices through flexible environments.

**Deployment Pattern:**
1. Deploy Microservices: Deploy each microservice as a separate App Engine service, which can have its own scaling and configuration settings.
2. Service Communication: Use HTTP requests or Cloud Pub/Sub for inter-service communication.

**Example:**
Deploy a set of microservices, such as a recommendation engine and an inventory management system, as separate App Engine services. Each service can be scaled independently based on demand.

# 2. Microsoft Azure

## 2.1. Azure Kubernetes Service (AKS)

**Description:**
AKS is a managed Kubernetes service that simplifies deploying, managing, and scaling containerized applications using Kubernetes.

**Deployment Pattern:**

**1. Containerized Microservices**: Package each microservice into Docker containers.
**2. Deploy to AKS:** Create Kubernetes deployments and services for each microservice on AKS.
**3. Scaling and Monitoring:** Utilize Kubernetes' auto-scaling and Azure Monitor for observability.

**Example:**
Deploy a microservices-based application on AKS, with services like user management, payment processing, and order fulfillment each running in their own Kubernetes pods. Use AKS for orchestration and Azure Monitor for tracking performance.

## 2.2. Azure App Services

**Description:**
Azure App Services is a platform-as-a-service (PaaS) for building, deploying, and scaling web apps and APIs. It supports deploying microservices through web apps.

**Deployment Pattern:**
1. Deploy Microservices: Deploy each microservice as a separate Azure App Service.
2. Service Integration: Use Azure API Management or Azure Functions for service integration and orchestration.

**Example:**
Deploy individual microservices such as a web front-end and a back-end API service on Azure App Services. Use Azure API Management to handle requests and route them to the appropriate service.

## 2.3. Azure Container Instances (ACI)

**Description:**
ACI allows you to run containerized applications without managing the underlying infrastructure. It's useful for simpler microservices deployments.

**Deployment Pattern:**

**1. Containerized Microservices:** Package microservices into Docker containers.
**2. Deploy to ACI:** Deploy containers directly to Azure Container Instances.
**3. Networking and Scaling:** Use Azure Virtual Network for networking and configure scaling based on demand.

**Example:**
Deploy lightweight microservices such as a data ingestion service and a report generation service to ACI. Each

service runs in its own container instance with network configurations for communication.

# 3. Amazon Web Services (AWS)

## 3.1. Amazon Elastic Kubernetes Service (EKS)

**Description:**
EKS is a managed Kubernetes service that simplifies running Kubernetes on AWS, handling tasks such as patching and scaling.

**Deployment Pattern:**
**1. Containerized Microservices:** Package microservices into Docker containers.
**2. Deploy to EKS:** Use Kubernetes manifests to deploy microservices to EKS clusters.
**3. Service Discovery and Scaling:** Utilize Kubernetes features for service discovery, scaling, and load balancing.

**Example:**
Deploy a set of microservices, such as a user profile service and an analytics service, on EKS. Manage containerized workloads and scale them based on demand using Kubernetes' native features.

## 3.2. Amazon ECS (Elastic Container Service)

**Description:**
ECS is a fully managed container orchestration service that supports Docker containers and is integrated with AWS services.

**Deployment Pattern:**
1. Define Task Definitions: Create ECS task definitions for each microservice.
2. Deploy Services: Deploy microservices using ECS services, which handle scaling and load balancing.
3. Service Integration: Use ECS Service Discovery for inter-

service communication.

**Example:**
Deploy a set of microservices such as a recommendation service and a user activity tracker using ECS. Define tasks and services for each microservice and manage scaling and load balancing through ECS.

## 3.3. AWS Lambda with API Gateway

**Description:**
AWS Lambda is a serverless compute service that runs code in response to events. API Gateway can be used to create APIs for Lambda functions, making it suitable for microservices that handle specific tasks.

**Deployment Pattern:**
1. Create Lambda Functions: Develop each microservice as a Lambda function.
2. API Gateway: Configure API Gateway to create RESTful APIs or HTTP endpoints for Lambda functions.
3. Event Handling: Use event sources such as S3, DynamoDB, or SNS to trigger Lambda functions.

**Example:**
Deploy microservices such as a user authentication service and an image processing service using Lambda. Use API Gateway to expose these services through HTTP endpoints.

**Deployment patterns for microservices architecture vary by cloud provider, but common strategies include:**

- Kubernetes-based deployments (GKE, AKS, EKS) for managing containerized microservices.
- Platform-as-a-Service (PaaS) options (App Engine, Azure App Services) for abstracting infrastructure management.
- Serverless options (Cloud Run, AWS Lambda) for running microservices with automatic scaling and minimal

management.
- Container instances (ACI, ECS) for simpler containerized deployments.

Each cloud platform provides tools and services that cater to different deployment needs, allowing you to choose the approach that best fits your application's requirements and operational preferences.

# APPENDIX: CLOUD SERVICES COMPARISON

| Functi on | AWS | Azure | GCP | Compariso n |
|---|---|---|---|---|
| **Compute** | | | | |
| Virtual Machines | EC2 | Virtual Machines | Compute Engine | All three provide highly customizable VMs, pricing models vary, but generally, GCP offers per-second billing, and AWS offers a variety of instance types. |
| Serverless Compute | Lambda | Azure Functions | Cloud Functions | All provide serverless computing where you pay only for execution time. Lambda has the most mature ecosystem, but GCP and Azure offer competitive solutions. |
| Container | ECS / | Azure | Google | All support |

| Orchestration | EKS | Kubernetes Service (AKS) | Kubernetes Engine | Kubernetes, with similar features. GCP's Kubernetes Engine is fully managed and closely integrated with their cloud-native tools. |
|---|---|---|---|---|
| Auto Scaling | Auto Scaling Groups | Virtual Machine Scale Sets | Managed Instance Groups | AWS has the most mature autoscaling service, but Azure and GCP provide similar features for managing scaling of virtual machines. |

## Storage

| Object Storage | S3 | Blob Storage | Cloud Storage | AWS S3 is the market leader, but Azure Blob and GCP Cloud Storage are close competitors with competitive pricing and similar features like tiered storage. |
|---|---|---|---|---|
| Block Storage | EBS | Managed Disks | Persistent Disks | All provide highly available and scalable block storage for VMs, with performance tiers (standard, SSD, etc.). |
| File Storage | EFS | Azure Files | Filestore | AWS EFS is popular for shared file storage, but Azure Files and |

| | | | | |
|---|---|---|---|---|
| | | | | Google Filestore offer similar performance for managing shared file systems. |
| Archival Storage | Glacier | Azure Archive Storage | Cloud Archive | AWS Glacier is a mature archival storage service, but Azure and GCP offer competitive pricing and features. |

## Database

| | | | | |
|---|---|---|---|---|
| Managed Relational DB | RDS | Azure SQL Database | Cloud SQL | AWS RDS supports multiple engines (MySQL, PostgreSQL, SQL Server, etc.), Azure SQL Database is built around SQL Server, and GCP Cloud SQL supports MySQL & PostgreSQL. |
| NoSQL DB | Dynamo DB | Azure Cosmos DB | Firestore, Bigtable | DynamoDB is highly scalable for NoSQL workloads, Cosmos DB offers multi-model support, and Firestore and Bigtable offer high throughput and low latency. |
| Data Warehouse | Redshift | Azure Synapse Analytics | BigQuery | AWS Redshift is a popular data warehousing solution, but BigQuery offers |

| | | | | serverless, highly scalable, and cheaper query costs, while Synapse integrates with Azure SQL. |
|---|---|---|---|---|

## Networking

| VPC (Virtual Network) | VPC | Virtual Network (VNet) | Virtual Private Cloud (VPC) | All provide logically isolated cloud networks to launch and manage resources, with flexible network policies and routing. |
|---|---|---|---|---|
| Load Balancing | Elastic Load Balancer | Azure Load Balancer | Cloud Load Balancing | AWS ELB supports multiple types (application, network, and classic), Azure Load Balancer is highly integrated with VM services, and GCP's load balancing is global. |
| CDN | CloudFront | Azure CDN | Cloud CDN | All provide a global content delivery network to cache data closer to users, AWS CloudFront is well-integrated with S3, while Azure CDN and GCP Cloud CDN are reliable. |
| DNS | Route 53 | Azure DNS | Cloud DNS | AWS Route 53 offers highly reliable DNS |

| | | | | with additional routing capabilities, Azure and GCP offer comparable services. |
|---|---|---|---|---|

## Security and Identity

| | | | | |
|---|---|---|---|---|
| IAM (Identity & Access Management) | IAM | Azure Active Directory | Cloud IAM | AWS IAM is highly granular, Azure AD integrates well with Office 365 and other Microsoft services, while GCP IAM is similar but more tightly integrated with GCP services. |
| Key Management | AWS KMS | Azure Key Vault | Cloud KMS | All provide secure key management services for cryptographic keys. AWS KMS has a large integration ecosystem, Azure Key Vault is strong for Microsoft services. |
| DDoS Protection | AWS Shield | Azure DDoS Protection | Cloud Armor | All offer protection against DDoS attacks, with AWS Shield providing the highest level of integration with AWS infrastructure. |

## Machine learning and AI

| ML Platform | SageMaker | Azure Machine Learning | AI Platform | SageMaker is a full-stack ML platform, while Azure ML integrates tightly with Azure services. GCP's AI Platform is known for TensorFlow and data-focused ML. |
|---|---|---|---|---|
| Managed AI APIs | Rekognition, Lex, Polly | Azure Cognitive Services | Vision, Speech-to-Text, etc. | All provide AI services for image recognition, text analysis, and speech processing. GCP's API ecosystem is considered very advanced for vision and natural language. |

## Analytics and Big Data

| Big Data Processing | EMR | Azure HDInsight | Dataproc | AWS EMR is based on Hadoop and Spark, Azure HDInsight offers similar big data tools, while GCP Dataproc is focused on cost efficiency and easy integration. |
|---|---|---|---|---|
| Real-time Data Streaming | Kinesis | Azure Stream Analytics | Dataflow | AWS Kinesis provides comprehensive real-time streaming, while Azure and GCP also offer real- |

| | | | | time processing with similar features. |
|---|---|---|---|---|
| Data Lake | AWS Lake Formatio n | Azure Data Lake | Google Cloud Storage | AWS Lake Formation is designed for creating and managing data lakes, Azure Data Lake and GCP Cloud Storage offer similar functionalities for massive data management. |

## Developer tools

| | | | | |
|---|---|---|---|---|
| CI/CD Pipeline | CodePipe line | Azure DevOps | Cloud Build | AWS CodePipeline integrates deeply with AWS services, Azure DevOps is popular for full CI/CD, while GCP Cloud Build is serverless and scalable. |
| Source Control | CodeCo mmit | Azure Repos | Cloud Source Repositori es | All provide Git-based source control repositories, but Azure DevOps offers more comprehensive project management tools. |
| API Managem ent | API Gateway | Azure API Manageme nt | Apigee (GCP API Gateway) | AWS API Gateway is popular for building REST APIs, Azure and GCP offer similar services with |

| | | | | close integration to their respective cloud environments. |
|---|---|---|---|---|

## IoT

| IoT Platform | AWS IoT Core | Azure IoT Hub | IoT Core | All provide scalable platforms for connecting, managing, and analyzing IoT devices, with slight differences in integrations and pricing models. |
|---|---|---|---|---|

## Monitoring

| Monitoring | CloudWatch | Azure Monitor | Stackdriver (Cloud Monitoring) | AWS CloudWatch is a mature monitoring service, Azure Monitor and GCP Stackdriver provide comparable features for logs, metrics, and alerts. |
|---|---|---|---|---|
| Log Management | CloudTrail | Azure Log Analytics | Cloud Logging | AWS CloudTrail offers comprehensive logging and auditing, while Azure and GCP provide similarly detailed logging solutions. |